The 15 Essential Marketing Masterclasses for Your Small Business

POWERFUL PROMOTION ON A SHOESTRING

Dee Blick

CAPSTONE
A Wiley Brand

Registered office

Capstone Publishing Ltd. (A Wiley Company), John Wiley and Sons Ltd, The Atrium, Southern Gate, Chichester, West Sussex, PO19 8SQ, United Kingdom

For details of our global editorial offices, for customer services and for information about how to apply for permission to reuse the copyright material in this book please see our website at www.wiley.com.

Library of Congress Cataloging-in-Publication Data

Blick, Dee, 1962–
　The 15 essential marketing masterclasses for your small business / Dee Blick.
　　　pages cm
　Includes index.
　ISBN 978-0-85708-440-8 (paperback) – ISBN 978-0-85708-439-2 (ebk) – ISBN 978-0-85708-438-5 (ebk)
– ISBN 978-0-85708-437-8 (ebk)　1. Small business–Management.　2. Marketing.　I. Title.
II. Title: Fifteen essential marketing masterclasses for your small business.
　HD62.7.B565 2013
　658.8–dc23

　　　　　　　　　　2013027976

A catalogue record for this book is available from the British Library.

ISBN 978-0-857-08440-8 (paperback)
ISBN 978-0-857-08438-5 (ebk) ISBN 978-0-857-08437-8 (ebk)

Cover design by Salad Creative Ltd

Set in 11.5/14 pt Adobe Caslon pro-Regular by Toppan Best-set Premedia Limited

Printed and Bound in the United Kingdom by TJ International Ltd., Padstow, Cornwall.

*To Alan Blick, an exceptional, loving and kind man,
and wonderful father-in law.*

Contents

About Dee Blick

Reproduced with permission of Dani Maimone

Dee Blick is a Fellow of The Chartered Institute of Marketing, the world's largest marketing body. Fellowship is the highest status any marketer can attain. Dee has 30 years marketing experience, the majority of which has been spent working with small businesses. She has a track record of planning and delivering successful campaigns for small businesses on a shoestring budget and is renowned for her practical approach to small business marketing. Dee has won many awards for generating the highest reader responses for her press releases, adverts and editorial features from ABC1 audited publications. She is also an established and successful business author. Her second book, *The Ultimate Small Business Marketing Book* entered the top 150 books on Amazon UK when it launched and became the No1 bestselling small business marketing book of 2012. Dee is a warm and engaging professional public speaker, regularly invited as a keynote speaker by organisations including Royal Mail and The Chartered Institute of Marketing.

Foreword

by Andy Fernandez, The Chartered Institute of Marketing (CIM)

We live in an era when more and more well-known high street brands are struggling to ward off increasingly popular on-line retailers. Retail brand casualties, particularly in the leisure and entertainment sector, are on the rise. Woolworths, HMV, Comet and Blockbuster are just some of the familiar brands who have been hit by the ever-increasing popularity of shopping from the comfort of your home. No longer is it easy to find the CD or DVD you are looking for in town centres. Who would have predicted 20 years ago that many would be picking up their favourite album or latest Hollywood release from the same store in which they carry out their weekly groceries shopping? Basmati rice, washing-up liquid, a free-range chicken and a copy of the latest James Bond DVD please!

Our buying habits are continuously evolving. We are influenced by what we see and hear and by those around us. But there are particular things which we as customers warm to. We like to be treated well. We like things to be straightforward, particularly if we're paying for a product or service. Businesses can still earn our loyalty whether it is through customer service, social media engagement, promotions or even PR. As humans, we naturally like to feel appreciated and it's no different when we're a paying customer. It's the things like the personal touch, gestures of goodwill or even the simplest "service with a smile" that endear us to those we buy from.

Many of us feel that we receive a more personal approach when buying from small to medium-sized enterprises (SMEs). Despite the major high street and on-line brands dominating the marketplace, it is still a breath of fresh air to have smaller companies competing in the marketplace. With over 4.5 million SMEs in operation in the UK alone, we still heavily rely on their services and they rely on our custom. But can they compete against the high street's big hitters? There are many different elements to running a business successfully – each element is a crucial cog. Maintaining the effectiveness of each of these cogs is paramount to the success of the business. Effective cogs form well-oiled machines.

In recent years, CIM coined the phrase "Keep calm and carry on Marketing" during its launch of a white paper on marketing during a recession. It showed that organisations that increase their marketing spend and activities in a recession are those who emerge the strongest in times of recovery. So does fortune really favour the brave? *Do SMEs need to be brave, or can some meticulous planning and shrewdness be enough to increase business?*

Dee's many years of experience in dealing with small businesses have really made her something of an expert. So much so that her last book, in which she provided straightforward but highly effective marketing advice and tips, was a phenomenal bestseller with thousands of small businesses benefiting from the secrets she has learnt over the years. A passionate marketer, Dee also has the wonderful and natural ability to engage you through her effortless writing which has inspired so many.

Many marketing books claim to have the answer to creating strategies that will in turn create demand. But how many books have you read that allow you to take away practical information and advice which will enable you to completely reinvent the way you target customers? The 15 masterclasses that follow have been selected by Dee as the crucial components which, by implementing and delivering with great care to your audience, will have a great impact on your business.

Read this book and be inspired by 15 masterclasses that will help you drive your business forward.

Andy Fernandez
The Chartered Institute of Marketing

Introduction

In the last 30 years I have been fortunate to work with hundreds of small businesses and have come across many more at my book signings and speaking engagements. During this time I have built a clear understanding of what small businesses *really need* when it comes to promoting their business, and the challenges they face on a daily basis in getting to grips with their marketing.

When I was planning the structure and content of this book, those needs were at the very front of my mind. I know that if you're a small business owner or are responsible for the marketing of a small business, you're more often than not light on budget and tight on time. What you do spend on marketing has to be invested wisely. You have to feel pretty confident that any funds put into marketing are going to yield a return that makes your time and effort worthwhile.

And that's why I am hoping that you'll find *The 15 Essential Marketing Masterclasses For Your Small Business* a treasure trove for helping you to develop robust and effective marketing campaigns that will drive your sales and build customer loyalty on the leanest of budgets. No more guesswork or wondering whether you're taking the right approach or not. In each masterclass I share the top tips and strategies that I have honed from working with small businesses on a daily basis and illustrate these with dozens of case studies.

I recognise that the topics covered by the masterclasses in this book are each worthy of a book in their own right. But I also recognise that as a small business owner you're probably not too concerned with the theory and science behind each marketing tactic, and are more interested in knowing how to put them into practice. *And it is the small business owner that this book is aimed at.*

So, in each masterclass, I have endeavoured to cover the practical principles behind each particular marketing tactic; providing tips and strategies that you can apply to your own business in the knowledge they have been successful for businesses like yours.

In 5 of the 15 masterclasses I have enlisted the help of renowned experts that I have known for many years, have immense respect for, and whose advice and tips I am confident will help you. Ben Locker shares his wisdom on how to write great web copy and Liz Barnes offers her insights on e-marketing and LinkedIn. Robert Clay reveals his top Twitter tips, Aneela Rose shows us how to write great press releases and Nicky Kriel explains how LinkedIn can be used to good effect. Short biographies of each of these experts can be found at the back of the book.

The 15 masterclasses are:

Masterclass 1 – The perfect practical marketing plan
Masterclass 2 – Your perfect positioning statement
Masterclass 3 – Why it pays to locate and research your target audience
Masterclass 4 – How to write copy that sells
Masterclass 5 – How to make your website a magnet for hot prospects
Masterclass 6 – How to write successful adverts
Masterclass 7 – How to get PR in printed publications
Masterclass 8 – Why it pays to do direct mail
Masterclass 9 – How to take the chill out of a telephone cold call
Masterclass 10 – The secrets of successful email marketing
Masterclass 11 – How to be a confident and engaging public speaker
Masterclass 12 – How to build your expert status
Masterclass 13 – How to wow your customers with genuine customer care
Masterclass 14 – Why you should be falling in love with LinkedIn!
Masterclass 15 – How to be terrific on Twitter

The idea behind writing the book as a series of masterclasses is for each one to cover an individual marketing topic in isolation, enabling you to dip into whichever subject you choose and in whichever order you like. Having said that, however, I recommend that you read "Masterclass 1 – The perfect practical marketing plan," before reading any of the others. The potency of any marketing activity is driven purely by its place in your marketing plan. With an efficient marketing plan in place, the significance and suitability of the subjects covered in the subsequent masterclasses will be more apparent. Once the marketing foundations for your business have been laid, the remaining masterclasses will help to inspire, motivate and guide you in creating inventive and effective marketing campaigns.

I wish you much success and happiness, and sincerely hope that this book enables you to take your business to the next stage!

Kind regards
Dee Blick

Masterclass 1
The Perfect Practical Marketing Plan

In this masterclass you will learn:

- Why a marketing plan is essential for your business.
- How to create an effective targeted marketing plan.
- The marketing planning mistakes to avoid.

Whilst many of the small businesses that have approached me for assistance with their marketing had not previously recognised the need for a marketing plan, they had certainly been experiencing the problems and challenges associated with not having one. These include:

- Overspending their marketing budget. This can be as a result of panic buying when business is slow, or of failing to keep within affordable limits when business is booming.
- Spending money on unsuitable marketing activities. Without a clear understanding of who they want to target and how they want to reach this audience, they are more likely to be wasteful with their budget, spending it on marketing ideas with only a slender chance of success.
- Writing sales communications that are not sufficiently appealing to their target audiences to elicit the required response.
- An over-reliance on generating business from existing customers rather than spending time and effort on increasing their customer base.
- Relying heavily upon word-of-mouth recommendations to bring in new business and consequently not engaging in any marketing activities.
- Sporadic marketing activity. As commitment to marketing wanes, so the momentum of previous campaigns diminishes.

It is understandable that small business owners do not automatically think of creating a marketing plan when they are in the early stages of establishing their business. A marketing plan suggests the need to become bogged down in theory at a time when the business owner wants to concentrate on the practicalities of generating sales. And then there is the concern of how much it will cost to create a marketing plan and whether it will require the expertise of a marketing consultant.

It's little wonder that so many small business owners steer clear of marketing planning and choose instead to dive straight into action and employ marketing tactics that are often unplanned, inconsistent, irrelevant and, as a consequence, ineffective.

Your marketing plan is your marketing satellite navigation system, guiding your business towards success in the most efficient way possible.

There are some things to bear in mind when creating your marketing plan:

- You do not have to be a marketer, nor do you have to work with a marketer, in order to create a detailed, informative and practical marketing plan. However, creating a worthwhile marketing plan does require organisation and self-discipline. You will need to allocate quality thinking time rather than snatching ten minutes here and there.
- You will need to carry out some research and be prepared to spend time documenting your thoughts. Your marketing plan has an important role to play in the development of your business and should not be rushed or dismissed as an academic exercise. It is fine to scribble the odd marketing idea on a beer mat but you can't take this laid back approach with your marketing plan itself.
- A marketing plan is most definitely not theoretical. It should never be regarded as a document that has been created only to satisfy the requirements of an investor or shareholder before being permanently filed away. It is a practical, informative and vital document; one that you should tweak, modify and improve on an ongoing basis.

Your marketing plan is the engine that drives your sales. Without a marketing plan you undermine your sales efforts.

If you understand your customers' needs and how to meet or exceed these needs, and are then able to use this knowledge to support your sales efforts, your conversion rates will soar. But you can only achieve this if you have put in the hard yards; researching your audiences, spending time understanding your competitors, analysing your products and services. Changes or improvements should be made before the selling begins. If you simply dive head first into selling, ignoring the questions that need to be answered in your marketing plan, you risk alienating your target audiences, targeting the wrong people or simply handing the sales initiative to your competitors.

What information should be contained within your marketing plan?

Here are the nine areas that your marketing plan should cover:

1. An audit of your marketing activities to date – what have you spent, how much new business has been gained?
2. Any improvements you're planning on making to your products and services.
3. A review of your key competitors.
4. Your realistic and achievable business goals for the next 12 months.
5. Your positioning statement – the compelling reasons why your target audiences should buy from you.
6. Your target audiences – why you want to reach them and how you plan to do so.
7. An audit of your marketing communications – are they outdated or no longer relevant to your current offerings?
8. Your tactical plan – a shortlist of your chosen marketing campaigns.
9. Any limitations or barriers – what is standing in the way of your marketing plan being implemented?

Where do you start?

I would like to share my small business marketing planning template with you. I developed it 20 years ago and in this time have refined it to the stage where I know from experience that it works for virtually any small business. It is a simple and straightforward document. You just need to invest some time and effort in completing it. It has the power to transform your business.

Imagine for a moment that you have contacted me and asked me to help you with your marketing plan. After agreeing a date for a one-day marketing planning session, I have sent you this marketing planning template and asked you to spend as much time completing it as you can before our session, jotting your thoughts down under each heading. When you arrive for our session, we work through this document, padding the answers out further still, using a flip chart for brainstorming. You go away, augment the document and start putting it into action.

Now, whilst you don't have me for the day, you can still use this template to create an extremely effective marketing plan. There is no need to pay a marketing consultant to help you and, as mentioned earlier, you don't need marketing experience to work through it.

Don't feel that you need to complete it in one sitting either. In fact, I would encourage you to allow time in your diary for a number of sessions in which to contemplate each heading, scope out your thoughts and document your answers. There is no requirement to emerge with a perfect, beautifully written plan, but you should create a thorough document that you believe will help you to formulate your marketing activity.

Be prepared to make tweaks, improvements and corrections as you start to implement it. Plan your activity over a 12 month period but regularly review your plan and adjust it to reflect any changes in the criteria upon which it was created.

The Small Business Marketing Planning Template

1. Audit Your Marketing Activities to Date. How Have You Have Been Promoting Your Business?

Why should you do this?

You don't want to continue a marketing activity simply because it's something that you've always done. Reviewing what you have spent in relation to the new business that you have gained will help you to identify and improve those activities that are still worth continuing, and to abandon those activities that are no longer working.

What information are we looking for here?

Look back over the last 12 months. Identify the different ways in which you have promoted your business (advertising, business networking, direct mail, social networking, exhibitions, seminars, cold calling etc.). Beside each activity, make a note of what you were hoping each activity would achieve for your business. Try to be specific and include the sales you were anticipating, the number of new customers you were hoping to gain, the number of existing customers that would spend more etc. Once you have gathered this information, answer the following questions:

- Did you fall short of your goals? If so, why do you think this was the case? Were your targets realistic? Did you expect too much for too little? How far short of achieving your goals were you?
- How much money did you spend on each activity and what were the results from each activity?
- Are there any activities that have been really successful and should be expanded, any that could be more successful with a little tweaking, or any that have fallen flat and need to be curtailed completely?
- Can you identify any weaknesses in your marketing thinking over the last 12 months? Have you developed planned campaigns and stuck to them well or have you tended to spend money on isolated marketing activities, such as the occasional advert, the odd exhibition, a one-off leaflet drop, social networking when you have a moment or two to spare? Were your target audiences always at the front of your mind when choosing your marketing tactics? What was your rationale for choosing each activity? Have you let your own personal likes and dislikes dictate how you market your business? For example, one business owner I worked with confessed that his marketing centred round business networking because he enjoyed meeting people in a semi-social setting. When he reviewed the cost of his networking activities and the business he had gained as a result, it was clear that some of the networking associations he belonged to were ineffective and he should not renew his membership of these. Another business owner had fallen into the trap of promoting her business exclusively through blogging and social media. Although these tactics were free (with the exception of the time she was spending) it became clear on review that her target audiences were not being reached in any discernible quantity. Although she continued to blog, she reduced the amount of time she spent doing so and used the time it freed up to run direct mail campaigns, accessing her target audiences in a more effective way.

Note

Do pause before completely abandoning any marketing activity that has not worked for you. One of my clients told me that direct mail did not work for them and that although they had run several mailshots, the business gained as a result had failed even to cover their costs. Upon review, however, we recognised that direct mail itself was not the reason for the lack of success; it was the way in which it was being used. A fresh approach to their sales letters and a new mailing list helped ensure that their next mailshot was profitable. So although there may be some activities that you are rightly convinced should be abandoned, be cautious of condemning others until you have looked closely at the reasons for the poor performance. It may be that the original approach was at fault.

2. Appraise Your Products and Services. Are You Planning Any Improvements over the Next 12 Months?

Why should you do this?

The small businesses that thrive and continue to be desired by their target audiences are the ones that place a value on continually improving what they offer. If you fail to consider this in your marketing plan, you risk being eclipsed by your more innovative and customer focused competitors. Your marketing plan provides the ideal opportunity for you to stand back and to review objectively what you offer. Consider and document improvements and changes that you would like to make that will benefit your customers.

What information are we looking for here?

Make a list of the changes, why you are making them, the impact you believe they will have on present and future customers and when they will be implemented. Will they give rise to an increase in price or can they be accommodated within your existing pricing structure? What impact will they have on your profit margin? Will these changes improve your ranking with competitors?

Note

Any product or service enhancement provides a perfect opportunity for inclusion in a marketing campaign. Any small but significant change to your offering is positive news and should be communicated to your customers and prospects.

3. Identify Your Key Competitors in the Areas in Which You Propose to Operate

Why should you do this?

Your customers are likely to be very aware of your competitors and this alone is a good enough reason for you to be aware of them too.

Why it is important to do this can be illustrated by the example of one particular business owner who approached me after the unsuccessful launch of his on-line training programme. He believed that the reason for his lack of success was insufficient media coverage. He had marketed his system to training managers as a unique product they would not be able to access from any other provider. However, had he done his competitor research beforehand, he would have discovered that several businesses were already offering something very similar, if not better. Before making claims about your products or services it pays to have completed your competitor research beforehand. Then you can say with confidence why you are better, special or different.

What information are we looking for here?

Carry out some research on those businesses you regard as your closest competitors. What can you learn from them? Compare your offering with theirs. Note those areas in which your products or services exceed those of your competitors (you can flag these in your marketing communications), and those in which your offering falls short in comparison (you may want to implement some improvements as a result).

Do you have competitors for all of your services or just for some? Are you really targeting the same audiences?

Note

This is one exercise in which you can learn a huge amount simply by reading the websites of your competitors. You may find it useful to compose a list of those details that you would like to know about each competitor so you can judge each one by the same criteria. It's always useful to be completely aware of your competitors and what they are doing, so revisit this part of your marketing plan every few months.

4. Document the Measurable, Realistic and Achievable Business Goals You Aim to Accomplish In the Next 12 Months

Why should you do this?

Judging the impact of your marketing activities is more straightforward if you have established goals against which to measure them. These goals do need to be specific, however, and simply stating that you want to "increase sales significantly in the next 12 months" is too woolly a target to be useful.

What information are we looking for here?

Start with your biggest goal – usually the level of sales you are hoping to attain in the next 12 months. Here are some examples:

- In my first year of trading as a business coach I want to generate £36,000 of fees (my previous salary). To achieve this, I need a minimum of 12 retained coaching clients, each spending £2000 to £4000 p.a.
- We must quadruple the sales of our hydraulic levelling systems with caravan owners in the next 12 months. To achieve this goal we must attain 60 new customers this year.
- We want to increase product sales from £500,000 to £600,000 in the next 12 months. To help achieve this we will need to increase the number of stockists that supply our products from 800 to 1000.
- We want to increase our annual turnover of promotional gifts and corporate clothing from £250,000 to £285,000 in the next 12 months with at least £28,000 of this increase to be achieved from promotional clothing sales.

Once you have documented your main goal, consider and document the smaller objectives that will help you to attain that goal. Here are some examples for illustration:

- This year I will exhibit at a minimum of two exhibitions that are attended by my target audiences.
- This year I will implement a quarterly marketing programme to communicate with my lapsed clients/existing customers.
- This year I will aim to increase the minimum amount that a customer spends with me from £250 to £400.

- This year I want to increase the number of hot prospects that I convert to clients from 17% to 23%.

Note

There's nothing quite like seeing your goals staring back at you in your marketing plan to persuade you that it's time to set about trying to accomplish them. Make sure that some of your business goals excite you when reading them, making the hairs stand up on the back of your neck and your heart beat just that little bit faster.

5. Define Your Positioning Statement

Why should you do this?

If you want to stand out in a crowded marketplace and become a magnet for customers, you need to create a positioning statement. So many small businesses undersell themselves because their communications – on-line, face-to-face and in print – fail to emphasise the benefits they offer. Looking at your business objectively and asking yourself the question "Why should customers buy from our business and remain loyal to it?" will help you to identify those positive aspects of your business that differentiate it from those of your competitors. Your positioning statement is the DNA of your business and should be reflected in all your marketing communications.

What information are we looking for here?

In addition to feeding into your marketing plan, your positioning statement performs a vital role in determining how you promote your business through all your communications. Due to its importance, the creation of your positioning statement and the information that should be contained within it is covered in detail in Masterclass 2.

6. Define, Research and Locate Your Target Audiences, Segment by Segment

Why should you do this?

Any marketing activity that you undertake is likely to be blunt and ineffective if you have not previously identified and investigated your target audiences. Your message may reach thousands of people but if few of them have any interest in what you are offering, it is unlikely that it will result in many sales. Only by understanding which audiences have the greatest need for what you offer and knowing how best to reach these audiences, will you be able to create marketing campaigns with a high chance of success.

What information are we looking for here?

As with your positioning statement, identifying and researching your target audiences is a vital aspect of your marketing planning as a whole and the process of doing so is an involved one. Consequently, Masterclass 3 covers this exercise in detail.

7. Audit and Develop Your Marketing Toolkit

Why should you do this?

It can be tempting to hang onto outdated marketing communications if you still have a large quantity of literature yet to be used. However, using these tired and old communications can actually sabotage a campaign and damage your brand. In fact, a communication does not need to be out of date to be redundant. It may still be accurate on a factual basis yet no longer suitably reflects the needs of the audiences being targeted or adequately emphasises the benefits on offer. Appraise your current marketing communications against your positioning statement and after completing the target audience exercise. Do they still pass muster? Your communications need to change as your business changes.

What information are we looking for here?

Auditing your marketing toolkit will help you to identify any improvements or changes that you will need to make to your communications in the next 12 months. Include all the communication tools that you use to market your business. For example, your website, newsletters, brochures, flyers, sales letters, bulletins, product sheets, seminar handouts, press releases.

When reviewing your current tool kit, consider the following:

- Did you enlist the services of a professional designer or copywriter to create your communications or did you take a more DIY approach? If the latter, do they still represent your brand in a positive way? Try to be dispassionate when analysing them. What would be your impression had you received them from a competitor? Impressed or underwhelmed?

- In light of your positioning statement, could any of your communications be improved to provide more depth, substance, relevance or reader appeal? Are your messages too generic to sufficiently engage your audience?
- How effective has each communication been? Did it have its desired effect? Have you received any feedback about it from customers or other third parties?

Answering the questions above will help you to decide which parts of your current marketing toolkit remain valid, which require improvement and which should be rejected. Don't decide yet upon which communications you will create in the next 12 months until you have studied the remaining masterclasses in this book. They will aid you in your decision making.

8. Create a Shortlist of Your Chosen Marketing Activities

Why should you do this?

Once you have identified your target audiences and understand where you can find them, the next step is to decide which marketing activities are going to help you to communicate with them effectively.

What information are we looking for here?

The marketing activities you choose for future campaigns should be influenced by the outcomes of your marketing activity audit and the research you have undertaken as part of your marketing plan. When you are confident that you understand the channels open to you for each target audience, you should draw up a shortlist of the marketing activities best placed to exploit these channels. You could consider the suitability of advertising (local, national, sector specific), face-to-face business networking, targeted direct mail, e-marketing campaigns, PR, on-line directories, webinars, social networking, partnership activities, seminars, exhibitions, launch events, media briefings.

Once you have decided upon the most appropriate activities, you then need to amalgamate them into specific marketing campaigns for each of your target audiences. These campaigns should be run over a 3 to 4 month period in order to produce the impact necessary to convert a prospect into a customer. This is the tactical part of your marketing plan.

To illustrate how a campaign can be established, let me use the example of VB-Airsuspension. VB-Airsuspension design and manufacture a range of air suspension products for motorhomes and light commercial vehicles and had identified one of their target audiences as being the owners of a motorhome worth in excess of £50,000. Having identified this audience, they examined how they could best reach them. The channels they established as being most appropriate included advertising in *Motorcaravan Motorhome Monthly* magazine (*MMM*), attending Motorhome Owners Club rallies and exhibiting at the leading annual Motorhome and Caravan Show.

Here's a snapshot of the marketing campaigns that were designed to attract this particular audience:

VB-Airsuspension

Target Audience: A UK Motorhome Owners Club. VB-Airsuspension identified this Motorhome Owners Club as being a priority audience because most of the club members own a motorhome that costs in excess of £50,000. Research revealed they hold a national rally every May.

- **March:** Phone the secretary of the Club requesting that we attend their rally in May. Advise that we will offer members at the rally free air suspension health checks, free refreshments and goody bags, and will award a 5% discount to any member who decides to have VB-Airsuspension installed on their motorhome.
- **April:** Prepare the sales literature for the rally. To include an expression of interest form so that we can gather as many home addresses and email addresses at the event as possible.
- **May:** Attend the rally – our goal is to carry out at least 30 motorhome healthchecks.
- **June:** Issue a direct mailshot to all members that expressed an interest in VB-Airsuspension, reminding them of the 5% discount and inviting them to visit our stand at the Motorhome and Caravan Show in October.

(Continued)

Target Audience: Readers of *MMM*. This magazine is regarded by readers as being the best place for information and reviews about products for their motorhome. It is a glossy, long established and well-liked magazine. It has the highest readership of all the motorhome titles.

- **March:** Meet the editor of *MMM* and the advertising sales team to discuss how best we can take advantage of advertising and publishing editorial in their publication. We want to aim our message at those readers with motorhomes costing in excess of £50,000 and starting in the May issue, plan to take out a half-page advert in six issues plus additional news and features in as many issues as possible.
- **April:** With ongoing half-page adverts and editorial agreed, submit an additional case study of a happy VB-Airsuspension client for publication in the June issue of the magazine.
- **May:** This month's half-page advert will promote the new features of our air suspension product and our national dealer network.
- **June:** Review the results from advertising. Do we need to change the advert for the remaining issues of the magazine? Prepare a special feature for the Motorhome and Caravan Show issue.

Target Audience: Visitors to the annual Motorhome and Caravan Show at the National Exhibition Centre in Birmingham. This event takes place in October and attracts thousands of motorhome owners every year.

- **September:** Contact those journalists that will be attending the event and invite them to visit our stand. Advise them of our offer of free refreshments, goody bags and a media briefing of our latest air suspension products for motorhomes. Follow up by phone the week before the event to remind them of the invitation to visit our stand.
- **October:** Attend the five day Motorhome and Caravan Show and make available to visitors that express a strong interest in air suspension our special show offer – a 5% discount if they have our air suspension fitted within 28 days. Hand out envelopes with our latest press releases, product sheets, special offer flyers and chocolate.
- **November:** Issue a direct mailshot to all visitors who completed our prospect forms reminding them of the expiry date of the offer and the benefits of air suspension. Follow up 5 days later with a telephone call.
- **December:** Review the results before making a commitment to attend next year's show.

By creating a 3–4 month action plan for each target audience you will find that your marketing as a whole is more ordered and effective. The activities scheduled for each month are documented and can therefore be planned in good time, and the regular communication with each target audience throughout the year, maintains the momentum towards an eventual sale.

9. Determine How You Will Put Marketing at the Heart of Your Business by Recognising the Challenges of Doing so

Why should you do this?

There's nothing more frustrating than creating a wonderful marketing plan but not being able to implement it. If you want to take advantage of this valuable body of information you may need to make changes fast! I have lost count of the number of small businesses that have told me that whilst they are keen to improve the results from their marketing, they don't have the time or the resources to put their marketing plan into action.

What are we looking for here?

Think about the barriers that you believe could prevent you from adhering to your marketing plan. Write them down, but try to be specific in what you write. "Not enough time in the day" or "too few resources" may appear to be genuine barriers, but can you break these down further? If so, you have a greater chance of taking steps to overcome them. I have included below as a guide a selection of barriers that were identified by a client of mine when completing this part of the marketing planning template:

- Frustration felt by the partners in dedicating time to marketing activities when they could be working on fee generating tasks instead.
- Insufficient staff resources to implement the plan and undertake the work.
- Reluctance among the staff to accept new ideas – out of comfort zone.
- Staff attitude – the work has always been there and has never really needed to be generated. Consequent lack of buy-in to marketing activity.
- Company structure – no business plan or real strategy, but good financial planning and fee/cost control.

By contemplating the restrictions they faced in implementing their marketing plan, the client realised that their business goals were unlikely to be achieved unless they committed to making changes in an effort to remove these barriers. Their subsequent actions included recruiting a part-time marketing administrator to address the resource issue and organising monthly marketing meetings between the partners and the staff in order to encourage the whole firm to embrace the marketing initiatives being undertaken. Be honest when considering those factors that may obstruct you from implementing your own marketing plan. Document each barrier as specifically as possible and, if feasible, take steps to remove them.

I hope that after studying this masterclass you recognise that it is your marketing plan that should determine where your marketing budget is allocated, and that spending money on networking, advertising, search engine optimisation or indeed any marketing activity before you have created your marketing plan, can lead to disappointing results.

Masterclass Summary

- A marketing plan should be a practical and evolving guide that forms the basis of most of your marketing decisions.
- You don't need marketing experience to create a marketing plan but you must allocate quality uninterrupted time.
- Look upon your marketing plan as the engine that fuels your sales activity.
- Begin with an audit of your marketing activities to determine how much it costs you to acquire business.
- Identify improvements to your products and services. List them in your marketing plan with a timescale for implementation.
- Establish realistic business growth goals that can be measured. Don't overlook the smaller action goals that will help you to achieve the big ones.
- Your positioning statement is crucial. Spend time creating and refining it.
- Know who you want to reach, why you want to reach them and where to find them.
- Your existing communications, including your website, need auditing too. Don't settle for out-of-date or poorly designed communications.
- Remove any barriers that stand in the way of you putting your marketing plan into action.

Masterclass 2
Your Perfect Positioning Statement

In this masterclass you will learn:

- What a positioning statement is and why your business needs one.
- The many benefits of having a positioning statement.
- How to create a positioning statement.

Whenever a small business owner is asked to describe what they do for a living, even the most reticent one will talk animatedly and enthusiastically about their business and what it has to offer. It can be hard to get a word in edgeways once they're in full flow. This all-too-familiar scenario is replicated at countless networking events the world over as business owners grapple for the opportunity to impress upon fellow networkers the values and capabilities of their business.

In most cases the listener cannot fail to be impressed by this passionate and inspiring endorsement and leaves the conversation with a very positive impression of the business. But this is just the first step towards that listener becoming a new customer or an introducer of new customers.

With that positive impression firmly implanted, it is likely the listener will want to find out more information about the business, perhaps by visiting the website, downloading the latest newsletter or browsing the social media profiles. And it is at this stage that things can go horribly wrong. Unless both the on-line representation of the business and the supporting literature fully reflect the animated presentation offered by the business owner, that positive first impression can quickly collapse.

The enthusiasm, vibrancy and passion with which the business owner spoke at the networking event must be replicated wherever the business is represented, be that on-line or off-line. Dreary, lifeless text may fill the white spaces on the website or newsletter, but will probably do more damage to the company brand than leaving that white space blank!

When standing in front of someone, with facial expressions and hand movements in our armoury, conveying passion and enthusiasm about our business can seem easy. Doing the same under the restrictions of the written word is not quite so straightforward.

That's why all small business owners should invest some time in creating a positioning statement for their business.

What Is a Positioning Statement?

A positioning statement is simply a clear, specific and unambiguous description of what you and your business offer – you may also have heard it referred to as a "benefit statement." It comprises of a series of bullet points detailing the genuine benefits that your business provides to its customers. It should be kept updated as your business changes to ensure it remains relevant, and constantly referred to when writing marketing material.

Look upon your positioning statement as the DNA of your business. The information within it will help you to stand apart from competitors and to build a strong brand identity. As you strive to be special and different, your positioning statement can act as a guide. It is also there to help provide impact to your written communications.

Your positioning statement provides an opportunity to spend some time determining exactly the benefits that your business offers. Once these benefits have been explored, appraised and documented, you will have created a powerful testimony to your business, a statement that reflects all that is good and great about it and one that provides an excellent reference point when struggling to add sparkle to your marketing communications.

One example of how a positioning statement helped rejuvenate a company's marketing material is that of BEL Signs, a family owned business that specialises in making exhibition banners, vehicle signage, and signs for the exterior and interior of buildings.

BEL Signs had fallen into the familiar trap of promoting their services by simply listing them on their sales literature, providing little information beyond brief product details. Their direct mail was uninspiring and lacked vigour and passion. The text was so generic that it could have been referring to any sign business.

By embarking upon the process of developing their positioning statement they unearthed a number of aspects of their offering that could be used in their promotional material, yet had not previously been communicated. These included:

- **A free in-house design service.** This service saves the client money as it removes the need for them to appoint a designer for their signage artwork.
- **A manufacturing team with over 50 years of expertise.** This fact alone should be enough to convince potential clients that they would be in the hands of an experienced and reliable team and would receive a high quality finished product.
- **The capacity to turn around complex jobs in as little as three working days.** From their own research, BEL Signs knew that the majority of their competitors were quoting three weeks for similar work. Given the urgency of many jobs, with clients often requesting their work be completed as soon as possible, this was another important benefit.
- **All parts of the sign production process undertaken in-house.** This enabled them to offer a 100% quality assurance guarantee to clients.
- **A client base that includes many recognised and successful local businesses and national brands.** Again, this benefit underpinned the fact that BEL Signs was a successful and popular business. When evaluating a company, potential clients will often look at the types of customers already being serviced before deciding whether to pass their own business that way.
- **The company celebrating its 30th anniversary.** This information was particularly relevant in the current climate as businesses are more inclined to engage a company with a long established track record, than to enlist the services of a newcomer. The risks are perceived as being lower and longevity in business is often seen as an indication that the company can be trusted and is an expert in its field.

By including this information and other benefits that had been brought to light during the process of building a positioning statement, BEL Signs was able to create marketing communications that contained real impact. In Masterclass 8, we see how the BEL Signs positioning statement was used to help develop one of their sales letters.

About You

What can you learn from the BEL Signs case study that could help you with your positioning statement?

1. Is the longevity of your business being highlighted?
2. Are you underplaying your expertise, or that of your team?
3. Is your client base worth shouting about?
4. Are there added value services that you are not charging for?
5. Are you offering any services that are valued highly by your customers but that you take for granted? (For example, the rapid turnaround of orders as in the BEL Signs case study.)

To further illustrate the value of the positioning statement in helping identify the various benefits that a company has to offer, let's review another example, that of Techmobility, a small business that adapts motor vehicles for disabled motorists under the Motability scheme.

Techmobility's target audience consists of motor dealers, disabled drivers and disabled passengers. The business is rich in customer benefits but, until they created their positioning statement, these benefits were not being adequately communicated to their target audiences. Their existing marketing communications, including their website, had not been:

- **Advertising their mobile workshop service.** This service had proved to be extremely popular with time-pressed motor dealers that resented taking time off from selling to customers on their forecourt in order to drive vehicles off-site for adaptation.
- **Highlighting their component-level qualified engineers.** This important point would emphasise to dealers that Techmobility's engineers were highly qualified and competent to handle the most complex of adaptations.
- **Promoting their use of high quality discrete adaptations.** With many adaptation specialists still fitting old-fashioned adaptations that take up more room in the vehicle, the positive impact that the cutting-edge adaptations installed by Techmobility could have on the driver or passenger experience was a benefit that deserved to be emphasised.
- **Accentuating the huge amount of positive customer and Motability dealer testimonial.** Along with the fact that over 800 Motability dealers used Techmobility for adaptations, this information would both reassure and inspire new dealers and their customers.

- **Publicising their dedicated administration team.** Many of their competitors were smaller companies and so did not have the resources to provide the indispensable "before and after adaptation" backup support that dealers and customers require.
- **Advising customers that they do not charge for return visits.** If the customer is not able to be present during the initial vehicle adaptation, a return visit may be necessary to make small tweaks to the adaptation to improve driver or passenger comfort. The fact that Techmobility did not charge for these return visits was a real benefit, for both the dealer recommending Techmobility and their customer.

About You

What can you learn from the Techmobility case study that could help you with your positioning statement?

1. Are you offering benefits over and above those provided by your competitors but failing to market these benefits effectively?
2. Are you overlooking the importance of gathering positive testimonial from customers?
3. Does your after-sales service compare favourably with that of your competitors?

Hopefully, by now, you can see that creating a positioning statement will help invigorate your marketing communications and prevent them from falling short. If you are not communicating the full array of benefits that your business can offer to potential customers, influencers and introducers, you're effectively handing the initiative to a more marketing-savvy competitor.

A powerful and effective positioning statement requires nothing more than time, focus and commitment. Once in place, it will act as an invaluable reference point for those times when you are composing your next advert or creating your next website page. No longer will you be struggling for ideas on what to write.

How Do You Create Your Positioning Statement?

1. **Allocate quality, uninterrupted time for the task in hand.** Initially set aside a minimum of two hours but be prepared to invest more if needed. As a general rule of thumb, I will spend three to four hours with a client developing and then documenting their positioning statement.

2. **Find an environment in which you can concentrate.** If this means hiring a hot desk or meeting room for a few hours because the environment in which you usually work is not conducive to concentration, make that small investment. Trying to focus when your phone is buzzing, other people are distracting you and your day-to-day work is calling out for attention is not likely to be a successful strategy.

3. **You can start the process alone, but you'll benefit by sharing your ideas.** You can often improve your positioning statement by discussing your thoughts with a person whose opinion you trust, a person not reluctant to challenge you. Don't shrink from doing this. The thoughts and ideas that can be generated from discussion with a friend or colleague can result in a really powerful, relevant and effective statement.

4. **Involve some of your clients.** Understanding why your clients choose you, which benefits they most appreciate and how you compare with competitors is valuable information that should definitely be included in your positioning statement. Whether you take a client out to lunch, pick up the phone and ask, create an email survey or do all three, obtaining your customers' views on the services that you offer is well worth the effort. Ian Brownbill, the Managing Director of Advent IT, decided to involve his customers before creating Advent IT's positioning statement. In Ian's words:

   We wanted to give an accurate answer to the question "what do you do?" so that we could market ourselves effectively beyond word-of-mouth recommendation. We recognised that the first step to achieving this was forming a positioning statement so that we could identify the needs we served, the benefits that clients appreciated and any obstacles to overcome. We knew our customers liked us but could not be specific enough to translate this adequately into our literature and website copy. We decided a telephone-based customer feedback project would help us to answer our questions and draft our positioning statement. Dee conducted this project for us, phoning our customers to

27

make it easier for them to answer our questions freely. What did we get from this exercise?

Our business is that we develop bespoke software. That's our product. What surprised us was that our customers take our good software for granted. They concentrated their feedback on the ancillary things we do that they value. This included our willingness to listen to them and to tirelessly explore what their requirements were beyond the initial project brief. They liked the fact that once on board we become part of their customer management team, proactively speaking up about potential issues and not shrinking from being involved. They all said it was a big plus that we didn't use techie speak, that we were always quick to respond to their enquiries and always available to help, even out of hours. Surprisingly very few had spoken to a competitor and, when they had, they said they preferred our approach of understanding their needs through listening and asking questions as opposed to selling to them with a slick presentation. They all said that we give value for money, that we stay within the budget quoted which again was favourable when compared to other IT companies they had worked with. This information has helped us to create a relevant and benefit driven positioning statement, one that we know is genuine because so much of it is from the mouths of our customers. But, apart from this, we were overwhelmed by the positive response from our customers to these questions. They really wanted to help us. It was a real eye opener that these busy people impressed upon Dee that they wanted us to keep in touch on a regular basis. This has led to a number of meetings since to discuss new projects; an amazing and unanticipated benefit of the research!

5. **Involve your team.** Whether you have one employee or several, you absolutely cannot overlook their input into your positioning statement. This is especially true of employees that act as front-line brand ambassadors. They are in regular contact with customers and prospects and so may have a very different perspective to you if you no longer work on the front line yourself. Arrange a team meeting and capture all ideas before deciding on those that will make it into your positioning statement.

6. **Transfer your notes and findings into your positioning statement.** You may like the format of your positioning statement to be that of a mind map, a selection of flip chart sheets stuck up around your office or simply an on-line text document – it boils down to your own personal preference. Bear in mind, though, that it must be easily accessible, easy to read and easy to understand. In all

likelihood it will take you two or three drafts before you arrive at the final statement. Look upon this as time well spent.

7. **Keep your positioning statement updated.** As your business grows, changes and improves, so should your positioning statement. It should be a dynamic, current statement that articulates the benefits that your business offers in one place. For example, you may win an award, gain new qualifications or join a trade association, all of which translates into providing customers with a better service. You may undergo further training, improve your payment terms, and so on. Whilst such changes are important, it can be easy to forget to include them in your marketing communications if you have not updated your positioning statement accordingly. Aim to review your positioning statement on a monthly basis.

8. **Be aware that not every single benefit in your positioning statement will be relevant to all your target audiences.** You may have expertise, experience and qualifications that are relevant to one type of customer but not to another. Include these benefits in your positioning statement but make it clear that they do not extend to all of your target audiences and so should therefore only be included in those communications aimed at the audience to which they apply.

What Kind of Information should Your Positioning Statement Contain?

As already established, this statement should be packed with benefits. Use these headings as a guide to developing one for your own business:

About you and your brand

This encompasses your experience, qualifications, expertise, track record, awards you have won and accreditations you have gained. It should answer the question, "Why should I choose you rather than a competitor?"

Your products and services

Do you offer innovative products and services that customers would be hard pushed to find to the same standard elsewhere? Do you offer tried and tested products and services with a no quibble, money-back guarantee? Why do your current customers buy your products and services? What are the specific benefits they cite as being influential in their decision-making process?

Your price strategy

How do customers benefit from your price strategy? Are you a value-driven provider, delivering more to customers than they expect for the price you charge? Is your price strategy simply to be lower than your competitors?

Your customer care policy

How do you look after customers, from the first introduction to the after-sales service? Be specific in the benefits you list. It is not enough to trot out clichéd statements such as "we are passionate about customer care," and "we put the customer at the centre of everything we do." Do you have a documented customer care policy? How many of your customers are repeat buyers and how many recommend you? Being able to state that 9/10 of your existing customers would happily recommend you is a powerful message, as is declaring that you receive repeat business from 9/10 of your customers.

Your service

How do customers benefit from the service you deliver? How reliable, swift to respond, fast to deliver and quick to resolve customer complaints are you? Can you provide statistics that will back this up?

Your social responsibility policy

The saying "people don't care how much you know until they know how much you care" is very applicable here. You build trust, credibility and integrity if you can demonstrate that you have a social conscience and care about your local or wider community. Do you support local causes or national charities, for example? Do you mentor young people or allow the use of your premises by local associations at no charge? Don't worry if this is new territory. Have a think about what you or your business could offer that is realistic and achievable and could kick start your social responsibility policy.

Your environmental policy

For some small businesses, an environmental policy is crucial; for others it is less so. For example, a printing company cannot get away with not having one, whereas a business coach is less likely to be judged as harshly. Use your judgement but be aware that an increasing number of organisations and businesses, especially those in the public sector, will ask for evidence of your environmental policy as part of the tendering process. If you recycle your unwanted stationery, printer cartridges and magazines, buy recycled letterhead paper and print your literature on environmentally responsible or recycled paper, you have an environmental policy. You just need to document it. Take this opportunity to consider also whether there is more that you can do in this area.

I would like to end this masterclass by looking at two different case studies that illustrate how the positioning statement can help you to market your business more effectively.

Case Study 1: Gabby Adler, the Property Specialist

Gabby Adler is a property buying and lettings specialist based in the Richmond upon Thames area in London. Before creating her positioning statement, Gabby was struggling to create the compelling messages she was eager to communicate to potential clients. She felt that her website, although attractive and professionally developed, was lacking rich and enticing content. It soon became apparent when running through the process of developing Gabby's positioning statement that there were a number of benefits that she was offering but were not being highlighted in her marketing literature or on her website. For instance, Gabby is well qualified in her role as a property buying and letting specialist, with a master's degree in property valuation and law. This was not even mentioned on her website or in her literature. She also had an attractive fixed-fee pricing strategy, but this again was something that was very much understated in all her communications.

By spending time developing her positioning statement, Gabby became more aware of the strength of her offering. Consequently, her confidence in her skills and abilities increased dramatically which, in turn, has led to her becoming a regular and trusted contributor in the national media, including the BBC, on matters relating to property buying and lettings. (These achievements have of course since been added to the positioning statement.) The copy on Gabby's website and in her printed communications is also now more powerful, relevant and targeted. Before completing the process of creating her positioning statement, Gabby was unwittingly underselling herself.

Here are four unedited extracts from Gabby's positioning statement. Note how, after revealing a fact about herself, Gabby accompanies it with an explanation of the way it benefits her clients as a result.

1. I have a master's degree in property valuation and law which means that I have been professionally trained to value residential and commercial properties. This helps my clients as properties often come on to the market overpriced. With my knowledge of the area's prices, and my professional qualification, I can advise a client on the precise value of a property and how this has changed over time. My client can be confident they are making a sound financial investment. My professional qualification also covers residential developments, planning law, landlord and tenant law, corporate finance, and accounting. My clients receive the added benefit of hiring someone with a wide knowledge base of all aspects of residential and commercial property. I am fully equipped and trained to deal with any situation that may arise on their property search. For example, my client may be interested in buying commercial property and obtaining planning permission to turn it into a residential dwelling. I have the knowledge and training to value the commercial property accurately and to guide my client through the planning procedure that covers the change in use.
2. My fair fee pricing strategy. I charge a fixed fee because it is fair. I do not do any more work for a £2 million budget than for a £500,000 budget so why should I charge my clients more when the process is the same? This means that my clients get exactly the same service, if not better, at a lower, fairer fee than a property finder charging a percentage fee which is the norm.
3. As I am a one-woman band, I can respond swiftly to clients' questions and requests. For example, I can meet a builder at the weekend to enable my client to make an offer first thing on Monday morning.

4. I specialise in one area (Richmond upon Thames) so that I can track property prices, what comes onto the market, what sells quickly or slowly. Having such a small area to work in makes me a real area specialist. My clients benefit from the fact that I know all the estate agents in the area and the types of property they are likely to get on their books. I spend most of my time in the area so it's easier for me to hear about developments in the local housing market, whether it's a new property coming onto the market or a property previously under offer falling through. Focusing on one area means I am able to have daily communication with the agents, and my clients can be the first through the door to see new properties coming onto the market.

About You

1. Are you guilty of underselling your assets, qualifications, expertise and experience because you have not paused for a moment to consider them? How do your clients benefit from your assets, qualifications etc.?
2. Do you have an innovative approach to your fee structure like Gabby and, if so, how are you advertising this fact?
3. If you are a one-person business, are you downplaying this believing it could count against you? The opposite could in fact be true.
4. If you were to audit your on-line and off-line marketing communications now, would you identify important benefits that you were not including?

Case Study 2: Optimum Kitchen Appliance Superstores

Optimum is a long-standing company in the kitchen appliance retail and servicing industry with two large showrooms in the south-east of England. Although it was investing in regular advertising and radio campaigns, it was pretty much undertaking the same marketing activities as its competitors. In such a competitive marketplace the company had to do more to stand out and, in order to do this, it needed to make potential and existing customers aware of the full range of benefits it had to offer. The process of creating the positioning statement led to benefit after benefit being discovered and documented.

Before committing to building a positioning statement, the team at Optimum were unaware that they had a robust and commendable environmental policy. Positive media coverage of the business has since been achieved as a result of this policy and it offers another reason for customers to use Optimum rather than a competitor. The positioning statement also proved invaluable in revealing Optimum's expertise in providing and fitting built-in appliances. It had not previously considered marketing this as a valuable and much needed service.

Overall the positioning statement exercise inspired a more positive and proactive approach to Optimum's marketing. (In particular, one powerful and effective advertising campaign was developed which you can read more about in the Masterclass 6.) It also prompted Optimum to establish a customer care training academy for staff. The exercise highlighted that, as previous training programmes were all of a technical nature and focused solely on products, the customer care aspects of the business were at risk of being neglected.

To provide a flavour of the type of detail contained in Optimum's positioning statement I have included here a small extract of the final document:

Our Service

1. We deliver appliances free within a generous postcode area. This is also the case for our economy lines.
2. We will unpack your appliance, and take away and recycle 90% of the packaging.
3. We will take away your old appliance at no charge if disconnected.
4. For Range Cookers, we supply up to four team members in order to transport your appliance safely from our warehouse to your home. You do not receive this service from on-line retailers. An Internet-only provider is likely to charge for delivery and, under certain circumstances, will not deliver at all (e.g. if the delivery team have to climb several flights of stairs).
5. If we discover a problem with your appliance when we deliver it, for example it is scratched or there is a fault with it, you don't have to do anything. We will take the appliance back immediately or if it is appropriate offer you a discount. We do not leave it with you for a different courier service to pick up.

6. We invest time in technical and customer service training and we do not pay commission on sales.
7. Delivery is flexible and more convenient for customers than the rigid delivery timescales on offer by the national brand chains. We don't use a third-party delivery company. If you want your appliance to be delivered before the school run, or at another specific time, we can accommodate this.
8. We can store your appliance safely for weeks, even months until your extension is completed or your new kitchen built/refurbished. There is no charge for this.

Our Price Strategy

1. Our strategy is to be competitive and open to a deal. Whilst we cannot always match the prices on the Internet, those prices usually do not include the extras that we provide free of charge, e.g. delivery and installation, storage, removal of your current appliance, recycling of packaging, easy returns and after-care servicing.
2. We regularly price match against one of our biggest local competitors and are cheaper on most lines.

Our Environmental Policy

1. We go beyond our legal duty to simply provide advice to customers about recycling options available to them. For anything that we sell, we take the old appliance back free of charge and recycle it within current legal guidelines.
2. We have invested in a machine that compacts polystyrene into small bricks which are then recycled.
3. We recycle 100% of our cardboard packaging and 90% of our product packaging.
4. Our environmental policy has had a dramatic impact on the number of skips we need to use. We have reduced our usage of skips for landfill from 15 per month to 3 per month.

About You

1. Are you pushing ahead with your business, making changes and improvements, operating in an environmentally responsible manner yet failing to communicate this to your customers and prospects?
2. Do you have a competitive price strategy and, if so, how clearly are you communicating this to prospects and customers? Are you highlighting just how competitive your fees, prices or rates are?
3. Are you measurably better than competitors in some areas but failing to communicate this? Is it time to document how and where you are better so that this body of knowledge can fuel your marketing communications?
4. Are you being generic when describing benefits, using sweeping terms that could equally apply to your competitors rather than going into the details of what you offer?

I hope that you can now see the many advantages that your own company will gain by creating a positioning statement, and that you understand the need to keep it updated with achievements, changes and new benefits. It is the DNA of your business. Don't stint on capturing everything – and put modesty to one side whilst doing so!

Masterclass Summary

- The enthusiasm and passion you exude about your business when face-to-face with a prospect or client should be replicated in your marketing communications.
- Your positioning statement comprises of a series of concise benefits under different headings.
- Your positioning statement should be referred to when planning your on-line and printed marketing communications.
- Regard your positioning statement as a document that captures the DNA of your business.
- Use it to inform and inspire your communications and it will help you tower above competitors.

- The case studies illustrate the value that the process of creating a positioning statement can bring to a small business.
- Spend time considering the questions at the end of each case study.
- Allocate time for creating your positioning statement. Turn your phone off, find a quiet space and let your mind wander.
- Share your initial efforts with your team. What is missing? Involve your clients. Why do they use you? Add their feedback to your positioning statement.
- Your positioning statement can be a series of flip chart sheets, a mind map, a text document etc. But it has to be easy to work from and easy to understand.
- Ensure your positioning statement is kept up-to-date as you make changes and improvements to your business, gain new awards, accreditations etc.
- When you have created your positioning statement, review your marketing communications and website in the light of the benefits you have captured. Have you been seriously underselling yourself? How many crucial benefits are missing?

Masterclass 3
Why It Pays to Locate and Research Your Target Audience

In this masterclass you will learn:

- The benefits of taking a targeted approach to your potential clients.
- How to research your target audiences effectively.
- The best ways to reach your target audiences.

One Saturday several months ago I received a call on my mobile phone. On the other end was Deenna who explained that she had launched an upmarket fashion boutique in Wales specialising in selling designer clothing, accessories and good quality jewellery. As a qualified colour and style consultant, Deenna was also offering first-class style advice to her customers. Keen to build her clientele, she was considering a leaflet drop encompassing all the homes in her local geographic area. However, after reading the tips in my first book on the importance of taking a targeted approach when marketing your business, she had decided to ring me for advice. We will revisit how Deenna changed her marketing activities as a result of that call later in the masterclass, but before that let's look at how a targeted approach to your marketing can be achieved.

Probably the most important marketing activity for your business, and indeed all businesses, is that of identifying your target audiences. Once these audiences have been identified it will be necessary to learn more about them by conducting some practical research. Not until you have accomplished these straightforward tasks can your marketing communications be constructed with confidence, accuracy, relevance and flair. And yet, although it is a crucial step towards marketing success, the process of defining and then researching target audiences is often one that is skipped by many small business owners.

So in this masterclass we're going to look at how you can identify and research your target audiences on a step-by-step basis, with case studies to illustrate what can happen when this process is followed.

Let's start by looking at some of the pitfalls that can be encountered when trying to sell with no specific audience in mind.

1. The marketing budget is often drained with little to show for it. By relying on very general advertising etc., the business owner is employing a tactic similar to throwing mud at a wall and hoping some of it sticks!

2. Some of the customers that are attracted can be far from ideal. In the absence of a targeted plan the new clients may turn out to be low profit and resource draining, rather than the lucrative and high value clients hoped for.

3. The lack of business focus can quite quickly sap the morale and the energy of the business owner and this can start a downward spiral. The business owner doesn't know who to target and so consequently does not know where to start. This can lead to panic spending – investing more money on non-specific and ineffective marketing activities, the lack of sales from which can further demoralise the business owner.

4. The marketing communications used to promote the business will lack focus and clarity too, and this can render them ineffective. For example, a decent chunk of money may have been invested in designing and building a website, with even more money spent on optimising it. But if the messages greeting a visitor are generic and intangible, they will lack the depth and relevance necessary to maintain the visitor's interest.

Let's compare those pitfalls with the benefits a business can enjoy by taking a highly targeted approach.

1. Businesses that know who they want to reach can invest their energies and resources on targeting only these specific groups. Consequently they are likely to fare much better in a challenging economy and will be more robust and resilient to knocks than any competitor operating a non-targeted approach.

2. By targeting specific groups, the business builds expertise and experience and is regarded as a specialist in these particular areas. Warm prospects will be attracted on the strength of this reputation.

3. Marketing the business becomes manageable. The business has focus clarity and direction and, as a result, the time and money being spent on marketing is channelled in the right direction.

4. The marketing collateral of the business – website, newsletters, blogs, brochures, flyers etc. is effective at converting cold prospects into warm leads and clients. Investment in business generating activities, such as telemarketing and search engine optimisation, is usually money well spent as the messages with which the prospect is greeted are relevant, clear and focused.

So you want to successfully reach your target audiences. Where do you start?

This is a two stage process. In the first stage you identify the groups that you want to reach and analyse them sufficiently to determine whether these groups warrant your time and energy in proactively marketing to them.

The second stage involves some practical research. You want to focus on understanding the needs of your target groups and how you can best place yourself to meet them.

This process can seem a little daunting and you may find it challenging to obtain answers to all the questions that are asked within each stage. However, don't worry if this is the case. By working through each stage the best you can, you will gather a body of really useful information. Every question does not need to be answered in order for the overall exercise to be useful. Any information that you can gather about your target audiences will help you to market your business to them effectively. And, as researching target audiences is a process that many small businesses fail to carry out, you are likely to be in a stronger position to convert your prospects into paying customers than your competitors.

So, let's look at the first of this two stage process in detail:

Stage One – Identifying Your Target Audience

Consider and document the type of customer group that your business will appeal to, e.g. dentists, accountants, local schools, hotels . . .

Beside each group, write down the reasons why you believe your business will appeal to them and why you should consider targeting them with your marketing communications. For example, do you have experience, qualifications or expertise that will be of value? Do you know some useful contacts that can help introduce you to this group? Do you have a strong reputation in the media, at exhibitions and on-line with this group? Write down every reason that you can think of.

The smaller each target group, the more manageable it becomes to reach them. This is especially important if you have limited resources or time for marketing. Therefore, in order to restrict the size of each group, consider the following options:

- Do you wish to place a geographical restriction? Will you only be targeting certain postcodes, towns, counties etc.?
- Do you only want to target businesses of a certain size? Is the number of employees, the number of partners, the annual turnover important?
- Can you further restrict the number of prospects in a group by being more specific about their type of business? For example, if you were targeting schools in a particular postcode area you may wish to refine your audience further still by either excluding or including primary schools, nursery schools, church schools and private schools. Spending time considering the detail of what constitutes your ideal customer in each group will help you to recognise the organisations that you want to reach and those that you don't.

It's time now to go into greater detail for each group. It's unlikely that you will be able to target every single group, especially if you're responsible for marketing your business with little or no help from others. Your ultimate goal may be to target every single prospect in every single group but, in order for your marketing to be manageable and to avoid overspending, I would encourage you to start by targeting only your priority businesses or individuals, regardless of which group they belong to. This will enable you to evaluate the success of your initial marketing campaigns and make improvements before rolling out further.

When considering your target audience, do not exclude strategic partners or introducers. These people may not buy from you directly but can carry influence in recommending you to their own customers or business acquaintances. For example, as well as marketing directly to businesses, an accountant could also build relationships with commercial insurance brokers, solicitors and independent financial advisers with the aim of being introduced to their client base. The type of organisations that could become useful strategic partners for your business very much depends upon what you do for a living. For a marketer, strategic partners could include designers, copywriters, web developers, search engine optimisation specialists and social media consultants. For a beautician, strategic partners could encompass hairdressers, nail technicians, style advisers, wedding organisers, photographers and fashion boutiques. Consider too whether any membership organisations or trade associations could be of value to you in this way.

Stage Two – Researching Your Target Audience

As a young marketer I failed to realise the importance of research and consequently some of my early campaigns were a little hit and miss. By relying on intuition and guesswork, rather than hard facts and research, my sales messages were not always as relevant and specific as they needed to be. As I grew in experience, however, I realised the importance of getting to know my target audience before sending out my marketing communications. Here are some suggestions of how you can gather a little more information about your own target audiences and so understand them better.

- Search on-line for forums or blogs that your target audiences may belong to. You may wish to join a forum yourself and ask questions that will help you better appreciate the needs of the forum members. Obviously you will not receive a warm reception if you start to peddle your wares, but if you make it clear that you are purely interested in understanding more about how you can shape your offering to better match their requirements you should find some people that are happy to help. Alternatively, you can pick up information simply from studying the topics and the responses of the forum posts.
- Subscribe to the printed publications that your target audiences read. Again, use the Internet to search for the relevant magazines or enquire whether your local library has a list of publications. By studying each publication in detail you will build a very good understanding of the topics that interest your audience. This can only help when you begin marketing to them in earnest.
- Study your competitors to see if there is anything that you can learn from their approach.
- Find the contact details of 15 to 20 businesses you would like to do business with, and then pick up the phone and call them. You may not like the sound of this but if you're polite and explain that you're simply ringing to book a convenient time to ask a few questions, you are likely to be given a fair hearing. For example, a few weeks ago I contacted 25 commercial vehicle bodybuilders, a target audience of one of my clients, Rosmia, a vehicle improvement specialist. Because we had not marketed to this sector before, the purpose of each call was not to sell Rosmia's services but to find out more about each bodybuilder's present arrangements. I was also interested in finding out if they were currently

working with any of our competitors. Without this information it would have been difficult to market to this group accurately. I made 25 calls, managed to speak to 15 decision-makers and did not encounter any hostility or resistance. Don't assume that people will not want to talk to you. On occasions you may be asked to send in an email detailing your questions but don't assume that this is just a ruse to get you off the phone. It may be the case sometimes but, on other occasions, you may be pleasantly surprised at the answers you receive.

- If possible, arrange a one-to-one meeting with your prospects in which you can discuss what they would require from your product or service to improve their current situation. These meetings are usually easier to arrange if the prospects have been introduced to you by one of your networking peers or if you have built a relationship with a membership organisation or an individual on social media. Be flexible with arrangements. This person is giving you their time so fit in with their agenda. Be ready to attend a meeting at any time of the working day or evening. Be well prepared, rehearsed and equipped to record every important detail. Make it clear that you are only after 30 minutes of their time and are interested only in understanding their needs. Don't underestimate people's willingness to help you once they know you are not trying to sell to them.

- If your target audience belongs to a membership organisation or group, find out if they have events, rallies, exhibitions, seminars and conferences and how feasible it is for you to attend any. For example, Mike Collins the MD of AccountAssyst, an on-line credit management system, asked to attend the regional member meetings of the British Promotional Merchandise Association (BPMA). Mike was hoping to market AccountAssyst to BPMA members and being able to chat informally to his target audience at these events was of huge value. Mike was able to understand firsthand the frustrations that many members were experiencing with their existing credit management processes and could therefore see how AccountAssyst would help resolve many of these problems and frustrations.

So what information should you look to collect as part of your target audience research?

Try to establish who makes the decision to buy and who influences the decision-making process. This will vary depending on the size of organisation you're looking to target. In a small organisation, it may well be that the managing director or owner is the only person involved in making such a decision. In a larger organisation it is more likely that a number of people play a part.

Can you determine the arrangements that may already be in place for what you sell? If an organisation has a strong need for your products, it is likely that they will already be receiving them from another source.

If the organisations you're targeting are already using the types of products or services that you provide, how straightforward will it be for them to move to you? For some businesses it may be very straightforward because there are no contractual agreements and they feel little loyalty to their existing provider. For others, however, there may be contractual barriers. This information can influence how you market yourself to the organisation. If a contract is in place you will need to bide your time, your emphasis being on building a relationship with the organisation over the remaining period of the contract. Rushing in and trying to acquire a commitment when an organisation has recently renewed a contract with a competitor would be a waste of time and energy.

Determine what might be preventing each organisation from doing business with you by establishing what really matters to them when buying the products or services you supply. Do you lack experience in an area that is particularly relevant to a certain group of businesses? Are you under-qualified? Is your business too small? Would you need to partner another business to service these organisations to the standard required? Are you unable or unwilling to match their price requirements?

Don't be disheartened if, after carrying out this research, you decide to rule yourself out for one of these reasons. Ask yourself "What are the deep underlying needs of these businesses and how can I meet them?" Document the needs that you identify and be honest about your ability to meet them. Again, this may lead you to eliminate some organisations from your target audience list because you recognise that your business would struggle to meet their requirements satisfactorily. Alternatively, you may decide to make improvements to your own business or form alliances with other businesses in order to be able to offer the services that your target audience is looking for.

Having worked through this process you will have emerged with a valuable core of information and intelligence on the organisations that you want to target. This information will be the bedrock of your future marketing. You will understand which organisations you should target, which aspects of your offering will appeal to them most, and how to make your communications accurate, relevant and specific.

Building Lists of Your Target Audiences

So with all this information to hand, your next step is to find out how you can reach a greater number of your target audiences beyond the handful of names you used for your market research. You may decide that you want to target all the dentist practices with an annual turnover of over £250,000 based within a 20 mile radius of your premises, but how do you actually discover the names and addresses of the practices that fit these criteria?

Let's look at how you can access list data.

- The Direct Marketing Association website (www.dma.org.uk) contains the details of DMA organisations that supply mailing lists. These lists can usually be obtained on a single or multiple use basis. Before deciding which list provider to choose, and the selection criteria for your data, read the tips on buying and renting lists in Masterclasses 8 and 10. Other considerations when choosing your list supplier include: Does the list supplier require a high minimum order of several thousand records? If so, this provider may not be appropriate for small businesses.
- Speak to several data providers comparing the service they are offering, the quality of their data, how they source their data and keep it up to date, their accuracy guarantees and costs. Some will provide special offers for new clients. Read the terms and conditions very carefully so that you are fully aware of what you're paying for and any limitations of use. Infringing these T&Cs may incur a fine. Ask for any quotations for buying or renting data, and the terms and conditions under which the data can be used to be provided in writing.

- Request a small sample of free data – half a dozen records so that you can check on the accuracy and quality of what they're supplying before you place an order.
- Don't let any special offers tempt you into buying more data than you actually need. Keep your target audiences at the front of your mind when specifying the data you need.
- If this is the first time that you're marketing to these particular groups, only purchase a relatively small number of names. It is advisable to measure the impact of your mailing against just a few hundred names before deciding whether the response level warrants the purchase of a greater number of names within that target group. If the response level is encouraging, you can purchase further data in the knowledge that this particular target group is receptive to your offering. If the response level is poor, you will not have wasted too much money on a list of names in a group of businesses that are not interested in your product or service.

When you've decided on your list provider, don't buy the data until you're ready to market to the list. Data ages quickly and, if you purchase a list but do not use it for several weeks, some of the data will be out of date by the time you start mailing.

The Internet is a rich resource for finding details of your target audiences and you may not have to buy or rent a ready-made prospect list from a third party provider at all. For example, I recently wanted to send a mailing to all the caravan clubs in the UK but had no details. Within a few hours of searching the Internet, I had built a list of 200 clubs. This information was further enhanced by calling each club and asking for the name and contact details of the person we should introduce our business to. A high quality list had been created that had cost nothing but time.

Most libraries in the larger towns include a well-stocked "Business Section." Ask your library if they also offer a list building service. The library I use provides a list building service at a very reasonable cost and many other UK libraries offer a similar service.

Let's conclude this masterclass by looking at the improved fortunes experienced by three very different businesses after they adopted a targeted approach to their marketing.

The Florist

David Costa, the MD of established florist, Flowers Unlimited, wanted to become much more proactive with his marketing. He had grown a successful business that included a large corporate account, some small business accounts and hundreds of local people using him regularly to send flowers to family and friends on special occasions. However, his business had grown primarily through word-of-mouth recommendation, something that he recognised was insufficient if he wanted to expand and take on more staff. He recognised that he needed to generate awareness of what he could offer to those audiences that he was not currently marketing to proactively.

He began the process by considering the types of organisations that had a regular need for his services. His list included:

1. **Between 20 and 30 new local corporate clients to target within 12 months.** David decided to target dentists, solicitors, accountants, serviced offices, design and marketing agencies – businesses that he knew usually offered a reception area in which a striking or unusual floral display could be displayed. After applying annual turnover and number of employee restrictions, he arrived at a list of 200 cold prospects in four local postcode areas.
2. **Large hotels within his town.** He drew up a list of seven independent hotels that he wanted to target. These were hotels that he knew, from personal visits, invested in striking floral displays that were replaced on a weekly basis.
3. **Premium motor dealerships in his home town and six surrounding towns.** Because David was already supplying flowers regularly to one of the motor brands, he understood their requirements and the level of budget they would have to work to. He selected the upmarket dealerships – Mercedes, BMW, Porsche, Jaguar etc.
4. **Funeral directors based in his town and the two towns closest to the shop.** David was already supplying flowers to one local funeral director and so had a good understanding of their requirements too.

With his target audiences identified, David employed a student from the local university to research each different group. She did this by examining the websites of some of the organisations and by calling others on the telephone. It became clear from the research that, although each group had the same underlying need for fresh, attractive and

(Continued)

competitively priced flower arrangements, they each had different requirements too. For example, funeral directors were especially interested in:

- **100% reliability and 100% accuracy.** When flowers are being provided for a funeral, there is absolutely no tolerance for lateness or error whereas, for a hotel, delivering the flowers for the reception display half an hour later than agreed is unlikely to cause a catastrophe.
- **Consistency.** A funeral director is often asked to recommend a florist and, when doing so, they have to be certain that the floral arrangement will be of the same high standards each time. The team had recently completed their Interflora floristry certificate, which included "single ended spray" training in order to guarantee absolute precision and accuracy when creating bouquets and displays for funerals. For a grieving relative or friend, ensuring the display they select from the photo is exactly the same as the one that is delivered is crucial. For a small business or hotel, replacing one type of flower with another is not so important.

Having read this case study, consider the following for your own business:

1. Have you been overlooking the potential of specific local target audiences? Could you generate local business by establishing the types of businesses that will have a need for your services, and then targeting them specifically in your marketing communications?
2. Could you benefit from the additional help of a student or a person returning to work? Would those extra few hours enable you to complete the necessary research into your target audiences? Completing that research can determine whether marketing messages are accurate and specific, or come across as generic and vague. If you cannot find the time to complete the research yourself, it may well be worth considering extra help.
3. Are you aware that it is unlikely that the groups you want to target share the same needs? Can your marketing messages be adjusted to take account of these varying requirements and so be even more specific and relevant?

The Fashion Boutique

So What Happened to Deenna?

The challenge for Deenna was that she was selling beautiful but expensive women's clothing in a predominantly low income area. She had advertised in a local paper which had only a limited impact and, at the point of calling me, she was seriously considering a leaflet drop in the local area. Instead, we spent a day together and identified the following target audiences:

1. Women that were losing or had recently lost weight. Such women would be in need of replacing a large percentage of their wardrobe and would welcome professional style advice to make the very best of their new shape. They would usually be willing to treat themselves to a number of new items of clothing and, even if on a tight budget, would be keen to buy at least one special outfit to celebrate their weight loss. (Group 1)
2. Affluent women – the "ladies that lunch" brigade. These would be image-conscious women, with time on their hands to spend socialising, going to the gym, playing golf and frequenting cafes and restaurants. This group would be happy to spend money on beauty treatments and have the money to spend on good quality and stylish clothing. (Group 2)
3. Professional women for whom looking stylish and well groomed was essential. These women would often be called upon to attend functions in the evening and would need to move almost straight from the working day into the working evening. For these women a capsule wardrobe, centred on a few good quality items, combined with qualified style advice, would be highly desirable. (Group 3)
4. Existing customers. This group would hold both those customers that would call into the boutique virtually every week and those that had not visited for some time. (Group 4)

How Were These Groups Found?

- **Group 1.** Deenna contacted the most prominent local weight loss groups in the area. After an initial meeting with the instructors a number of fashion shows were arranged, both at the boutique itself and off-site at special events, supporting local charities. As hoped for, these fashion shows appealed to many members and were well attended.

(Continued)

- **Group 2.** Deenna approached the lady captain at the local golf club and arranged a fashion show at the golf club, inviting each member to visit the boutique to receive some free personal style advice. This also proved to be very successful, with several members visiting and buying clothes. Deenna also approached the deluxe beauticians and hair salons in the local area, inviting them to a series of open evenings at the boutique at which they would be able to enjoy a relaxing time browsing the latest fashions. She also encouraged them to invite their customers. In return, their services were promoted at the boutique on these open evenings. These events were very well attended.

- **Group 3.** Deenna contacted a local legal practice and invited the female employees to an exclusive fashion and style evening at the boutique. Very cleverly Deenna also offered to style the local female MP. The MP was pictured in several local publications which yielded much positive PR in the local papers.

- **Group 4.** Deenna launched a newsletter, and included in it offers to encourage existing customers to visit the boutique more often with previews of new stock. The newsletter performed the task of reminding those customers that the boutique was still there and well worth a visit, as well as providing the incentive to pop in. A customer referral campaign was launched, asking the customer to "recommend your best friend" or "recommend us to a stylish female relative".

The feedback I received from Deenna was that within six weeks of implementing her targeted approach she had enjoyed hundreds of new customers visiting her boutique. She explained that the biggest investment had been that of her time which was taken up with organising the fashion shows and style evenings. The original planned leaflet drop was abandoned; this would have cost several hundred pounds and would have included households unlikely to have the budget to spend at the boutique.

Using Deenna's case study, consider the following for your own business:

1. Are you overlooking the benefits of partnering with other businesses in order to reach their customers?
2. Don't forget the importance of communicating with your existing or lapsed customers. Include these customers when drawing up your target audience plan. You may want to segment your existing customers into different groups based

on the value they deliver to your business, their loyalty and how much you actually value them as a customer. Some customers will have a much higher lifetime value than others. Not all customers are equal. Some warrant more attention, time and care than others so don't be afraid to segment them. Doing this should enable you to focus your attention on those customers that really matter to you.

3. Are there any high profile potential customers in your local area that you can offer a discounted or free service to, in exchange for them endorsing you and using the opportunity for you both to benefit from PR coverage?

4. Identify the different needs of your target audiences. The women that were losing weight had very different needs to the solicitors. Although the underlying needs of Deenna's entire target audiences are to look and feel good, they all have different motivations when it comes to actually purchasing. Try to tap into those motivations.

The On-Line Credit Management Specialist

As mentioned earlier, AccountAssyst is an on-line credit management system, aimed at businesses selling products or services to other businesses. Ideal target clients are businesses with an annual turnover of up to £3m that are vulnerable to suffering from bad debt. This could be because their debtors can switch quite easily to another business offering the same service, or the services being provided are not essential to the day-to-day running of the debtor's business. In either case, there will be little impact on the debtor's business if the supplier cuts them off. As part of the target audience exercise several groups were identified, two of which were:

1. **Businesses that specialise in selling promotional gifts and corporate clothing**. Historically, these businesses suffer high levels of bad debt. Any system that could reduce bad debt should be well received by this audience group.

2. **Trade associations and Chambers of Commerce** representing businesses doing business with other businesses. As the leading membership association for businesses specialising in selling promotional gifts and corporate clothing, the British Promotional Merchandise Association (BPMA) was to be approached, as would the Bradford Chamber of Commerce (BCC). The aim in both cases was that the BPMA and the BCC would endorse the system and recommend it to their small business members.

(Continued)

If this worked successfully, the system could then be rolled out to other Chambers of Commerce and trade associations.

Before the trade associations and Chambers of Commerce were approached, an experienced telephone researcher was brought in to learn about the problems that a selected number of businesses from the target audience groups were experiencing with unpaid debts. She started by contacting businesses selling promotional gifts and corporate clothing but found that even though she was not trying to sell AccountAssyst on her calls, the business owners were unwilling to talk about their credit management policies or the issues they had with customer debts. Although these businesses had a strong need for more effective credit management processes, they were not going to admit it! However, when she approached the members of the BPMA as a recommended partner of the association (the same target audiences she had been calling on the phone), not only would they talk freely about their problems, over 70% expressed an interest in having a demonstration of the system. This was achieved on the back of just one telephone call and a follow-up email. The endorsement of the BPMA was pivotal in persuading members to open up and express their interest. It opened the door to a dialogue.

The experience was exactly the same with members of the Bradford Chamber of Commerce. Because AccountAssyst was promoted in the Chamber newsletters and magazines, it meant that, when a phone call was made to a member, most responded positively to the questions being asked and many went on to express an interest in a demonstration of the system.

Using the AccountAssyst case study consider the following for your business:

1. When you have drawn up your list of target audiences, spend a little time on researching the membership associations, Chambers of Commerce, trade organisations and even interest groups that they may belong to. Within this list could be several important introducers or strategic partners.
2. Within your list of priority target audiences, ascertain how open each group is to communicating with you and whether you will need to market your product or services via an introducer or strategic partner. In my experience, you may find that you receive a good reaction irrespective of the approach you take and that's great. But, as with AccountAssyst, you may find that the only way to successfully

reach and convert organisations within some of your target groups is through the endorsement or introduction of a third party connected with and respected by the group. Until you uncover any such barriers through your research, you won't know this.

Identifying your target audiences is definitely the most important part of your marketing plan. Although some hard work is involved, once those audiences have been established they should be used to determine every step you take with regard to marketing your business.

Masterclass Summary

- If you try to sell to everybody you can attract the wrong type of customer and drain your marketing budget with little to show for it.
- Think about the types of customer you want to target.
- Be clear on the reasons why these potential customers would want to do business with you.
- Consider restrictions you want to place on your targeting e.g. excluding some postcode areas, only targeting businesses of a certain size.
- Consider the vital role that strategic partners, introducers, trade associations etc. can play in promoting your business to your target audiences.
- What can you learn from your competitors? Ten minutes spent on each competitor's website can yield valuable information.
- Compile a small contact list. Pick up the phone for that crucial and revealing grass roots research.
- Build a detailed picture of your target audiences including the decision-makers and influencers.
- There may be existing contractual arrangements or barriers to a sale. You might have to play a waiting game.
- Only buy or rent lists from reputable list providers. Compare services, ask for a free sample and scrutinise the terms and conditions.
- Use the Internet to collate lists.
- Consider what you can learn from the three case studies and apply to your business.

Masterclass 4
How to Write Copy that Sells

In this masterclass you will learn:

- Why your sales communications play a vital part in the sales process.
- The best tips to help you to write sales communications that are engaging and charming.
- How to review and improve your existing communications.

Your sales communications play an important part in promoting and growing your business, acting as powerful ambassadors for your brand and building trust with customers and prospects alike. A sales letter eloquently describing the benefits your business has to offer can ensure that you receive a warm reception when you next contact the recipient. A well-written, thoughtful and targeted communication, sent as a follow-up to a telephone conversation can be instrumental in closing a sale. You can't be in front of every prospect or every customer representing your business face-to-face, so you have to rely on your sales communications to carry the torch and deliver the right impact.

And yet, despite their many advantages, sales communications are often treated as being of relatively little importance, with the task of copywriting being delegated to the office junior. The lack of priority afforded to sales communications is then reflected in the quality of those produced, and many can end up being little more than paragraphs of text taken from the website or brochure. When communications are written with a lack of care and attention to detail, any chance of generating feelings of goodwill towards a business are lost. The response from customers and prospects will not be good and, as a result, the business owner can be tempted to conclude that written communications no longer work.

But they do.

If people are interested in buying, they want to be sold to. You can't afford to treat your sales communications with disdain. They have to be clear, concise, attractive and benefit driven. If a prospect requests information after seeing your advert or visiting your website and you follow up with a hastily scrambled sales letter or email, rather than building on that initial interest, you will risk stopping it in its tracks.

In order to write sales communications that sell, you need to know who you're selling to and how you can meet their needs. (Masterclasses 2 and 3 will help you to compile this information.) Your communications need to be specific and engaging. There is no room for bland or generic statements; leave those to your competitors.

Your Copywriting Planning Guide

Before starting to write your next sales letter, newsletter, flyer or brochure, read the following Copywriting Planning Guide to establish the foundations of the communication. It will help you to focus on your audience, on the messages that will encourage them to respond, and on what you would like them to do. Once you have determined what to include in your communication, writing the actual content should be a relatively straightforward task.

1. **Who am I writing to (my target audience)?**
   - Cold prospects – with no awareness of our business.
   - Warm prospects – they have some interest and awareness of our business but are yet to buy.
   - Lapsed clients – we have had a trading relationship in the past.
   - Existing clients.
   - VIP existing clients – treated as VIPs because of the value of the relationship.
   - Strategic partners – they have the potential to introduce clients to us.

2. **What do I know about each one of my target audience groups?**
   - How do they arrive at the decision to buy (or recommend me)?
   - Why would a cold prospect buy from me?
   - Why would an existing customer continue to buy from me?
   - What are the deep underlying needs of each audience group for what I am offering?
   - What might deter cold or warm prospects from forming a relationship with me?
   - What competitors are operating in my field?

3. **What do I want my communication to achieve?**
   - Generate enquiries for our new products/services?
   - Generate orders for our new product/service?
   - Encourage sign-up to my blog?

- Stimulate interest in our new website?
- Create awareness and interest in preparation for a follow-up telephone call?
- Sell places at our seminar/networking event?
- Am I being realistic with my objectives? (Consider the relationship you have with the recipient of the communication and set your expectations of what you want to achieve from this communication accordingly.)

4. **What are the compelling messages my communication should include if my objectives are to be achieved?**
   - How can I adequately convey our experience and expertise?
   - What are the benefits that I should focus on and why? (Revisit your positioning statement for inspiration.)
   - Will I add more credibility to my message if I include client case studies?
   - Can I include unedited customer testimonial or third party endorsements?
   - Are there impressive facts and figures that I can use to underpin the benefits I am showcasing?
   - Do I have any qualifications, accreditations and expertise that should be included?
   - Can I include any evidence that our offering is superior to competitors?
   - How can I confidently address the barriers that could prevent this person from wanting to do business with us?
   - Would including any tables, graphs or comparison charts better highlight the benefits we offer?

5. **Would it be appropriate to include a special offer in this communication?** (If you decide that a special offer would work, please read the tips in Masterclass 6.)

6. **What is my call to action?** Do I want the recipient to call me, make an appointment, visit my website, contact our local representative, visit our exhibition stand or simply send an email expressing an initial interest?

When you have worked through this guide, spend a few minutes reading your responses. Are there any areas that you feel are weak and that could benefit from some more research? Are you now confident that you can begin writing? Be inspired by other communications too. I keep dozens of samples of literature that have been sent to me or that I have picked up on my travels. I will often refer to some of these, making a note of what I like (and don't like), what's relevant to the sales communication I am writing and what I feel I can improve on. You may find it useful to save examples of good and bad sales literature yourself and to refer to them when at the early copywriting stage of gathering ideas. Similarly, rather than deleting emails you don't like, print the ones that irritate you and those that motivate you to respond. When a newsletter or sales letter is sent to you that you really like, keep it. Make notes on each one about what appealed to you and what put you off. This can help you develop ideas before you begin writing your own sales communications.

Reviewing Your Existing Communications

If you want to perform a swift but effective appraisal of your existing communications, the following will help you to decide whether it is time to scrap or improve!

1. Read the communication out loud. How does it sound?
2. How current is the communication? Are any of the services, products, prices, or team members you mention outdated or inaccurate?
3. What's missing? Have you undersold any benefits? Did you forget to include information about your accreditations and qualifications?
4. Does the communication include chunks of text that you have copied from other communications to save time, or is it projecting a truly relevant and targeted message?
5. Has the communication achieved its objectives? If its purpose was to generate leads, to build the loyalty of existing customers, to generate immediate sales, did it succeed?

Be bold and decisive. If on the strength of this exercise you conclude that the communication is no longer fit for purpose, ditch it.

The Content – Some Copywriting Tips

Having worked through this process, it is time now to write the communication. Here are some proven tips that will help you come up with some sparkling material:

1. Find the "Write" Space and Time

It's unlikely that you will be able to write a killer sales letter, a brilliant newsletter or an engaging case study if you have begrudgingly allocated a few minutes in an area of your office or home that is awash with distractions. Instead, take this exercise seriously. Allow sufficient time to complete the task comfortably, and find a part of your working environment that's free from disturbance or interference in which to do so.

The time spent on copywriting should be divided into three stages; the first is the "ideas" stage. As you work your way through The Copywriting Planning Guide, or the tips on reviewing your existing communications, capture your ideas as they occur and pull out those samples mentioned previously.

The second stage covers the actual writing. Whilst I can't say how long it will take to write the first draft of your sales communication, I can reassure you that as you begin writing and your confidence grows, the time you spend on each communication will reduce. At this stage, don't worry about the length of the communication. It's more important that you write freely using the ideas recorded in stage one to guide you so that your content is relevant and aligned to the needs of your audience.

The third stage is the editing stage. At this point you take your red pen to your communication and run through it meticulously, rooting out spelling and grammatical errors, removing any waffle or repetitive text, and double checking that the message you want to convey is clear and concisely presented.

Copywriting should not be rushed. It requires your full concentration. So allocate sufficient time in your diary and find that quiet space in which to work.

2. Forget the B2B and B2C Distinctions

Your writing style does not need to change based on whether you are writing to business people or directly to consumers. Don't think B2B (Business to Business) or B2C (Business to Consumer) when writing, instead think M2Y (Me to You). At the end of each communication is a human being reading your message.

3. Write for Your Reader

Although this has been covered throughout this book, it's such an important subject that I hope you don't mind me covering it here too! Your communication should be full of references to "you" and "your" with far fewer references to "we," "us" and "our." When you have written the first draft of your sales communication, circle the references to "we," "us" and "our" and consider how you can rephrase those sentences to include "you" and "your" as the preferred alternatives. In this example I have taken a paragraph from a letter I wrote to a selection of headmasters, marketing my client's free music sessions. As you can see, there are only two references to "we" but seven references to "your."

How can we work with your school?

At no charge we can:

- **Offer free musical workshops** at your school, morning or afternoon. These can be included within your specific activity weeks or at other times within your school term.
- **Run free musical sessions** within your school assembly. Every tutor has been CRB checked and they come with bags of enthusiasm too.
- **Work with your PTA** at events such as your school fetes, offering free taster sessions.

Now look at how the copy becomes impersonal when I rewrite it with "we" as the dominant phrase, and remove the previous references to "you" and "your."

How do we work with schools?

At no charge we can:

- **Offer free musical workshops** which we can run in the morning or afternoon. We can include these in a school's specific activity weeks or at other times within the school term.
- **Run free musical sessions.** We often run these in the school assembly. Every tutor has been CRB checked and they come with bags of enthusiasm too.

- **Work with a school's PTA** at events such as school fetes, offering free taster sessions.

4. Be Friendly and Conversational

Try to avoid writing in a style that may come across as pompous or boastful to the reader. For example:

"Established for over 15 years, we are the leading independent recruitment agency in the South of England and beyond. YourRecruit can boast exceptionally competitive fees . . ."

This may be true, but the style is a little self-satisfied. Much better instead to write in a conversational and friendly way and, in doing so, draw your reader closer to you. Don't irritate them by overplaying your successes but instead explain how your success can benefit them as follows:

"If you're recruiting in the South East or nationally but don't have a big budget, we can help you! YourRecruit is an independent recruitment agency with over 15 years' experience, recruiting talented people for businesses like yours."

Read your sales communication out loud at each stage of writing. Doing so will allow you to "hear" the tone of your writing and help identify whether you're achieving the friendly and informative style you are aiming for.

5. Talk about Benefits and Features

A feature is a fact about your product or service. The benefit is how your customer gains from that feature. Wherever possible include both features and benefits in your communication and link them together. The feature often adds extra credibility to the benefit. For example:

"K-Seal is a one-step permanent coolant leak repair product for motor vehicles." (Feature) "You just shake the bottle; pour it into the cooling system and drive. A repair made with K-Seal is guaranteed for the lifetime of the engine." (Benefits)

"Our promotional mouse mats are made from recycled material and measure 15cm × 15cm." (Features) "This means they are environmentally friendly, small enough to be enclosed in an A4 envelope but large enough to advertise your marketing messages." (Benefits)

When writing about the features of your product or service, consider the benefits that accompany each feature and include them in your sales communication.

6. Don't Become Sidetracked Searching for a Unique Selling Point if You Don't Have One

When writing this masterclass, I received a newsletter from a local business in which there was an article including the sentence "what makes our business unique is that we are fanatical about delivering fantastic customer service." I doubt very much that the delivery of fantastic customer service is a unique selling point, given that millions of other businesses are similarly keen to do just that. It is a fallacy that all small businesses need to find a USP in order to stand out from the crowd and it's often this mistaken belief that encourages a business owner to come up with disingenuous statements in their marketing literature, such as the one above. Don't become hung up on finding your unique selling point if in reality you don't have one. Your customers won't respect you for claiming unique selling points which are anything but. It is much better instead to focus on communicating your features and benefits clearly and concisely, and delivering these in that friendly and conversational voice.

7. You Can Write Long Copy as Well as Short Copy

Is it true that you should only write a few paragraphs because "nobody reads any more?" No. When a person is genuinely interested in finding out more about what you offer, and wants to know how they can benefit, long copy can be very effective. In fact, in most copywriting tests it tends to outperform short copy. The principle is the same, however, whether writing a short or long communication; it should be well-written and relevant. There is a greater risk with a long communication that it can deteriorate into a rambling, long-winded and repetitive piece, and ruthless editing is therefore particularly important. Decide what you feel is the most appropriate length for the specific communication that you are writing. If you are sending out a covering letter to accompany your newsletter or brochure, a few hundred words may be sufficient. If issuing a sales letter to announce a new product or service, however, you may need several paragraphs to explain fully the features and benefits now on offer. Do not be afraid of writing long copy if the communication demands it.

8. Are You Asking Questions?

When you're standing in front of a prospect you can build rapport through your body language, your tone of voice and by expressing a genuine interest in that person. With a written communication, holding the attention of your reader is much more of a challenge. You can arouse your reader's interest by asking questions periodically throughout the communication. A question provides the reader with an opportunity to pause and take stock, to reflect on the point you're making, the benefit you're revealing. You can even grab their attention immediately by asking a question in the very first sentence:

> "When did you last attend a workshop that really motivated you?"
> "If you could make one change to your marketing today, what would it be?"
> "If you were given a budget of £1000 to spend on improving your website, where would you start?"

To stimulate your reader to think about the different messages and benefits within your communication, ask a question as though you were standing in front of them. For example:

> "Can you see how this would benefit your business?"
> "Is this something that would be of interest to you?"
> "How does that sound to you?"

You can also ask closed questions provided that you are confident that the answer to each one will be an emphatic "Yes."

> "I'm sure you would like to spend less time on administration and more time on sales, wouldn't you?"

> "Am I right in thinking that you would like to reduce the amount of money you're spending on office stationery?"
>
> "Wouldn't you like to have a higher standard of washroom servicing but not pay any more for the privilege?"

Start with a list of the different questions you should include in your sales communications – those that will make the reader think and engage with your message. If, at the editing stage, you realise that you have asked very few questions, identify any statements that could be turned into a question with a few tweaks. "We help you to spend less time on administration and more time on sales" easily becomes a question when you replace "We help you to" with "Would you like to . . .?"

9. Are You Telling a Story?

If you can weave a story into your sales communication, you will generate the interest of your reader by taking them on a journey. From an early age we have been captivated when listening to stories, and including stories in your sales communications will add that extra bit of warmth to the message you want to convey.

For example, if you wanted to promote a particular service in your sales letter, why not tell the story of a customer who has benefited from this service? In this example, a copywriter is telling a story to illustrate his skill at writing copy!

> "I had a phone call today from a customer that really made my day. Stephen was calling to tell me that the sales letter I had written promoting his bookkeeping services to small businesses had been a huge success. He had mailed it to 75 small businesses and, within one day, eight business owners had contacted him to arrange a meeting."

Should you feel that by telling a story in this manner there is the risk of sounding boastful, why not ask the client to tell the story in his own words?

With this in mind, one of my clients recently asked me to interview a selection of his customers to understand why they used his services and why they were loyal to him etc. I asked each customer the following questions, scribbling their answers down, and then transcribing them into individual documents using their words as much as possible. Each customer shared freely and at length, and was later asked to review the story we produced to confirm they were happy with its accuracy and felt that it properly represented their personal relationship with my client.

- Tell me the first words that spring to your mind when I mention the XYZ Company?
- What do you use them for?
- Do they deliver added value? Do you feel that they provide more than you pay for?
- How do they compare to competitors?
- How would you describe their customer care?
- How would you describe your relationship with them?
- Are there individuals in the business that stand out for particular praise?
- If you had to sum the business up in just one sentence what would it be?

The feedback from this straightforward exercise was used to improve the copy on the website and to create a number of new client case studies.

You could begin your story in much the same way that you would tell a traditional tale, for example:

> "Can I tell you a story about one of our longest standing customers, Jean, and why despite being approached many times by competitors, she has never been tempted to leave us? In Jean's own words . . ."

You can also use the same technique to tell your own story, why you founded the business, the values that underpin everything you do.

10. Break It up

If you want your sales communications to be readable you must focus on the layout as well as the copy. Big slabs of text in a tiny typeface are too much like hard work for your readers and so will be skipped over. Break your text up with bullet points, headlines, sub-headlines, and paragraphs to ensure it appears an easy read.

Look at these two pieces of text. The content is exactly the same but you're only likely to want to read one of them.

Here's a solid block of text in tiny type:

I would like to introduce our business, Flowers Unlimited to you because we work with many of the hotels in the Brighton and Hove area, supplying the most exquisite vibrant and fresh floral arrangements that really do meet a wide range of budgets. Who are Flowers Unlimited and how would we work with you? Flowers Unlimited are fanatical about sourcing the most beautiful flowers and luscious foliage so that your arrangements are anything but standard and your clients are never disappointed when you recommend us for their special occasion. Whilst we source contemporary and unusual flowers and foliage from around the world, we also shop in our own backyard, selecting stocks, roses and chrysanthemums from Sussex. But, of course, it's not just about flowers is it? Service is important too. We will replace any bouquet or arrangement you're less than delighted with. We are confident in offering you this guarantee because we select only the highest quality, fresh flowers and store them in a cool room, not a fridge so they don't prematurely wilt when displayed at your hotel. Our floral designers are trained and accredited to the highest standards from luminaries including Jane Packer. They understand the importance of attention to detail and have the flair, skills and creativity to create gorgeous arrangements that fit your requirements and your budget to a tee.

And here's that same text in a larger font and laid out more appealingly:

I would like to introduce our business, Flowers Unlimited to you because we work with many of the hotels in the Brighton and Hove area, *supplying the most exquisite vibrant and fresh floral arrangements that really do meet a wide range of budgets*.

Who are Flowers Unlimited and how would we work with you?

Flowers Unlimited are fanatical about sourcing the most beautiful flowers and luscious foliage so that your arrangements are anything but standard and your clients are *never* disappointed when you recommend us for their special occasion.

Whilst we source contemporary *and* unusual flowers and foliage from around the world, we also shop in our own backyard, selecting stocks, roses and chrysanthemums from Sussex.

But, of course, it's not just about flowers is it? Service is important too.

- **We will replace any bouquet or arrangement you're less than delighted with.** We are confident in offering you this guarantee because we select only the highest quality, fresh flowers and store them in a cool room, not a fridge so they don't prematurely wilt when displayed at your hotel.

- **Our floral designers are trained and accredited to the highest standards from luminaries including Jane Packer.** They understand the importance of attention to detail and have the flair, skills and creativity to create gorgeous arrangements that fit your requirements and budget to a tee.

11. Include Clear and Appropriate Calls to Action

It would be a real shame for you to go to the trouble of presenting a dazzling array of benefits, blended with some thoughtful questions, interesting stories and some arresting facts and figures, only to stop short at the final juncture – the rallying cry that encourages your reader to contact you. Do not assume they will pick up the phone; send an email or sign up for your newsletter if you have not asked them to do so. Spell it out and, when possible, combine your call to action with the benefits they will enjoy by heeding it. Here are a few examples of calls to action I have used for clients.

"To book your complimentary 'Get up and Grow' meeting with one of our small business specialists, please contact the Perrys branch closest to you today."

"This free and comprehensive guide can be ordered by emailing xxxxxx or calling xxxx. It is a must-read if you want to learn more about the tax issues relating to buy to let."

"We would love your feedback on our website. And if you're one of the first ten readers to subscribe to our blog and email your feedback to xxxxxxxx you'll receive a sample of Café du Monde's divine coffee, absolutely free."

"Are you in need of inspiration for your point of sales and partner promotions? Contact us today. We deliver miracles locally, nationally and globally on lean budgets."

"Would you like a free full-size sample? Complete our three question survey now."

"To sign up to our free weekly training tips simply respond to this email with the word "Yes" in the title of the email."

"If you would like a genuine 15% discount on your next order of promotional desktop items, ring Paul Sheldrake on his direct number now."

Don't feel that you're limited to just one call to action in your sales communication. In a newsletter, each article could feature a call to action. Even a sales letter could include a number of different calls.

12. Be a Ruthless Editor!

If the extent of your editing is to rely on spell-check and scanning your screen for obvious mistakes, you run the risk of producing a sales communication that contains a number of grammatical and linguistic errors. Consequently, your compelling message will not be delivered in the way you would like. Don't sabotage a great communication by sending it out containing mistakes that could have been identified and corrected had time been spent on editing. Editing and checking your document at the end of the process is as important as the planning you carry out at the beginning. I always perform at least two document edits on a printed sheet rather than editing on screen.

Other than grammatical considerations, you may also want to bear in mind the following during your final review of your piece:

- Read the communication out loud. Does it flow well or falter in places? Does it sound conversational and friendly, or stilted and starchy?
- Is the language being used a little too technical for the audience? Are you using jargon that the reader will struggle to understand or may become irritated by?
- Have you made the benefits sound attractive and appealing?
- Have you presented the benefits, facts, figures and questions in a logical order?
- Is it clear to the reader what you want them to do next? Is your call to action appropriate for the relationship you currently hold with the reader?
- Pass the communication to a friend or colleague for appraisal. Do they find it interesting?
- Is there anything missing? Is there an argument for including a case study, or some testimonial?
- Is the layout of the communication attractive and easy to read? Does it look professional and welcoming or a little cramped and off-putting?

If you arrive at the conclusion there's more work to be done, this is a good sign – it shows that you are looking at your work critically. Realistically, you should expect to complete more than one draft before you're happy. This does not necessarily mean rewriting your document each time, but it may include identifying further tweaks in order to refine it, changing the odd word here and there or polishing your punctuation.

Look upon the editing process as time well spent. It may seem a little wearisome and to be adding a delay to you getting your message out there, but these final tweaks can be vital in the success or otherwise of your marketing communication. Once editing has been completed you should be left with a relevant, attractive and well-written document that your reader will appreciate and respond to.

I hope you feel after studying this masterclass that the time you lavish on planning, writing and editing your sales communications is time well spent.

Masterclass Summary

- Before embarking on writing your sales communications ensure that you understand your audience, their needs and objections.
- Craft relevant communications that are rich in benefits using The Copywriting Planning Guide.
- Review your existing communications. Are they suffering from a lack of care?
- Allow yourself time, free from distraction to plan and write your communications.
- Remember that a person, not a brand will be reading your communication.
- Replace references to "we," "us" and "our" with references to "you" and "your."
- A friendly, conversational style is more effective than a starchy, traditional style. Read your copy out loud.
- Focus on the benefits. Yes, readers are interested in features, but ultimately they want to know how they will benefit from those features.

- You don't need a unique selling point to stand out and be successful so don't make one up!
- Asking questions will help you to break up your copy and will encourage your reader to consider your message.
- A slab of unbroken text is uninviting. Break up your text by using questions, headings, subheadings and bullet points.
- Don't forget to include calls to action in your copy. Let readers know the options open to them.
- Always edit your copy. If you can't edit your own work, hand it to someone who can.

Masterclass 5
How to Make Your Website a Magnet for Hot Prospects

By Ben Locker, web copywriting expert and Professional Copywriters' Network co-founder

In this masterclass you will learn:

- How to research who your customers are, and what they are searching for.
- How to write on-line copy that gets found and inspires people to act.
- How to turn strangers into friends, and friends into customers.

I first met Ben Locker on Twitter. Intrigued by his excellent copywriting tips, I followed the link through to his blog and spent a few hours immersing myself in his brilliant advice. Several telephone conversations ensued and, in the last few years, Ben has been a keynote speaker at my copywriting boot camps and marketing summits. The response from the audience always, "more please!" Ben has many years' experience of writing website copy for both small businesses and global brands. He is not only a great copywriter but also a web copy troubleshooter, often brought into a business to identify why their website copy is failing to convert a visitor into an interested prospect. He's full of expert copywriting common sense and so I leapt at the opportunity to include his words of wisdom on writing for the web in my book.

Tell someone you're planning to write your business's website and they'll be asking you about search engine optimisation (SEO) in two seconds flat.

SEO is the art and science of getting your website found by people who use search engines. Your aim is to work out which phrases – or keywords – your customers type in when they're looking for products and services like yours, and to optimise your pages so they are among the first to be found.

Getting a good ranking can be easy or difficult, depending on how competitive your industry happens to be. It also depends on many factors other than your copywriting, such as the number of other sites that link to yours, how often your pages are mentioned on social media and even the way your web pages are built.

There are plenty of books that tell you about the technical aspects of SEO, but what you're going to learn in this chapter is a bit more special.

Yes, it will give you techniques that will help your website get found. But it will also show you something more important – what the marketing guru Seth Godin calls:

Turning strangers into friends and friends into customers.

Because, no matter how much effort and money you chuck at SEO, every penny is wasted unless your website makes people want to buy from you.

The key to doing this is by writing great pages that customers want to read, that make it easy for them to browse, buy and subscribe, and which use some of the words they type in when they fire up their favourite search engine.

Sound good? Then let's start.

Step 1: Get Your Customer in Your Sights

Dee has already told you how important it is to write with your customers in mind. You need to do this so you write with their interests at heart – showing them the benefits of buying from you or working with you, and avoiding all the stuff they're not interested in (like your mission, values and other corporate nonsense).

The first steps in writing great on-line copy are to work out who your customers actually are – and then create a list of pages you need to write for them. These are some of the ways you can do it.

- **Be certain who you're writing for.** Before you write a word, work out which groups of people you're writing for – men, women, pensioners, small businesses, vegetarians, local pet owners, classic car enthusiasts, supermarket buyers. These are your audiences. When you buy clothes on-line, you don't want garments for men, women and children to be jumbled together on the same pages. So, if you're a solicitor, don't mix up your services for businesses, charities and individuals.
- **Step into your customers' shoes.** Think about each service and product from your customers' points of view. Different audiences often respond to different benefits. If you think they do, create a separate page that's tailored to each. Don't copy chunks of copy from one to the other – duplicate content can make your pages sink like a stone in the search engine results.
- **Create a site plan.** Draw up a list of all the pages you need to write, then arrange them into sections targeted at each audience. As well as your product and service

sections, think about other pages or documents that your customers will find useful – such as a contact page, buying guides, a blog, a news section and a page about your company. If you write an "About Us" page, don't bang on about your history or create a list of every Managing Director since May 1973 – instead, explain why customers will benefit from doing business with you.

- **Get the right readers to the right pages.** Half the trick of turning visitors into customers is getting them straight to the information that interests them, and keeping them away from pages written for a different audience. Trade visitors to a builder's merchant website don't want to see pages aimed at home DIY enthusiasts. Use your home page to point people to the section of your site that's written just for them.

Step 2: Keyword Research. What Are Your Customers Looking For?

Now you've got your audiences in mind and created your site plan, you need to work out some of the phrases (or keywords) customers type into search engines when they're looking for products and services like yours. You will use this information to make your pages easier to find.

Use the tips in this step to create a list of keywords for every page in your sitemap – you'll be using these as the basis for detailed customer keyword research in step 3.

- **Start your keyword research by talking to your customers.** Ask them what they would type into Google to find products and services like yours – their answers will give you a valuable starting point. Use a simple on-line survey (try www.surveymonkey.com) to gather their ideas, offering a prize as an incentive to fill it in.
- **Remember each page will need separate keywords.** This is particularly important for your products and services – research keywords that are relevant to each page, and not just for your home page.
- **Find out how people are already reaching your website.** If you have a website, use an analytics program to measure how many people visit your site, the pages

they read, and the keywords they use to find you. Look for keywords they are already using, and find out whether some result in more enquiries or sales than others. Add effective keywords to your list. (Note: if you don't use an analytics program, install Google Analytics today. It's powerful, free and you can set it up at www.google.com/analytics/).

- **Work out which keywords your competitors are targeting.** First look for relevant words they use on their pages or which appear in the top of your browser when you visit – like these ones:

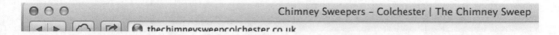

Next, look at the words in their "meta" tags. (See Step 6 for a quick explanation of what these are.) To do this, select "view source" in your browser menu and look for a description and/or keywords section that looks a bit like this:

```
<meta name="description" content="Chimney sweepers
throughout Colchester. Chimney sweeping and troubleshooting.
Pots and cowls. Wedding services offered. Call The Chimney
Sweep on 01206 766 891"/>
```

```
<meta name="keywords" content="chimney sweepers,
chimney sweeping, troubleshooting, colchester, the chimney
sweep"/>
```

Again, add the keywords you unearth to your list. The chances are your competitors have done some thorough research before choosing them.

- **Discover which keywords your competitors are succeeding with.** The quickest way to do this is to head to http://www.semrush.com and type in the addresses of your competitors' websites. You'll get a free list of 10 keywords they rank well for in Google or Bing.
- **Think up related keywords of your own.** Sell classic cars? Think up alternatives like "classic cars," "retro cars," "old cars," "car auctions," "classic cars for sale" or even "cheap second-hand cars"

- **Don't forget about problem solving.** If you sell hair straighteners, not every person will be searching for things like "hair straighteners," "straightening irons" or "best hair straighteners" – they'll be looking for a solution to a specific problem, such as "How can I get rid of curly hair?", "Can you straighten permed hair?" or "How can I straighten my hair?"
- **Use on-line keyword tools.** When you have created your list of keywords, it's time to get some detailed insights into how potential customers use search engines. Unless you pay for access to specialised research tools, your first stop should be Google's on-line keyword tool. You can find it at http://adwords.google.com/KeywordTool.

Step 3: Find out What Customers *Really* Search for

On-line keyword tools are worth their weight in gold. They analyse what huge numbers of people search for every day of the week, and they can reveal proven keywords, stop you wasting time on keywords few people use, and even give you ideas for new products and services that your target audience is looking for.

Some of the best keyword tools cost money to use – Wordtracker is the best known of these (see www.wordtracker.com). But Google's own keyword tool is both free and effective, giving you access to data from its own search engine. Make a point of using it, using the tips below.

- **Research related keywords in batches.** Type in keywords for related products or services – don't paste all the keywords you have researched into the box or you'll be overwhelmed. On the opposite page you can see how an Independent Financial Advisor has typed in related keywords relevant to pensions advice and retirement planning.
- **Weed out unpopular keywords.** You'll see that the keyword tool tells you how many people search for each phrase during a month. There's no point targeting phrases that no one types into Google. In this example, "Saving for my pension" and "Where can I get pensions advice?" will attract few or no visitors – so discard them.

- **Create realistic targets.** Some keywords generate a lot of searches – that makes competition high. There's nothing wrong with targeting competitive keywords, but it will take more time and resources to achieve results. So be sure to look for more specific (long-tail) phrases that are less competitive. In this example, the financial advisor has discovered that "Planning for retirement UK" and "How can I save for retirement?" are relatively popular search terms, and not among the most competitive.
- **Analyse Google's suggestions.** When you type keywords into Google's tool, it suggests relevant alternatives. If you haven't logged in using your free Google account those suggestions appear in a list, as in the example shown.
- **But if you have logged in** (head to http://accounts.google.com to set up your account), you get results that look like those on page 82.

The 15 Essential Marketing Masterclasses for Your Small Business

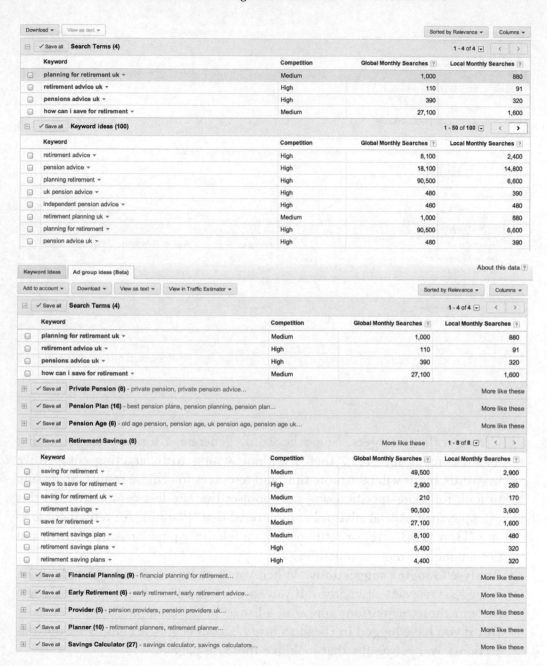

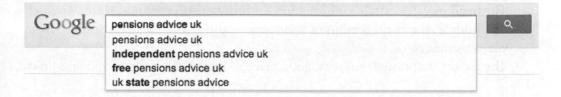

- **When the Google tool lumps keywords together in categories like these**, it not only helps you decide which keywords to target or refine, but it also gives you ideas for new pages or even on-line services. Using the information above, the financial advisor might decide to add a new page or section for individuals who are aiming for early retirement, or position his pension products at people looking for a "retirement savings plan." He might even add an on-line savings calculator as a way of drawing people into his site.
- **Try out your chosen keywords in Google.** If you're going to target keywords, it's a good idea to see who is already on the first page of the search engines for those search queries. You can then analyse the websites you find to see how they use the chosen keywords. There's also another benefit: as you work, Google's autocomplete function throws up new ideas for keywords (see above), which you can then analyse in the keyword tool.

Step 4: Bring Your Keywords and Site Plan together

At this stage, you will have researched keywords for every page in your sitemap – bring them together in a spreadsheet so you can tick them off as you write each page. If your keyword research has given you ideas for new pages or services, incorporate these into your sitemap too and then get ready to write!

Step 5: Divide Each Page into Three

Every web page has three sections you need to know about: the head, the body and the footer. When you write a web page, it's a good idea to address each of these in turn.

- **The head** mostly contains information for browser software and search engines.
- **The body** is the main section of your page – and is the bit that's important to your customers.
- **The footer** is optional, but it's a good place to put useful information and links.

Step 6: Sort Your Head out

The head of your page contains information you can't see on your actual webpages. But don't worry – you need next to no technical knowledge to do a good job.

- **The head of your page has two elements you need to worry about, and one you want to ignore.** The important two are the title that appears at the top of your browser, and something called a "meta description." The one you want to forget is the list of keywords like the one you saw for the chimney sweep in Step 2.
- **The title at the top of your browser** is controlled by an HTML tag called <title>. Don't worry – you don't need any coding knowledge to use it. In most content management systems (websites you can update using your browser) there'll be a box you can type it into. On my agency's site, we use these well. Here are two examples.

One for our on-line copywriting page:

And one for our copywriting blog:

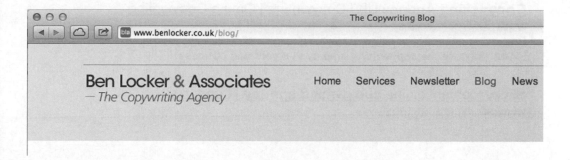

At the time of writing, our website appears on page one of Google if you type in "Online Copywriter", "Online Copywriting", "Copywriting Blog" or "The Copywriting Blog". Getting the right titles has helped to make this happen.

The keywords come first in the title, followed by the company name if you choose to use it. If you do include your company name in the title tag, always put it last – unless your company name is very generic, you should rank well for it anyway. And whatever else you do, make sure that each and every page on your site has its own, unique title.

- **The meta description is like a mini sales pitch that appears in Google's results.** There'll probably be a box to type this into your content management system. Put relevant keywords in this space, but use them to grab your reader's attention (using the copywriting techniques Dee has taught you) and encourage them to click through to your site. If you look at this search result, the main text under my agency's entry is a meta description – it's reproduced by Google to help the reader understand what the page is about.
- **If your content management system has a "meta keywords" box, ignore it.** In the early days of the web, search engines used these keywords to help decide what your page was about. Filling it in these days does little more than reveal your keyword strategy to your competitors (QUICK – check theirs! You can see the keywords in the source code by selecting "view source code" in your browser).

of professional UK **copywriters** are ready and waiting to take your order!

Copywriting Agency UK | Copywriters | Online Copywriting
www.benlocker.co.uk/
Copywriter needed? For online copywriting, bright marketing copywriters and sales
letters - choose the **copywriting agency** that gets you business.

Sticky Content online **copywriting agency** | London UK
www.stickvcontent.com/

Step 7: Flaunt Your Body. Write Copy Your Customers Can't Take Their Eyes off

This is where you start writing. Remember – good on-line copy is like a conversation with your customer, not a shouty block of keyword-infested text that looks like it has been written by a machine. You have to write pages that people want to read.

- **Never forget that you're writing your copy for customers first, and search engines second.** If you do it the other way round, the best you'll manage is to attract a lot of visitors who don't want to buy from you.
- **Don't throw away 150 years of copywriting knowledge, just because you're writing for the web.** Everything Dee has told you about grabbing your readers' attention, using words to charm, bewitch and cajole them into buying, still holds true. AIDCA (Attention, Interest, Desire, Caution, Action) is as powerful on the web as it is in print.
- **Use headings to structure your writing.** Your website system should let you use heading tags to structure your pages. Sometimes you'll find a dropdown menu saying "heading 1," "heading 2" and so on. These apply the heading tags <h1>, <h2>, <h3> and so on as you need them. Put your headline in the <h1> tag and only use it once. Use <h2> onwards to break up your page with eye-catching subheadings as needed.
- **Remember what Dee said about headlines.** It can help your search engine rankings if you put keywords in your headlines, but put your reader first.

Legendary ad-man, David Ogilvy found the best headlines contained news, stimulated curiosity or promised a benefit – or a combination of the three. That's still true, whether your headline is in print or on a screen.

- **Write for your reader, then worry about the keywords for your page.** One of the biggest mistakes some writers make is to worry endlessly about the keywords they should be including in the page. Write simple, clear copy that focuses on the benefits to your reader, and only then revise it to include the keywords that will help it get found.

- **Don't get too hung up about keyword percentages.** Some people will tell you that your writing needs to contain a certain density of keywords: 1%, 3%, 7% or more. Ignore them. Yes, you need to include keywords, but don't stick slavishly to arbitrary percentages. Use the keywords where they help explain your product or service, and certainly use synonyms to give your text variety. But don't try and make each page contain exactly the same quota of keywords – Google will smell a rat.

- **Do be wary of using the same keyword too many times.** Sometimes you'll have to use the same keyword many times, especially if you are writing about technical products and services – after all, there are only so many ways you can say "correlative microscopy" – but if the search engines think you have stuffed a page with keywords, it will probably fall down the rankings.

- **Do a "you"/"we" count.** The great direct marketer Drayton Bird points out that the more you use "you" words, the more your messages get read. It's because people prefer to hear about their own interests. He has this vital piece of advice that holds true for web pages or any other sales communication:
  Go through your messages – in whatever medium – and do a "me"/"you" count. If the "you" words don't outnumber the "me" words two-to-one, change things.

- **Do make your pages accessible.** If you insert an image, give it a text description using the "alt" tag for the benefit of visually impaired users – your content management system will allow you to do this automatically. If you add in a link, avoid doing so on phrases like "go to this page". Use the link to describe what users will find when they click on it.

- **Give each page a call to action.** Before you write a word, ask yourself what you want readers to do when they've finished reading your page. There's nothing more frustrating for customers to read a page and find nothing to do at the bottom of it – so give them a call to action, whether you want them to buy, subscribe, comment or get in touch.

Step 8: Exploit Your Footer (Then Have a Bit on the Side)

The bottom of your web page – the footer – is like a visual full-stop that helps users know where a page ends. It also gives you a chance to hand them useful information and extra reasons to buy – a bit like a postscript in a sales letter.

If your site has a sidebar, you can use it in the same way, and often better.

Here are some of the things to put in your footer or sidebar that can help keep your customers interested, or encourage them to click through to other parts of your site.

- **A sign-up form** for your newsletter or other updates. There's a great piece of software called Mailchimp that allows you to build up an email list of people interested in your products and services. It's easy to integrate its forms into your site, which means subscriptions will take care of themselves (see www. mailchimp.com).
- **Links to your most popular blog posts or products.** Drive people to content that has a proven success rate.
- **Testimonials.** Use these at every opportunity. Customers believe other customers much more than they believe you. One word of warning – always make testimonials relevant. Testimonials for engine repairs won't work on a page that sells a car respraying service.
- **Awards and media coverage.** Flaunt your success and bolster the trustworthiness of your brand.
- **Social media links.** Encourage people to connect with you on Facebook, Twitter and LinkedIn – forging these relationships will give you many more chances to sell to your visitors in future.
- **Legal info.** Increase trust with links to your privacy policy, disclaimers, returns and refund policies.
- **Contact details.** Never waste a chance to make it even easier for your customers to get in touch with you.

- **Your Analytics code.** This bit won't be seen, but put the code for Google Analytics or similar programs into the footer part of your page – it gives you a goldmine of information about the people who are visiting and interacting with your website.

Step 9: A Step out of Order. Not All Web Pages Are the Same

It might seem odd to put this step here, but I wanted you to get comfortable with the nuts and bolts of writing web pages – any web pages – before I sprang these ideas on you.

So far, we've talked mostly about product and service pages, which are the mainstay of any business website. But there is plenty of other content you can write that can help you build up an audience and get the cash register ringing.

Here are some examples, along with tips on what you can use them for.

- **Blog posts.** If you write a blog that's relevant to your business, you can win subscribers, engage readers via their comments and establish yourself as an authority in your field. Be sure to keep posts regular so readers get into the habit of coming back, but don't fall into the trap of putting quantity over quality.
- **Product descriptions.** Photos sell, but great descriptions inflame the desire to buy. *Never* post a picture of a product without giving the customer good reasons to buy it.
- **Landing pages.** These are pages written to make your reader do something very specific, such as buy a particular product or service. They're normally written for people who reach your website after clicking on a paid advert in the search engines or elsewhere on the web. Some are written like sales letters, others are short and with a strong call to action. It's often a good idea to declutter these pages – so get rid of sidebars or footer links that send visitors anywhere other than the shopping cart or the subscription page.
- **White papers and guides.** People are always looking for help. Offer advice in the form of practical "how to" guides, right through to industry papers. These can create your first interaction with a client or customer – and if they give you

their email address as a condition of downloading your guide, you can develop the relationship until they're ready to buy.

Step 10: Monitor Your Progress

Once you've written your copy, you need to monitor how well your pages rank for their chosen keywords. You can do this by regularly typing those keywords into a search engine, but frankly life's far too short.

- **A better option is to use a tool like SEOMoz (www.seomoz.org) or Raven (www.raventools.com).** These allow you to enter all your keywords, and will then give you regular reports on how well your pages are doing. Take time every week to see which pages are rising through the rankings, and which are sinking.
- **If you find some pages aren't ranking well** after a few months, try making small tweaks to them – like adding an extra keyword to a headline or heading. Then leave the page for a few weeks and see what happens (remember Google doesn't update its index instantly. It takes time, so don't make lots of changes in quick succession).
- **Finally, use Google Analytics to find out how many visitors are coming to your site, and how many act** – whether it's to contact you, subscribe to news-letters, download guides or buy products. If you find a page gets lots of visitors and hardly any of them respond to your call to action, the fault is with your page. Remember, page rankings depend on many factors, including external links – so don't immediately blame your copy if you don't rank well.

That's the real beauty of website copywriting – you can measure exactly how well it works, in a way you can't with a poster or a TV advert. So if you find you're not getting the number of visitors you need, or they're not responding in the way that you intend, put them back in your sights and try again.

And don't forget that injection of charm Dee recommends so highly. All the clever techniques in the world won't get you anywhere unless you write with the warmth and authenticity to turn that stranger into your friend, and then into your customer.

Masterclass Summary

- Identify your customers and step into their shoes.
- Tailor your site structure and copywriting to your target audiences.
- Use on-line and off-line techniques to research the keywords your customers are using.
- Use your keywords to write copy that gets found by search engines and is relevant to your customers' needs.
- Genuine testimonials from happy customers work as well on your website as they do in your printed communications.
- Create page titles and meta descriptions that act as mini sales pitches in the search engine results.
- Build up a loyal and engaged audience to help keep the cash register ringing.
- Monitor the success of individual web pages and refine them so they encourage more of your visitors to act.
- Don't overlook the importance of having a friendly and conversational style.

Masterclass 6
How to Write Successful Adverts

In this masterclass you will learn:

- **How to avoid the common and not so common advertising mistakes.**
- **About AIDCA, why it's your ultimate copywriting tool when writing adverts.**
- **How to write adverts that generate responses and sales.**

I began my marketing career writing full page adverts for a life insurance company, for publication in tabloid newspapers. From this early experience I became fascinated by advertising and have become a lifelong student of the subject, reading books from the advertising greats and trying out new techniques to improve the responses to my adverts. Since those early days I have written hundreds of adverts promoting many products and services, including pest control, accountancy, kitchen appliances, promotional gifts, motor products, training, copywriting and financial services. I have made my share of mistakes (most notably in the early part of my career when I was high on confidence but low on experience), but have managed to amass a wealth of knowledge on the topic, and a practical understanding of what it takes to write adverts that work. And that's what this masterclass centres on – the sharing of practical, effective and proven tips to help you to write successful adverts.

There is more to achieving success from advertising than simply writing a great advert, however, and I also cover how to find the right publication in which to advertise, how to negotiate a good rate with the publication and share a fantastic tool used by copywriters called AIDCA.

But first let's look at the more common advertising mistakes that small businesses make:

- **The wrong publication is selected.** For example, if a bookkeeper hopes to attract sole traders, then placing an advert in a publication aimed at and read by large companies is likely to result in responses that they cannot service.
- **The call to action is missing or too vague.** The advert does not make clear to the reader what they should do next to progress their interest.
- **Competitors' adverts are more attractive or attention grabbing.** Or perhaps too many competitors are advertising in the same publication.
- **The timing is not right.** The business owner has picked the wrong time of year to advertise their products or services, such as advertising chimney sweeping in April.

- **The advert includes spelling mistakes,** grammatical errors or blurred images. The reader is unlikely to see past these and may well conclude that the product or service being advertised is of similarly sloppy quality.
- **The advert** contains too much text and appears unreadable.
- **The advert is bland.** It does not highlight the benefits that will make the reader stop and read on.
- **Too much is expected from a very small advert.** An advert of this size is unlikely to have sufficient impact to be noticed and therefore should not be expected to generate a high level of response.
- **The advert looks good but doesn't get the message across.** The designer has had a field day at the expense of the copywriter! The advert is stylish but it's not clear what is being advertised.

With thought and planning, these mistakes can be avoided. Let's start by considering how to identify the publications that are suitable for you to advertise in.

The most beautifully crafted, benefit-crammed, attention-grabbing advert in the world won't work if the publication in which you choose to advertise does not attract the audiences you're looking to target. Before you think about actually writing an advert, you need to research the publications that may or may not be suitable for it to appear in. Search on the Internet and browse the shelves in your local supermarkets to identify those publications that you think are appropriate. Visit the website of each one to find out more, and if you're still interested, follow this process:

1. **Request a hard copy of the publication plus the features schedule and rate card.** The rate card will provide details of the costs of advertising based on the size of the advert with information on any premium spots, such as the front cover, back page, inside back page etc. The features schedule will provide you with details of the various features scheduled to be published in the coming months. This information will enable you to choose which issues will contain features that will complement the message in your advert and which issues are planned to include features that are unrelated or may even conflict with the theme of your advert.

2. **Ask for information about the readership profile and the distribution of the publication.** If you're a business that gains most of your custom locally, do you want to be advertising in a magazine that is mainly distributed outside your operating area? Find out as much as you can about the readers. This means pressing the advertising salesperson for facts and figures in writing. For example, before placing the Kalimex advert included at the end of this masterclass, I ascertained that the majority of readers of *Commercial Vehicle Workshop* magazine were either managers of commercial vehicle fleets or managers of commercial vehicle workshops. As these were two audiences I wanted to target, the readership profile of this magazine was perfect. The distribution pattern of the magazine was less relevant as K-Seal, the product being advertised is available throughout the United Kingdom.

3. **Although the distribution area of the magazine was not so important, the distribution method certainly was.** Determine the estimated readership and how the publication reaches those readers. I discovered that *Commercial Vehicle Workshop* was sent to 9000 technicians, suggesting that advertising in this magazine was not going to be a big risk. Had the magazine been left in public places to be picked up by passers-by, I would have judged the level of readership to be unclear and not have advertised in the magazine, despite the audience it was aimed at.

4. **Study the publication using the tips in Masterclass 7 to guide you.** What does the publication look and feel like? Would your business be well represented within these pages? Can you spot opportunities for additional editorial coverage? Aim for a powerful combination of paid-for advertising and free editorial. The advertising salesperson may have influence with the editorial team, so mention your desire to complement adverts with editorial and make them aware that this is a critical factor in your decision to advertise. The *Commercial Vehicle Workshop* editorial team agreed to match every advert bought with a piece of high-quality editorial including Kalimex's newsworthy articles and features. However, if you're aiming to secure editorial alongside your advertising, make sure that your submissions are genuinely newsworthy and of interest to readers. No amount of paid-for advertising will persuade an editor to include a press release or sales pitch dressed up as an article.

5. **Negotiate!** The rate card is usually a price guide and not set in stone. Most publications will offer a discount from the rate card if you're a new advertiser, are planning on booking more than one advert or are proving resistant to their overtures! If the publication will not budge from the rate card price, ask for additional editorial coverage and get this in writing.

6. **It has been proven that readers subconsciously focus** more on the content shown on a right-hand page of a publication than they do on a left-hand page. Placing your advert on a right-hand page is therefore a good idea. However there are other considerations. Where will your advert be located in the publication? Will it be alongside competitors' adverts? Will it be alongside an editorial feature that will complement or reduce its impact? If the publication has sections, which section will your advert be in? Don't commit to advertising until you're happy with the answers to these questions.

7. **What size should your advert be?** The size will be determined by the dimensions of the publication in which you're advertising, and of course your budget. The bigger the space, the more you pay. Community magazines are usually around A5 size, with trade and consumer magazines A4 size or greater. Your advert has to be big enough to grab the reader's attention and to convey your powerful benefits. Ideally, aim for a minimum size of a quarter page advert and if your budget can stretch, go for a half-page. The balance of the page could well be filled with your editorial, so providing the impact of a full page. If you're buying a number of adverts over several weeks or months in the same publication and have already managed to negotiate a good deal, be cheeky and ask for a size upgrade on one of the adverts – a quarter page to a half-page, half-page to a full page etc. at no additional charge.

8. **Don't commit to advertising unless you're confident** that at the very least you will recover your costs. there are, of course, no guarantees with advertising but if you've studied the publication and have arrived at the conclusion that its readers are the audience you want to reach and the publication is an appropriate vehicle in which to promote your business, there's a far greater likelihood that your advert will achieve its goal than if you take a more "hit and hope" approach.

9. **Don't design your advert yourself.** The most brilliantly worded advert can fail because of poor design. I have seen full page adverts in magazines, costing £2000

or more, that are little more than a block of text and a series of blurred images. Your advert is your shop window. It has the challenging job of either familiarising the readers with your products and services or of reminding them you still exist. Don't waste a valuable opportunity and your budget by dismissing the importance of professional design in attracting readers to your message.

Why Your Advert Must Have an Impact

For your advert to be successful, it must have impact, something famously defined by Raymond Rubicam, the American advertising pioneer, as *"that quality in an advertisement which strikes suddenly against the reader's indifference and enlivens his mind to receive a sales message."*

How do you achieve impact? AIDCA should help you.

AIDCA is a tool that many copywriters use when writing copy. It stands for

- **A**ttention
- **I**nterest
- **D**esire
- **C**aution
- **A**ction

Let's look at each one of these stages in more detail.

Attention

Your advert has only a few seconds to grab the attention of the reader and stop them in their tracks as they flick through the publication. This is usually achieved with an eye-catching headline or image.

Interest

Once you have gained the attention of your reader, your next job is to interest them in your proposition. A selection of compelling facts and figures about your offering or a quote from a very satisfied customer should do the trick.

Desire

Having built sufficiently on the reader's interest, you need to generate a need for what you are offering. Referring to the powerful benefits that come from purchasing your product or service can do just that, especially if accompanied by a special offer.

Caution

This is an important stage that can often be overlooked in the creation of an advert. The reader is now interested in what you're offering and is considering a purchase but probably still has doubts. If these doubts remain unchecked, they may prevent them from going any further. Think about the doubts you have heard expressed when chatting to prospects. What are the questions you've needed to address before that prospect has become a customer? Can your understanding of the thinking process of a prospect help you to address any common concerns with a few lines of text in your advert?

Action

If the four previous stages in the AIDCA model have worked, there is just one final hurdle to overcome before your advert can be termed a success – your reader must understand what to do next. Ensure that your advert includes details of how your reader can progress their interest further. Clearly state your contact details, the terms and conditions of any special offers, how to book a meeting, request a quote, take advantage of your free session etc. Encourage the reader to visit your website if you believe that after doing so they will be more likely to get in touch.

Before taking your advert to the design stage, review it against each of the five stages of AIDCA. Are you successfully moving your prospect through those five crucial stages? If any stage is skipped, the chances are that the advert will be less successful than hoped.

Writing Successful Adverts

All aspects of marketing can be embraced when putting together a winning advert. A friendly, conversational style is as important in your adverts as it is in your sales letters. The benefits identified in your positioning statement could be what are needed to move a prospect from "Interest" into "Desire." Consider what you want to promote in your advert and how much information can be conveyed in the advertising space that you have bought. For example:

- If you want to promote an event you're organising, readers will need to know enough about your event for it to sound attractive and relevant to their needs. Your advert, however, will only be able to convey a smattering of information about the event, so encouraging the reader to find out more on your website is probably the best purpose for your advert.
- If you want the readers to know that your new business is now open and would like to promote this with a limited opening offer, consider the type of offers that you believe work well. Revisit the magazines in which you'll be advertising and study the offers promoted by other advertisers for inspiration.
- You may want to promote a successful product or service to a new audience. If so, don't assume that the benefits and marketing messages you've been using to woo your existing target audiences can be replicated with this new audience. Research this new audience so that you understand how to target the readers with the right message. Run through Masterclasses 2 and 3 for assistance.
- If you want to offer your existing products and services to the same target audiences but are using advertising to extend your reach in this market, remember the benefits and messages that proved effective in attracting your existing customers when they were only lukewarm prospects.

Let's now look at how to write each element of your advert.

The Headline

To be honest, you will struggle to emulate the headlines that appear on billboards and that adorn the adverts of blue chip brands. These headlines are usually written by incredibly talented individuals from advertising agencies, paid enormous sums of money to create something special. Because the headline can often be the most challenging part of their advert, many small businesses resort to using their business name as the headline. Unfortunately, this is unlikely to have the impact necessary to move the reader's attention from what they are reading to their advert.

With a little know-how, however, headlines can be relatively simple for anyone to write. Here are some tips:

1. Your headline should be relevant to the subject matter and not one contrived in order to be catchy. If the reader is attracted by a headline that has no connection with the content that follows, they will simply turn the page.
2. If you choose a short headline of just a few words, consider including a sub-heading that expands further on the message. For example, I recently came across this headline in a magazine promoting a special reading lamp: "Reduce Eyestrain Instantly," followed by the sub-heading, "Enjoy breathtaking clarity when you read at home, risk free for 30 days." The main headline caught my eye immediately and the sub-heading expanded the promise suggested in those first three words.
3. It doesn't have to be short and sweet. It can run into one or more sentences. One of my adverts had the headline "At the Optimum sale you can save up to £300 on a built-in or freestanding appliance. Prices have been slashed on range cookers, fridges and freezers, dishwashers, washing machines and all built in appliances!"
4. Your headline should stand out. Make it larger than the body text, or embolden it. You can further highlight it by adding speech marks or using italics to emphasise a particular phrase or word. It can be a different colour or a different typeface to the body text. RESIST THE URGE TO PUT YOUR HEADLINE IN CAPITALS because this can be irritating to some readers. AND AVOID USING QUIRKY TYPEFACES THAT WILL MAKE IT CHALLENGING TO READ.

Let's now look at some ideas for your headline.

- **Use a testimonial from a delighted customer.** If you have received a fantastic, up-to-date customer testimonial, consider using it in your headline, especially if you believe that readers will identify with it. Put the testimonial in quotes and include the full name or initials of the relevant customer. Let the reader know the quote is genuine. You can see this in action in the Ashley Law Mid Sussex advert at the end of this masterclass. Testimonial can be as little as six words or stretch to several sentences. Make sure it has credibility. For example, a headline such as: "Dee is a fantastic trainer" is vague and provides me with an ego boost rather than offering anything of interest to the readers. Whereas:

> *"Dee quickly builds up a rapport with her delegates, using plain language they all understand. Everyone likes her presentation style and finds it a breath of fresh air that she does not use PowerPoint slides."*
>
> John Corcoran, Regional Education and Training Manager,
> Electrical Contractors Association

. . . has impact because it's a genuine quote. It conveys some of the benefits of hiring me as a trainer, and by including the name and title of the person who wrote the testimonial it produces a headline that is attention grabbing, credible and genuine.

- **Use your headline to promise a benefit.** These types of headlines are popular because readers are motivated by what your product or service can do for them. At this stage of writing your advert, you should be confident about the benefits that will make the reader interested in finding out more. Here are examples of headlines promising a benefit. Which ones could you successfully adapt for your own business?

> *"Become an accomplished, confident presenter in just four sessions."*
> *"Save up to 40% on our range of luxury, handmade organic soaps."*
> *"Join our business improvement club in April. Save £250 and watch your profits soar!"*
> *"Keep your kids happy and safe in our new soft play area whilst you catch up with friends in our juice bar."*
> *"Visit our exhibition stand at the National Caravan Show and, if you're one of the first 50 visitors, receive a free touring goody bag."*

- **Headlines that ask a question are effective** because they can grab a reader's attention if they're sufficiently interested in what you're asking. They will be considering their answer while reading your advert. Here are some examples of questions that have been used as effective headlines.

"Is it time you outsourced your payroll?"
"Would you like to reduce your stationery bill by as much as 50%?"
"Do you want to start your own business but don't know where to begin?"
"Would you like to be a fearless and confident public speaker?"
"Do you need an amazing magician for your next event?"
"Did you know the average financial adviser listens for just 82 seconds before interrupting?"
"Why do 98% of our customers recommend us?"

- **Including your business name within a headline can be effective too.** For example, if you're advertising in a local publication you may want to include your business name in the headline because some of the readers will already be familiar with it and will read on for that reason alone. As mentioned earlier, however, the headline should consist of more than just your business name. Here are some examples taken from a community magazine, *Horsham Pages*, distributed in my local area:

"The greatest small butchers shop, New Street Butchers"
"Bishops Move – local knowledge, nationwide service"
"Lost in the Loft, the video transfer specialists"
"The Window Wizard for all your double glazing repairs"
"DP Roofing Ltd – your first call for flat roofing experts"
"Horsham Business Club. Are you looking for effective networking?"

Have a go at writing headlines for your own business in the various styles covered before deciding which work best for promoting your business.

The Content

Most of the space in your advert should be taken up with communicating benefits. Although you may be tempted to share several benefits, you're unlikely to have enough space in which to do so. If this is the case, concentrate instead on sharing just a few that you feel confident will appeal to the readers. When you study the five adverts at the end of this masterclass, you will see two approaches to describing benefits. One is to list them as bullet points, the other is to write a few concise paragraphs. Remember the purpose of your advert and the picture you've built up of your readers when contemplating which benefits to include.

Consider making a special offer

Your advert doesn't need to include a special offer but it can certainly help to increase responses. Try including one in your next advert. You can always tweak or remove the offer in future adverts if it does not have the desired effect. Here are some ideas to consider:

- Include a voucher within the advert or, if space precludes this, make the entire advert a voucher.
- Limit your offer to the first 10, 20, 30 people to get in touch to encourage prompt response. Perhaps include a time limit too.
- Drive people to your website with the promise of a special offer awaiting them there.

To give some ideas of the sort of offer you could consider including in your advert, here is a selection of offers that have been successful in generating a good response:

- A hairdresser offered a £1 haircut for brand-new customers only.
- A fish and chip shop offered a second portion of fish and chips for £1 when the first portion was bought at the full price.
- A motor repair product specialist offered prospects a limited edition mug filled with jellybeans when they placed their initial order of a product.
- An air suspension specialist offered prospects a free nodding dog mascot when booking a free air suspension health check for their motorhome.
- A personal fitness trainer offered the first training session free.
- A cake maker offered six free cupcakes when clients commissioned a special celebration cake.

Or, if you offer a professional service, maybe the following examples will seem more appropriate:

- A printing company offered prospects two high-quality mugs filled with organic chocolate for businesses booking an audit of their printing.
- A promotional gift specialist offered prospects free artwork worth £60 on their first order of promotional gifts or clothing.
- A company specialising in providing software for libraries offered a five piece desk set to journalists visiting their exhibition stand.

- A commercial interior designer offered a discounted price for their conference if delegates booked by a certain date.
- A business coach offered a 60 minute complimentary coaching session for prospects to determine if coaching was for them.
- An independent financial adviser offered a free retirement road map to prospects booking on their retirement planning seminar.
- A copywriter offered to write up to 300 words free for a prospect to evaluate her style with no commitment.

Including an offer in your advert can be very effective but do spend some time determining what is appropriate and, of course, what you can afford.

How about a teaser ad?

Sometimes a small, text-only "teaser style" advert in a publication can be effective in creating intrigue and encouraging readers to look for your main advert. This should be located in another place in the publication. Here are some examples of teaser ad wordings:

- Where can you enjoy a superb meal prepared by a Michelin Star chef for just £15? Page 34 reveals all.
- Would you like more targeted website traffic? Dan Purchase from Britweb shows you how to achieve this on page 43.
- Need to get more sales from your sales literature? Ben Locker shares his ten copywriting commandments on the inside back page.

Ask the publication what they would charge to run a small, text-only teaser advert in addition to your main advert, and if they have run these adverts before and so can provide examples.

Visuals

Photographs and illustrations can bring a real energy and allure to your advert. If you do include images with your advert, always accompany any illustrations, photos or images with a short description. You may want to show examples of your work, before and after images, pictures of you, your team, suppliers or customers. These images will add authenticity and credibility to your business and make your advert appealing to look at.

If your visuals are unaccompanied by a short description the reader may not be aware of their significance or their connection to you. Increasing the reader's connection with the brand was something that we aimed for with the Optimum Kitchen Appliance Superstores adverts. We replaced the previous images of washing machines, fridges and cookers with a large smiling visual of a member of the Optimum team, accompanied by their name and title.

Ensure any visuals you use are of good quality and are appropriate for the size of the advert. For example, an image included in a small advert for an interior designer is unlikely to be large enough to be able to adequately represent an entire redesigned room, and as such the impact of the image would be reduced. Better instead to include an illustration of just one aspect of the room that could be properly represented in the size of image available and signpost readers to the website for a dazzling array of glorious images!

The call to action

This is the all-important "Action" stage of the AIDCA model. Do you want readers to visit your website, sign up to your blog, download your white paper, enter your competition? Should they call you for an informal chat, contact you via email to find out more, book on-line for your free initial session, email to confirm they will be visiting your exhibition stand? Your advert must make clear to readers how they can get in touch with you and how they can take advantage of your special offers. Ensure your contact details are very visible.

Design

As mentioned earlier, don't design your advert yourself – unless you're advertising your design services, of course! Instead, pass the content of the advert to your designer along with your pantone colours, high quality images of your logos and your business name. Spend time briefing your designer on the purpose of your advert. Provide them with as much information as possible about the publication and its readers so they can design your advert with the audience in front of mind too.

Be Ready to Respond to Those Responses!

Depending upon the specific call to action in your advert, you may need to put in place some arrangements in order to cope with the expected increase in enquiries. If you have asked the reader to visit your website to sign up to your newsletter, the advert is unlikely to generate any direct increase in your workload. You have placed the advert to raise awareness of your company and to encourage the readers to find out more about you. Numerous document downloads and signups from your website can take place without any additional involvement from you or your team. If, however, you have asked the reader to call or email you, it may be necessary to make plans to accommodate the additional activity. Consider changing your answer phone message so that prospects calling outside your working hours will receive a helpful and friendly message that lets them know when you'll be in touch. Similarly, if you're unable to monitor your email account constantly, think about adding an automated response to acknowledge email enquiries. It will be a waste of your hard work and budget if your advert creates the interest that you crave but, through being unprepared for the additional activity, these new prospects are left with a poor first impression of you.

Measure the Performance

Having decided upon the design and content of your advert and the publication in which to place it, you must now monitor whether it's successful or not. Some businesses do this by asking all enquirers to quote a specific code printed in the advert. This helps the business owner to identify how many new enquiries have come directly from the advert. Again, how you measure the success or otherwise of your advert will depend upon your call to action. Use your website analytics to determine whether there has been a significant increase in web traffic and downloads, for example. If making a special offer in the advert, make a note of how many times this offer is taken up. Don't decide to continue or to abandon advertising until you know how successful your advert has been.

Five Successful Adverts to Appraise

Here are five adverts representing five very different businesses – a firm of chartered accountants, a kitchen appliance superstore, an air suspension specialist, a financial adviser and a supplier of motor repair products. Each advert also included the full contact details of the business and was professionally designed.

When perusing these adverts you should spot many of the tips mentioned in this masterclass in action. Hopefully you will also recognise how your own adverts can be adjusted to embrace the tips we have covered.

Example Advert 1 – Perrys Chartered Accountants

This was a full page advert that appeared in a glossy consumer magazine called *Kent Life*. It was placed in the business section of the magazine and was accompanied by a full page of editorial in which one of the partners shared six practical accountancy tips for businesses. The purpose of the advert was to attract those readers who were contemplating moving accountants, hence the headline and sub-heading. Perrys client base comprises businesses of all sizes and we wanted to make this clear in the advert. We did not want to deter readers from contacting Perrys because they believed their business may be too large or too small to benefit from Perrys service.

Is It Time for Change?

Changing accountants can be a hard decision to make. But did you know that as one of our clients you have the best of both worlds?

We offer a local, highly proactive accountancy service with the reassurance and expertise of an established and trusted brand.

Whether you're just starting out in business or have been established for many years, you will benefit from our dedicated business and tax planning experts and competitive fees. If you're interested in having a proactive accountant on your side, contact us today to arrange an informal, first meeting at no charge.

With seven branches throughout London and the South East, there's a Perrys branch close to you.

Example Advert 2 – Optimum Kitchen Appliance Superstores

This full page advert appeared on the back page of the television guide enclosed in a local newspaper. The purpose of the advert was to attract those readers looking to buy built-in appliances, either as part of a new kitchen or to replace an existing faulty appliance. The advert was published in the six weeks leading up to Christmas. As mentioned earlier, rather than including a number of small images of kitchen appliances, it was accompanied instead by a smiling picture of Ben, one of the directors of the company.

"Have your new built in appliance in time for Christmas!"

Ben, Installation Specialist at Optimum, 20 years' experience.

Optimum is your local trusted specialist for supplying *and* expertly fitting built in appliances.

You benefit from

* Free measuring up for your new appliance
* Free removal and recycling of your old appliance
* Free storage of your new appliance until you need it!
* Free local delivery
* The widest range of built in appliances *and* range cookers available
* The best prices

Optimum – where first class service is standard.

Example Advert 3 – VB-Airsuspension

This half-page advert was published in *Motorcaravan Motorhome Monthly* magazine (MMM), a glossy magazine read by motorhome owners as a source of independent advice. It was accompanied by a full page of editorial in which the MMM team reviewed VB-Airsuspension. In this example the advert was designed to support the editorial and included the contact details of each VB accredited dealer. The headline was a genuine quote from the Caravan Club, another trusted organisation to which thousands of motorhome owners belong.

"A wonderful suspension setup that delivers a softer more comfortable ride."

Caravan Club comment on the market leading VB-Airsuspension system.

(Continued)

- FullAir systems, SemiAir systems and uprated Coilsprings to accommodate most budgets.
- Raised ride height and improved stability in cross winds and when cornering and overtaking. An altogether smoother, safer and infinitely more enjoyable ride.
- Low maintenance and user friendly. Enjoy miles of carefree on-the-road driving with optional Full Air Auto-Level and Ferry loading functions.
- Backed by a 2 year warranty and a comprehensive European service network.

Example Advert 4 – Ashley Law Mid Sussex, Independent Financial Advisers

This was also a half-page advert and appeared in three issues of a monthly community magazine. The magazine is posted through the letter boxes of houses in some of the more affluent postcodes within the operating area of Ashley Law Mid Sussex. The advert had to convey a lot in a small space without appearing cramped. In each issue the advert was accompanied by a half-page of editorial introducing the Ashley Law Mid Sussex team and explaining their service ethos in more detail. This was negotiated free of charge when booking the adverts. The wording of the call to action was important as we had to convey that in booking a meeting, the reader would not be pressured in any way into a sale.

The Right Financial Advice . . . Worth Its Weight in Gold

- Personal Pensions/SIPPS
- Investing for Income/Growth
- Inheritance Tax Planning
- Financial Planning
- Mortgages

> "A sincere and friendly service without undue jargon. The team at Ashley Law Mid Sussex consistently go beyond my expectations and always have an answer to issues raised." *
>
> JM *unedited testimonial

To speak to an experienced and ethical independent financial adviser contact a member of the Ashley Law Mid Sussex team today. An initial meeting is informal, unpressured and without charge.

Example Advert 5 – Kalimex

This full page advert was published in *Commercial Vehicle Workshop* magazine. The headline was designed to attract the attention of those commercial vehicle workshop managers who had experienced, or were experiencing, problems with coolant leaks in their commercial vehicles. These managers would be only too aware of the significant repair costs associated with such problems. The advert included a large image of the product and the bullet points were designed to share benefits and remove the main barriers to a sale – that the product might only have a limited application, could be hard to apply or was expensive. The testimonial was from a stockist supplying K-Seal HD to commercial vehicle workshops.

Coolant Leak Repair?

Big or small, K-Seal HD seals them all

K-Seal HD is the proven one step total permanent coolant leak repair for HGVs and LCV's – guaranteed to last

- **Permanent Coolant Leak Repair.** K-Seal HD permanently seals virtually all types of coolant leak including cracked heads, head gasket failures, cracked blocks, radiators, heater cores – even water pumps.
- **Simple to use – just shake, pour and go.** K-Seal HD requires no special preparation. Add directly to the cooling system whether you're on the road, on site, in the depot, in the workshop.
- **Excellent value for money.** Compared to the cost of having a vehicle off the road, K-Seal HD is a drop in the ocean.

Autumn offer: we've got 10 limited edition Kalimex K-Seal HD T-shirts to give away. Complete the reader link NOW for a chance to get yours!

> *"K-Seal HD is the most proven one; everyone says that the stuff is marvellous."*

> *JD Motor Factors*

Masterclass Summary

- Be realistic in your expectations. A tiny advert tucked away amongst many others is unlikely to generate hundreds of responses.
- Before committing to advertising, research the publications you are interested in. Use Masterclass 7 to help you.
- Don't just think advertising; think about additional editorial opportunities. Your latest news, a giveaway, a competition, your press release.
- Is the space you're buying big enough to have impact? Look at other adverts of similar size.
- Use a graphic designer. Stand out with a great looking, professionally designed advert.
- Work through the AIDCA process when writing your advert.
- What should your advert focus on? What's needed to grab a reader's attention?
- Your headline is important but can be written in a variety of ways. Consider using testimonial, facts and figures, a few words followed by a longer subheading.
- Always use "you" and "your" more than "we" "us" and "our."
- Benefits all the way! How will readers gain more, save more, be even happier or have their problems taken away?
- Don't overlook the pulling power of a special offer. Readers are looking for more, something extra, something of real value.
- Make sure that any images are captioned, good quality and reinforce the benefits.
- Teaser adverts can work well – always signpost to the page that features your main advert.
- Measure the impact of your advertising, asking people how they heard of you.
- Be ready to handle all those responses.

Masterclass 7
How to Get PR in Printed Publications

In this masterclass you will learn:

- How to avoid common PR mistakes.
- The many benefits of gaining relevant PR coverage for your business.
- How to build a powerful PR presence for your business on a shoestring budget.

I was contacted several years ago by Penny who ran a business that specialised in providing software for libraries. Penny had found it challenging to get any coverage in the printed media subscribed to by her target audiences despite these same magazines regularly carrying content from competitors. She had been sending press releases and articles to the journalists and editors, but to no avail. When I appraised her press releases they were accurate and well written, so the quality of what she was submitting was not the problem. However, for some reason they had not been hitting the spot. And so we spent an entire day combing through the contents of every publication to which Penny felt she could make a worthwhile and relevant contribution. Our mission was to form an opinion about the look, feel and content of each publication in which we wanted to feature. We considered:

- The style and focus.
- The amount of space allocated to editorial content and to advertising.
- The number of regular columns and features, news pages, business articles, top tips and reviews.
- The number of contributions by guest business writers.

By getting under the skin of each publication and understanding its mission, its readers and its structure, Penny was able to answer the pivotal question, "Where can I add real value to this publication, and how?"

It changed her focus from sending out well-written but fairly random press releases to all the publications in which she wanted to gain coverage, to a much more bespoke approach, taking into consideration the profile, content and readership of each publication.

From this exercise we drew up a list of potential "hooks" that we were confident would be of real interest to each publication. Rather than simply sending in a press release, Penny approached each editor with her ideas, explaining how she believed that she could add value to the magazine and the specific topics that she aimed to cover in her articles. The results were wonderful. Every single publication commissioned Penny to contribute an article and she became a regular columnist for several leading magazines in her sector.

Why had Penny been so successful? Because she had studied each publication in detail, viewing it from the perspective of the editorial team, what they would welcome and what would fit their approach and editorial style. Previously, Penny had treated all the publications in which she was interested in appearing as one general group. Consequently she had written very general press releases, focusing mainly on what she wanted from press coverage rather than on what she could offer.

The purpose of this masterclass is to illustrate how you too can gain PR coverage for your business in printed publications such as special interest magazines, trade magazines, newspapers and glossy consumer magazines. These same tips apply should you want to boost your profile in on-line publications too.

Let's start by looking at the benefits that can be gained from PR coverage.

1. **A rapid increase in sales.** It may surprise you to read that, but it is possible to gain sales from new customers quite quickly as a result of PR coverage as you will see in the case studies accompanying this masterclass.
2. **A big reduction in the time it takes for a prospect to do business with you.** PR is excellent at compressing a cold prospect's decision-making process. By establishing a good reputation you will find that the time you need to spend converting a potential customer's interest into a sale reduces dramatically. And it also helps retain your existing customers, reinforcing their loyalty and encouraging them to buy more from you.
3. **An increase in the number of business opportunities offered to you.** This can include invitations to speak at prestigious events, to judge competitions and to attend awards ceremonies. Each can lead to forming high-value strategic partnerships with other businesses. The perception you build through PR is that you're a successful person with an equally successful business.
4. **Competitive advantage.** Ongoing positive PR exposure separates you from your competitors. You become less likely to find yourself competing with other businesses for a prospect's custom. In many cases you will be the only business

approached simply because you have built the impression through your PR exposure that you're a safe, respected and risk free proposition at the top of your game.

5. **Brand building.** Whether you have been around for many years and recognise that now is the time to accelerate recognition of your brand or you are starting out and want to generate an awareness of what you can offer, PR will help you to achieve this.

The Mistakes to Avoid

Researching the style of a publication and then writing a press release or article does not guarantee it will be published. There are a number of reasons why it may not be accepted. Let's look at some of the more common ones:

1. **The quality of the submission is poor.** An editor or journalist is not going to spend time correcting spelling mistakes or grammatical errors. When communicating with the media, make sure every email and accompanying attachment you send is accurate and clear. A spelling mistake to an editor is like a red rag to a bull, no matter how insignificant it may appear to you.
2. **The submission is unsuited to the publication.** It is always advisable to spend time reading the publication with a view to understanding its tone and focus before writing your article.
3. **The article is submitted either too late or too early.** It is important to check the copy deadline and the forthcoming features schedule in order to ascertain the right time to submit your piece.
4. **The submission is lost amongst a sea of articles and editorial ideas from other small businesses.** Aim to build a relationship with the relevant editor or journalist before submitting anything for publication. This way you are more likely to secure their buy-in to your idea.
5. **Some publications have a policy of not accepting any press releases or features from third parties other than their own editorial team.** Their entire content is written by their own commissioned features and articles team. Try to discover if this is the case before wasting time submitting anything to these types of publications.

6. **A publication may have a policy of not accepting any press releases from a small business that clashes with their regular advertisers.** This can often be the case with community magazines that are wholly dependent on revenue from advertising. They will not jeopardise a relationship with an advertiser by including editorial from one of their competitors. Again, it is worth finding out if this is the case before wasting time writing a piece for the magazine.

7. **A publication believes they have commissioned an exclusive article, only to see it reproduced in rival publications.** If this happens, the editorial team are unlikely to publish any further material from that contributor again. If you are given a decent amount of space in which to share your expertise, make it clear that you will not be offering the same article to another publication. This will appeal to the editor.

Recognise Your Market

Aim to identify all the publications read by your target audiences and then study each one to determine which ones warrant your time and attention. You may already be aware of a few titles, but is that enough? These titles may not be the best ones for you to approach. There may be other titles aimed at the same audience but with a higher standard of editorial content and attracting a greater number of readers.

Here are some simple and cost-effective ways to go about doing this. The only expense is the purchase of the publication and your time.

- **Pay a trip to the library** and ask if they provide business support services. If they do, they may be able to provide you with a list of publications that fit your criteria. Recently I wanted to find out how many magazines existed in the UK aimed specifically at small businesses. I used the market research service at my local library and, at no charge, was provided with a list of 30 magazines including the contact details of the journalists and editors. This information had been compiled by one of the business librarians.
- **Search the Internet.** This is by far the most effective approach. Most printed periodicals have a website and this is likely to include the contact details of the advertising and editorial teams as well as information about the publication

itself. Take screenshots of the details of each publication so that you can study them at leisure. Also, make a note of the editorial team and how they like to be communicated with. A growing number of editors now specify that you should contact them by email only, but some still prefer the telephone.

- **Browse the racks in your local newsagent or stationer.** The big superstores also now carry thousands of titles. Purchase the publications you would like to appear in.

- **Search on Twitter or Facebook.** In my experience, many publications, especially those aimed at professional trades, do not yet wholeheartedly embrace social media. But it's still worth spending a little time searching for any publications that do have a social media presence and that serve the audiences you're interested in reaching. For each one you find, visit their website so you can gather more details. And follow them on the social media site so that you can respond to any editorial requests swiftly.

Initial Research Completed, What Are the Next Steps?

Contact each publication you're interested in and ask for the latest copy, including their rate card and, if they have one, their features schedule. The features schedule is always useful information as there may be features planned to appear in the future that complement your ideas. The rate card should provide you with useful information on circulation and readership in addition to the advertising rates. If you have to telephone for a copy, do not disclose that you're interested in editorial coverage at this stage. Express a general interest as a potential advertiser if you're forced to disclose the reason why you're calling.

When you have received all the copies you need, adopt the same approach that Penny and I took and study each publication. Consider:

- **How is the publication structured?** Does it include regular features and columns, guest writers, reader contributions? Can you see a potential opening for you to write a column or share tips as a guest writer?

- **Does the publication contain competitions and giveaways and, if so, can you tell if they are sponsored by businesses?** Is there scope for you to offer a competition?

- **How much editorial is included in the publication?** This comprises of informative articles, features and tips that have not been supplied by an advertiser paying for the privilege. Could you provide useful editorial that complements the existing material?
- **Does the editorial outweigh the adverts, or vice versa?** If the publication is full of adverts with only the smallest amount of editorial, you will struggle to get any PR in this magazine unless you are willing to advertise too. By contrast, a publication that is packed with editorial suggests that with the right approach and an enticing "hook" you will have a better chance.
- **What is the general tone of the publication?** Is it quirky, friendly, an easy read with interesting content? Is it technical or official looking? Can you see a synergy between the tone of the publication and your own brand?
- **What is the readership of each publication?** Look in the first few pages to see whether the publication is ABC1 certified. This provides a guarantee of the net distribution of the magazine. Within the first few pages you will usually spot the ABC1 logo. Read the rate card accompanying the magazine to determine how the publication is distributed and who reads it. Does this match your target audience?
- **How is the publication distributed?** The distribution of a free community magazine, for example, is likely to be delivered directly through letter boxes in specific postcode areas or left for pick up in cafes, libraries, public places etc. For a magazine aimed at small businesses, distribution will usually be by subscription with the magazine being posted to the business or home address. Bear in mind that subscription magazines have a more loyal readership than publications left at distribution points. Ideally you want your submission to be in a publication which has loyal readers.
- **What is your overall assessment of the publication?** If you had to rank it in a beauty parade where would it sit?

What Can You Bring to the Table?

Having completed your research on each publication, you are now able to draw up your shortlist of those that you consider ideal for your articles and news features.

Having done that, you need to switch the focus from it being all about you, to it being all about the editor and their publication. There will be many perfectly legitimate reasons why you want to feature in these publications, but unfortunately an editor is unlikely to share your enthusiasm! They are already being targeted by many businesses like yours, keen to secure free PR coverage.

By asking yourself the following questions before submitting your article or press release, you will be elevating your chances of publication above those businesses that do little or no research before pitching an ill-considered idea. Answer each question in as much detail as possible, and make notes. These notes will help when you send that first email or pick up the telephone to the editor.

1. **Having studied the contents of this publication, why do I think that my business is suitable for featuring in it?** Achieving worthwhile PR coverage takes time, so you need to be confident that this publication is read by a significant number of the audiences you want to attract.
2. **Why would the editor of this publication be interested in featuring me rather than one of my competitors?** What can I bring to the table that is new, different or interesting? What's in it for the editorial team? Where can I add real value to the publication for both the editorial team and the readers?
3. **What is my initial approach?** Could I sponsor a competition prize, write an articulate letter for the letters page in response to an article or feature? Could I suggest an article on a subject that has already featured in the magazine, but one that views the topic from a very different angle? Could I offer to run a competition with the prize being some free products/consultancy? Is there scope for a top tips article or potential for a question and answers column? If I have news to share, is it interesting to readers or just to me? How could I complement any forthcoming features? Could I offer myself as a trusted voice, someone the journalist can approach for an insightful comment to include in an article?

Having answered these questions, you're now going to have to pitch what you believe is your best idea for each publication. Make sure that you have expanded your idea sufficiently to be able to articulate it to the publication confidently. This will entail practising your pitch before you pick up the phone, or drafting several emails before sending the final one. Use the templates in the case studies later on in the masterclass to help you.

But first of all, who are you going to call or email? If you are happy that you know who you need to contact and how they like to be contacted, it's straightforward. However, with some publications your initial contact may be made purely to ascertain the details of the person you need to speak with in order to pitch your idea. In some instances, the gatekeeper will provide you with the email address of the editor or journalist, on other occasions you may be put straight through to the editorial contact. This is when being prepared with a concise introduction that includes who you are and your winning idea for editorial coverage in the publication, pays off. Practise delivering it in less than two minutes because this is probably the most time that you'll be allowed before judgement is pronounced!

If you're emailing, you need to present your idea in approximately 300 words with the most attractive part of your idea encapsulated in the first paragraph. The journalist or editor reading your message receives hundreds, if not thousands of emails. A long and rambling email about your ideas or an equally long and rambling press release is overkill. Your fantastic idea may be dismissed simply because you failed to present it concisely. Use the email template in the Kalimex case study to guide you.

A Good Telephone Introduction

Here's how I introduce myself to an editor or journalist that I have not spoken to before. In this example I am promoting my own business, not a client's. Simply replace the text in italics with your own details and include a memorable and impressive fact about you.

"Good morning. My name *is Dee Blick and I am a Fellow of The Chartered Institute of Marketing and a small business marketing author*. Can I briefly present an idea for an editorial feature that I believe, having studied your magazine in some detail, your readers would enjoy reading and be inspired by. Is now a good time to talk?"

If the answer is "yes," that's a good start. Sometimes the answer is "no;" not always because the editor or journalist is disinterested, but because they have more pressing things to attend to. When confronted with this, I suggest that I provide a summary of my idea in an email and call back at a more convenient time. If I am greeted by an answerphone, I will not leave a message but will keep on trying until I eventually get to speak to the editor or journalist.

Be aware, too, that when speaking to an editor or journalist, they may like your idea but will have their own thoughts on how they want it presented in their publication. You may be thinking of a press release, they may be thinking of a question and answer column. You may have thought of a competition, they may want to do a giveaway instead. Be flexible. You may end up with more coverage than you had initially anticipated simply because you were able to articulate your idea and its relevance to their readers with flair and precision.

What Happens When You're Given the Thumbs up?

I work with many journalists, editors and feature writers and can attest from our discussions that what most frustrates and irritates them is when they agree to an editorial idea only to be let down in one of the following ways:

1. **The instructions provided to the contributor detailing the way in which a feature should be written have been ignored.** If you're asked to write a piece for a publication, follow the editorial instructions to the letter. These instructions will usually include:
   - Word count for your submission – do not stray from this figure.
   - The tone of your submission – you will probably be advised about the tone of the article they're expecting you to write. They may also request specific emphasis on particular aspects, including certain facts, figures or quotations. Again, follow these instructions closely. Don't try and sneak in some selling points about your business. This is editorial, not paid-for advertising.
   - The general accuracy of your submission – you'll be expected to submit a piece without spelling or grammatical errors. Using spell check on your laptop is insufficient. Ensure your article is double-checked by a person that is pedantic about these matters.

- Accompanying images – if you've agreed to supply images with your submission, make sure they are to the standard required and provide any relevant captions, such as the names of people shown. Sending blurred, poor quality images could lead to your submission being sidelined.

- The copy deadline date – don't miss it! By sending a well-written, accurate submission within the copy deadline date you will be helping the editor and proving yourself a reliable contributor. Be late and the publication will need to fill the space allocated for your article at the last minute. Not something they will be pleased about, or likely to forget.

- Exclusivity – if the publication commissions an exclusive article, do not subsequently submit it to other publications. There exists an understandable degree of rivalry between publications vying for the loyalty of the same audience. Therefore, rather than aiming to gain coverage of the same article in a number of publications, try to build high-value relationships with a small number of publications and offer each one original material. By offering exclusive articles, you're likely to be viewed as a trusted contributor and this should in turn lead to further editorial coverage in the future.

2. **They are unable to get hold of the contributor at the agreed time or on the contact numbers provided.** Make sure that if an editor or journalist has agreed to interview you that you're available at the agreed time and can give your undivided attention to the interview or talk. It's also advisable to make yourself available in the hour before and after the interview to allow for changes to their schedule. Confirm your mobile and landline details once agreement has been reached for the interview.

Remember to thank the journalists and editors that have featured your business. Believe it or not, very few receive a personal email message of thanks or an enthusiastic phone call expressing gratitude for the coverage. Don't take that coverage for granted.

See These Tips in Action with Three Small Business Case Studies

As you read each one of these case studies consider how you too can use the different PR approaches for your own business.

Case Study 1 – Cocoa Loco

Cocoa Loco is a multi-award-winning artisan chocolate business based in West Sussex, specialising in organic and Fairtrade chocolate products. When they were exhibiting at the Speciality Fine Food Fair in London they wanted to attract as many journalists as possible to their stand, the goal being to showcase their new branding and to highlight the fact that their range was now organic and Fairtrade. With hundreds of exhibitors to compete with, this was a tall order.

They needed to stand out from the other exhibitors by doing something a little different. Therefore, rather than simply sending out a press release to the journalists they knew would be attending the event, they sent the following letter instead, accompanying it with a jumbo bar of their chocolate in their new packaging and one of their new eco-bags. Everything was tissue wrapped, enclosed in a recyclable gift box and sent by recorded delivery to each journalist. Within just one day of the letters hitting the mat, two journalists had contacted Sarah Payne, founder of Cocoa Loco, to confirm they would be visiting her stand. These journalists then took to social media to express their admiration of the new packaging and Cocoa Loco's organic and Fairtrade status. On the day itself, many of those journalists targeted with the mailshot turned up at the Cocoa Loco stand resulting in a significant amount of media coverage of the company in both printed and on-line publications after the event.

Here is the letter . . .

Dear (journalist name)

I would like to invite you to visit our stand at the Speciality Fine Food Show at Olympia in London. Cocoa Loco will be exhibiting at the show from Sunday 2 September to Wednesday 5 September.

We do have genuine news to break!

*We now have the largest range of organic **and** Fairtrade artisan handmade chocolate products anywhere in the UK and at the show we will also be unveiling our new packaging and rebrand.*

We would also like to thank you for your time with one of our absolutely divine jumbo handmade chocolate slabs, personalised with a message of your choice and presented in a beautiful fully recyclable gift box trimmed with Cocoa Loco ribbon. It will be waiting for you!

A few facts about Cocoa Loco . . .

Here are just five reasons why many national brands including Abel & Cole, John Lewis, Oxfam, Jamie Oliver and many purveyors of fine food emporiums and delicatessens the length and breadth of the UK choose to sell our handmade organic and now Fairtrade chocolate.

1. Our chocolate is single origin, lovingly handmade in small batches by skilled chocolatiers. It is superb quality, artisan, tasty, scrumptious and multi-award-winning. Of the many awards we have scooped, the most recent is for our chocolate eggs in an Easter competition run by the *Daily Telegraph* this year.
2. Made in Britain. We are proud to be a British business operating in the heart of West Sussex at our premises, the purpose-built and aptly named, Chocolate Barn.
3. You won't find Cocoa Loco in any of the major supermarkets.
4. As you would expect, we make bittersweet velvety dark chocolate, the most luscious smooth and creamy white chocolate, plus milk chocolate so more-ish that you will need to ration yourself. But recognising that today customers want it all, we also make a range of divine, naturally-flavoured bars including . . . white chocolate and raspberry; white chocolate and rose geranium, with a whisper of geranium oil; milk chocolate and orange, with zingy Italian oranges; milk chocolate and brazil nuts (whole brazils, never slivers); milk chocolate with our handmade sesame snap and honey; dark chocolate and nibs, packed with antioxidants, plus the intriguing dark chocolate and sunflower seeds with sea salt.
5. Our range extends beyond bars and into exquisite truffles, big fat milk, dark and white chocolate buttons, intensely rich and dark chocolate brownies, baking kits in gorgeous Kilner jars, nutty flapjacks and cookies and so much more. Everything is made by hand with the same painstaking attention to detail.

Unveiling our new rebrand and Fairtrade accreditation at the Speciality Fine Food show

At The Speciality Fine Food Show we are unveiling our new rebrand and packaging and celebrating that, after months of hard work, we now have Fairtrade accreditation for each one of our recipes.

In the next few days you'll receive a phone call from one of our team asking for the details of the special message you would like on your free chocolate slab. We can personalise it with a message for a friend or relative if you're feeling generous! In the meantime, I hope that you enjoy one of our handmade, Fairtrade and organic jumbo bars, contained within our new packaging.

(Continued)

Kind regards

Sarah Payne

Founder, Cocoa Loco

PS: Our stand number 25 is located near to the restaurant. My mobile number is xxxxxxxxxxxxx and it will be switched on throughout the show. You can also email xxxxxxx

What can you learn from this case study?

1. If you would like to draw journalists to your exhibition stand why not send an imaginative but appropriate alternative to a straightforward press release?
2. What could you add to your letter or press release to make it intriguing? Visit Masterclass 8 to study the benefits of lumpy mail.
3. Consider what message would grab the attention of journalists. Have you recently launched a new product or service? Are you entering into a new market? Have you recently gained an award or qualification that you could shout about?

Case Study 2 – Kalimex

Kalimex supplies high quality motor repair products for the professional motor mechanics and the DIY enthusiast. These products are sold through motor factor stockists. Although Kalimex had been extremely successful in building PR in the trade magazines that were read by motor factors and mechanics, they wanted to target end users – the DIY motor enthusiast looking for a proven, cost-effective motor repair solution to their problem. Three of the biggest motor enthusiast magazines were identified as the ones in which Kalimex should to try to gain coverage, but it was only after following the process outlined in this masterclass that this coverage was achieved.

The content of the three magazines was studied in order to identify how Kalimex could add value without conflicting with existing advertisers. As each editor of the magazines had specified on their website that they preferred to be contacted electronically, an email was sent to them. Within 10 days, two of the editors had responded confirming that they would be happy to feature some coverage of K-Seal, Kalimex's permanent coolant leak repair product. One magazine was prepared to run a giveaway of K-Seal, the other to have an editorial feature on K-Seal. This coverage was worth its weight in gold given that the reach of the magazines was in excess of 500,000 readers. Less than 300 words inspired the editors sufficiently to persuade them to give Kalimex thousands of pounds worth of free coverage in their premium publications.

Here is one of the successful emails:

Dear (editor's name)

I am writing to you because one of our products, K-Seal permanent coolant leak repair, is very popular with performance car owners – it permanently fixes most leaks in the block, head, head gasket, and radiator and heater matrix in one application. It can keep an ageing vehicle on the road for many more years without the need for a costly work-shop repair.

Could I ask if it would be possible for us to give away some K-Seal goody bags in *XXXXXXX* magazine for your readers comprising of a full size bottle of K-Seal, a T-shirt and key ring (worth £40 each). We would be more than happy, delighted in fact, if you would allow us to give away 10 goody bags in exchange for name checking K-Seal in your prestigious publication. Because K-Seal is exceptionally popular with car enthusiasts I would hope that it would be a very popular promotion. Two million bottles have sold worldwide and it is the Number 1 bestselling permanent coolant leak repair with profes-sional motor mechanics. You simply shake, pour and go.

If you would like me to send you a goody bag initially with some information on K-Seal as a precursor to running a give-away, please let me know. I did not want to take the liberty of sending you a sample without asking, as I am sure you are deluged with busi-nesses sending you products on an unsolicited basis. Please let me know the address that you would like the goody bag to be sent to.

I look forward to hearing from you.

Kind regards

Dee Blick FCIM

Chartered Marketer

Kalimex Ltd

Some Points to Note . . .

1. One well-written email can sometimes be all that's needed to achieve the coverage you're keen to secure if your proposition is sufficiently appealing to the editor.
2. A concise message can often be more appealing and persuasive than a lengthy description of an idea.
3. Offering your product as a give-away or competition prize is highly effective. The product will be described in some detail in the publication and the feature will usually include a high quality image.

Case Study 3 – Dyno-Pest

Dyno-Pest specialises in pest prevention and pest control for businesses and homes in the Greater London area. When its membership association, the British Pest Control Association (BPCA), launched a high-quality magazine called *Alexo*, targeted at facilities managers and other purchasers of pest control, Dyno-Pest was keen to be featured. After asking for a copy of the features schedule, we were able to put forward ideas for an article that would complement the forthcoming items. In the particular issue in which Dyno-Pest was keen to secure PR coverage, the focus of the magazine was on proactive pest control for businesses involved in the production and storage of food. The BPCA was also keen to promote the benefits of readers using their members' services; something that Dyno-Pest was already aware of.

An email was sent to the editor of *Alexo* explaining that Dyno-Pest was ready to provide an article supporting the editorial stance of the magazine. This proposal received an immediate positive response and Dyno-Pest was allowed to contribute two full pages of editorial. The article was objective and did not promote Dyno-Pest's services directly. The expert featured in the article, however, was Dyno-Pest Managing Director, Ralph Izod.

Here is the main section of the email I wrote pitching the idea for the feature to the editor.

"I would be happy to write a full page article on the importance of businesses involved in food production and storage obtaining expert consultancy (and not just treatment and traps) from a BPCA member. I would explain in the article why advice at all stages of the growth of the business is crucial – more plant, more goods and more staff also

Increases the potential for pest problems and so simply continuing with the original pest treatment regimes is flawed. My advice to the readers would boil down to, "Don't take a mechanical tick box approach to pest control; put pest management at the heart of your business with an ongoing dialogue with your BPCA pest controller".

I would however need to write 600 words to make it a meaty article and not just a sweep over."

What Can You Learn from This Approach?

1. This case study shows the value in studying the features schedule of a publication and considering whether you can contribute an article that would strengthen a planned feature in the magazine. If so, suggest this.
2. When approaching your media contact, always consider what they will gain from your proposal. Note how the email empathises with the need to promote the service of BPCA members; an objective that Dyno-Pest was aware that the BPCA takes very seriously.

No masterclass on how to get PR in printed publications would be complete without expert top tips on how to write a press release. Here are some fantastic ones from Aneela Rose, founder of the award-winning business to business PR agency, Aneela Rose PR.

How to Write an Effective Press Release – by Aneela Rose

Communicating with the media is an art in itself. Who you contact, what you say, when you say it – all have a bearing on whether your news is printed or not.

Preparing and distributing a press release, also known as a media release, news release or press statement is the globally accepted format in which to send out news to the media. If you want to whip up a media storm, a professional-looking press release is the way to go about it but it must be factual, concise, interesting and use pertinent facts. A real life press release example of a Sussex landscape machinery company called Tracmaster is included and referenced in this section.

1. Your Story Must be Newsworthy

Does your news affect other people, customers, countries, the local area or the world? Be realistic. If your company has restructured and has a new Technical Director, this will be of interest to trade publications not the BBC! Our example story is of a Sussex company moving into new offices, which is not breaking news, but the investment and expansion angle is our hook.

2. Build a Targeted Media List

Know who to send your release to, and know your publication. Before writing your release, research and build a specific list in order to shape your release and define your approach. Who will this story be of interest to? Is it purely of local relevance or is it of industry significance with national interest? The Editor is the best contact on a local paper or the Features Writer on a trade magazine if your news is for a niche market. The Tracmaster story was crafted with specific local business and trade journalists in mind.

3. Write a First Class Press Release:

3.1 The headline is the hook

The headline must be compelling and create immediate impact as it is sometimes the only thing the journalist will read. State your most exciting news, finding or announcement succinctly. Think of headlines you notice in the local papers or trade publications you read every week. Puns work well but not too much cheese!

Bad press release headlines

- Tracmaster opens new office
- Tracmaster celebrates new office
- New larger office for Tracmaster

Good press release headlines

- Investment Shapes the Future for Tracmaster
- Tracmaster Celebrates: Larger Premises. Expanded Services. New Future.
- Innovation Through Growth. Tracmaster Diversifies and Celebrates Opening of New Premises.

In our example headline, *"Tracmaster Invests in the Future and Celebrates Opening of New Premises,"* the attention grabbing keywords are **"invests," "future"** and **"celebrates."**

3.2 A must-read opening paragraph

Get right to the point in the opening lines, you must answer Who? What? Where? How? and Why? in one snappy paragraph, as in our example. Your release will be accepted or rejected on the basis of your headline *and* introduction so make sure it's packed full of newsworthy content.

3.3 KISS! keep it short and sweet

One page is ideal, two pages is maximum. There's a natural tendency to be salesy. Resist this! It would have been easy to plug the product range more in the Tracmaster release but this isn't the news. Remain objective and stick to the facts. Look at your story from the journalist's perspective and what the readers will find interesting and relevant in as few words as possible.

3.4 Make it grammatically flawless

As Dee said earlier, a single mistake will put off a journalist as your professional image is compromised. Ask a colleague or friend to look over your release as a second pair of eyes. Don't rely on your computer to pick up mistakes.

3.5 Include hard numbers

Support your announcement with figures; your news will be more compelling. Tracmaster's story is given more gravitas with the inclusion of numbers, *"Since moving to an appointed dealer network, its sales through dealers have increased threefold; whilst its market share for two wheel tractors has grown to an estimated 60% in the UK."*

3.6 Get quoted

Insert a catchy statement from yourself or an industry expert to add further interest. Try not to repeat what you've already stated in the release, include new data and don't be afraid to be bold. We've concluded our release with a strong closing remark, *"new opportunities and international markets have opened up for us," said Alex Pitt.*

3.7 Editors like notes

At the foot of your release add a background statement with a mini-biography and website link. Only include information that isn't already mentioned in your release. Also known as a "boilerplate," this is standard and reusable information that includes contact details for editorial follow-up.

Power words that will grab attention		
Discover	Guarantee	Results
New	Improve	Proven
Simplify	Boost	Stop
Future	Profit	Discover
Intensify	Transform	Achieve

Words that are over-used in press releases and should be avoided		
Unique	Best of breed	Revolutionary
One of a kind	Seamless	Customer-centric
Organic growth	Solution driven	Next generation
Value added	Outside the box	End user

4. Supply an Outstanding Photograph

Readers first notice an image then the headline and, if interested, they'll continue to read the article. Photographs are powerful and persuasive and, as first impressions mean everything in PR, supply a photograph that is print-quality, high-resolution and ready to be published with an articulate caption to help get your story noticed. Two images were supplied with the Tracmaster release; one of Nicholas Soames MP cutting the ribbon and the other of the proud Tracmaster team outside their new building.

5. Distribute Your Press Release to a Select Group of Journalists

Plan the distribution of your release to a small group of researched and correct journalists rather than sending it en-masse to random contacts; this will give your story more prominence and will achieve better quality coverage. Email is the preferred method nowadays, with the release embedded within your message as opposed to an attachment as this will be deleted or caught up in spam filters.

6. Make Journalists Care about Your Story

Following up your release is essential, contrary to what you may have been told! The general rule is three interactions with 3–4 days in between. Instead of asking the journalist if they received your release, explain why the news is interesting. In our example, I phoned the journalist and said, "I sent you some information about a local company investing in its business which contradicts the current manufacturing trends." I got his attention immediately and he wanted to know more.

Getting Results

Even if you don't get coverage first time, spending all that time and effort will not have been in vain – far from it! You will have brought your name to the attention of journalists which allows you to start forming relationships, which is at the very heart of PR.

With the Tracmaster release, the main objective was to get the story printed in the four local newspapers and five key trade publications including *Horticulture Week* and *The Landscaper*, all of which was achieved. As a result, the news was exposed to a readership of around 195,000 people.

Example of Actual Press Release

Press Release

<insert date you send the release out>

Tracmaster Invests in the Future and Celebrates Opening of New Premises

Sussex-based Tracmaster, a leading landscape and groundcare machinery specialist, celebrated the opening of new larger premises in the Victoria Business Park, Burgess Hill, on Friday 9 September 2011. To honour the occasion the RT Hon Nicholas Soames MP officially opened the building, cut the ribbon and spoke to staff and guests at the launch event. Guests toured the new modern facilities led by Tracmaster's expert guides and explored behind-the-scenes.

The opening event, co-hosted with the Burgess Hill Business Parks Association, celebrated Tracmaster's launch of its substantially larger offices, warehouse facilities and the introduction of a new trade counter facility. The move allows expansion of its manufacturing capability to further develop its own CAMON brand and range of machinery.

Tracmaster's investment in the new building follows a period of growth for the company. Since moving to an appointed dealer network, its sales through dealers have increased threefold; whilst its market share for two wheel tractors has grown to an estimated 60% in the UK.

Key to Tracmaster's growth and expansion is the continued development of two machinery brands, CAMON and BCS, both of which have become widely known and respected for their performance and durability. In addition in recent years, Tracmaster has shown its innovation through diversifying its product range, adding to its core lawn and groundcare machinery with the launch of snow clearing equipment and micro crushers.

At the event, sales and marketing director, Alex Pitt announced that Tracmaster had just been appointed by Spanish agricultural and groundcare manufacturer, Ribas, as the sole UK distributor for its ploughs and workshop machinery. Alex also revealed that Tracmaster is currently in talks with a major UK company in regards to becoming the local mid-Sussex dealer for a newly launched range of lawnmowers and ride-on tractors.

"Today we are looking forward to a positive future as our expansion marks the beginning of many new developments for Tracmaster. The larger premises gives us the space to actively work on our Camon range which we first launched in 1994; open a trade counter for the first time; and expand our in-house production capability. As the new UK distributor for Ribas ploughs and workshop machinery, new opportunities and international markets have opened up for us," said Alex Pitt.

– ENDS –

Notes to Editors: (www.tracmaster.co.uk)
West Sussex based Tracmaster has been successfully supplying lawn and groundcare machinery to a wide variety of customers across the United Kingdom for over 25 years. Established in 1984, Tracmaster has grown and developed two brands of machinery, CAMON and BCS that have become widely known and respected for their performance and durability.

For more information & images, please contact our media representative:
Aneela Rose at Aneela Rose PR
Tel: 01444 241341
aneela@aneelarosepr.co.uk

Thanks to Aneela for providing such useful, proven and experienced advice.

So, finally, having secured all this fabulous PR coverage, let's consider how your business can benefit from it. You should try to take advantage of every drop of that positive exposure.

Putting Your PR Coverage to Good Use

Make sure that you increase the impact of your PR coverage beyond the initial publications in which you and your business are featured, in the following simple ways:

1. When writing sales letters, use the back of the letter to include snippets of your press coverage. Or, if that space is already earmarked for other messages, use the space usually reserved for a postscript. Include a line such as: "As featured in *XYZ* magazine."
2. Where can you include the details of media coverage on your website? Could you provide a selection of articles or news that you have secured for visitors to download? Perhaps a list of your media coverage accompanied by the logos of the publications (make sure that you get their permission beforehand) would be more appropriate. Do you need to beef up your "About Us" page to include your media coverage?
3. Could you add some of the details of your media coverage to your email signature? For example: "Dee writes a monthly marketing column for the *District Post* business pages." Or "Read our feature on pest control and food production in the September issue of *Alexo* magazine."
4. When networking, make your networking peers aware of your media coverage. They will then hopefully be able to use this to good effect when introducing your business to their pool of contacts.
5. Include details of your press coverage in any credentials documents for cold prospects. Whether it is true or not, the perception of people is that you're doing very well if they see you getting good media coverage. Conveying this to cold prospects will therefore increase the likelihood of them wanting to do business with you.
6. Use your media coverage to get even bigger and better coverage. You may start out with a smattering of coverage in a few publications such as the odd news feature in the business section of your local newspaper, but as your confidence and experience of working with media people grows, you can aim higher. Use the coverage you have gained to demonstrate to other journalists that you know the media ropes and can be trusted to deliver.

7. Let your followers on social networking sites know about your coverage by posting the details of it and providing any links.
8. Let your audience know when you are invited to speak in public. A few minutes at the start, establishing your credentials and alerting your audience to the publications that they can find you in, all helps in building their perception of you as an expert in your sector.

Masterclass Summary

- High-quality PR exposure is within your reach and it will lead to an increase in sales for your business.
- It takes more than just a well-written press release to guarantee PR coverage for your business.
- Use the Internet and your local library to search for publications read by your target audiences.
- Analyse each publication in detail; where could you contribute news stories, press releases, competitions, perhaps an expert column?
- Gather information on the readers of the publication. Are they your ideal clients?
- Ask yourself "What can I offer that a journalist or editor will be really interested in covering?"
- Before sending an email or picking up the phone, prepare a concise introduction, focusing on how readers will benefit from what you have to offer.
- Be flexible and prepared to abandon your own idea to accommodate alternative suggestions from the editor or journalist.
- Deliver on time and to the exact word count. Your article must flow, be grammatically perfect and read well.
- Thank your contact at the publication when your piece goes live.
- Be creative when trying to attract the attention of a journalist. Send a printed letter, a gift or a goody bag.
- Press releases still work. Make sure yours consist of genuine news and not sales spiel.
- Gain maximum value from any media coverage by promoting it when public speaking, on your website and in all communications.

Masterclass 8
Why It Pays to
Do Direct Mail

In this masterclass you will learn:

- Why direct mail is here to stay.
- How to successfully use direct mail to grow your business.
- The answers to the most frequently asked questions on direct mail.

Recently, The Chartered Institute of Marketing has heralded direct mail as a comeback kid. In my own experience, direct mail has always been a cost-effective marketing channel for small businesses, providing an ideal method in which to communicate with lapsed customers, existing clients, cold prospects, potential introducers and even journalists. So, in this masterclass, we're going to look at how you too can use direct mail effectively.

If you have previously tried direct mail and have been disappointed with the results, you are probably tempted to dismiss it completely as an ineffectual marketing medium. It may be, however, that a different approach is all that's required to start seeing a more positive reaction.

Let's start by looking at some of the reasons why direct mail campaigns can fail:

1. **Insufficient time is spent on developing compelling sales messages.** As a result they can come across as weak or vague. Benefit messages, facts and figures, case studies and testimonial that could inspire recipients to read the letter and other enclosures from beginning to end are not present.
2. **A "cheap as chips" approach is taken.** A flimsy flyer, a letter printed on poor quality paper with a blurry faxed signature, addressed with an impersonal printed label; if something this cheap looking pops through the letter box, most recipients will quickly consign the package to the recycling bin, unopened and unread.
3. **The contents are unprofessional and unattractive.** No matter how compelling or targeted the message, it will undoubtedly be diminished by spelling mistakes and poor formatting.
4. **The mailing list used is out of date.** Large numbers of returned, unopened envelopes are a tell-tale sign of this being the case and suggest an unsuccessful campaign.
5. **The customer database is unfit for use.** It may have been originally built for administrative or invoicing purposes but to use the same list as a marketing

database without any close inspection or refinement is unwise. It can result in some customers receiving several copies of the same mailing because they have more than one record on the system, others being mailed with an incorrectly spelt name or address and some not receiving any mailing at all because it has been sent to a previous address. Every customer database should be regularly cleaned and customer details checked to ensure they are still up to date to prevent the risk of loyal customers becoming irritated.

6. **The request made in the letter is unrealistic.** For example, asking a cold prospect with no awareness of your business to immediately become a customer on the back of one letter is unlikely to be successful. Instead, a planned and integrated campaign will probably be required.

7. **The mailshot is rushed.** No time is invested in crafting a timely, relevant and charming message; no money spent with a designer to ensure that the accompanying literature looks attractive.

So, assuming you avoid these mistakes, why can direct mail be such a powerful and cost-effective medium for you and your business?

1. **You gain a share of your reader's mind.** The people you want to reach are busy. Capturing their attention is a challenge. However, there is every chance that a well-written and timely direct mailshot, will lead to the recipient affording you some of their undivided time as they read your message.

2. **You can build a strong proposition to buy.** Decision-makers, whether business people or consumers, need sufficient information to persuade them to move from the early buying stages of "awareness" and "interest," through to "evaluation," "desire" and then "action". Direct mail provides the space and the freedom to provide this information and to present your business in an articulate and compelling fashion.

3. **Low-cost but with the potential of a high return.** It is possible to spend very little on a direct mail campaign and still enjoy high returns. (The three case studies covered later in the masterclass will illustrate this.) One letter printed on your letterhead paper, one business card and one envelope are your basic direct mail ingredients, and often this is all that you will need.

4. **Fast with impact.** Within days of making the decision to send out a mailshot, your message is hitting door mats. Direct mail is ideal for promoting your latest seminars, your product launches, your improved services or even last-minute offers. It is also the perfect medium for including samples, giveaways, vouchers and running special promotions.

5. **Loyalty building.** Direct mail enables you to communicate cost-effectively with your existing customers and consequently to build on their loyalty. Your latest newsletter or customer-only offers are just a couple of examples of mailings that will help achieve this.

6. **Engages all the senses.** Direct mail is a highly tactile medium and, because of this, has been proven in many cases to have more impact than a message conveyed electronically.

7. **Highly targeted.** Direct mail enables you to target your audience very precisely, irrespective of whether you are targeting five key decision-makers in five different businesses or mailing 20,000 cold prospects.

8. **The perfect blending tool!** Direct mail can be successfully used as a stand-alone marketing tool but, ideally, should also be integrated with other marketing activities to increase response. A telephone call made before or after your mailshot can help improve response rates. A follow-up email sent a few days after your mailshot has landed will remind those interested recipients to get in touch with you. A message on Twitter, Facebook or LinkedIn alerting the recipient that something special is in the post will ensure it's singled out for attention when the post arrives.

9. **The perfect partner to on-line promotion.** Direct mail can motivate cold prospects, warm prospects, lapsed customers and existing clients to visit your website, sign up to your blog, download your latest offer or to connect through social media. It can follow up your LinkedIn introductions and your email marketing campaigns.

Some strong reasons there for giving direct mail a chance, but who should you be sending direct mail to?

Direct mail can be used to:

- **Reconnect with your lapsed customers.** Just because a customer has not bought from you for several months doesn't mean they're no longer interested in what you have to offer or that they've gone elsewhere. You won't know until you update them on what they have been missing. Why not create a special offer to woo them back? Why not update them with the improvements in your products and services, new benefits, added value initiatives and your value-for-money pricing structure?

- **Build a relationship with warm prospects.** Warm prospects are simply those people who are interested enough to contact you but are yet to become paying customers. They may have completed a form on your website, telephoned, sent an email or held an initial meeting with you. A thoughtful letter acknowledging this, combined with some compelling benefits and a genuine new customer offer may be all that is required to convert the "interested but too busy to get in touch" prospects into new customers.

- **Contact your existing customers.** As you will see with the BEL Signs case study, you should not assume that your customers are aware of all your services or products. Keeping them updated will help build their loyalty and increase sales.

- **Maintain contact with exhibition visitors.** It's tempting to return from an exhibition with delight at the number of people that visited your stand and completed your enquiry form, only to be sucked back into the day-to-day running of the business and to let the dust gather on those leads. A charming follow-up letter could be all that is needed to arrange those important face-to-face meetings.

- **Introduce yourself to cold prospects, strategic partners or influencers.** Good quality lists are effective when you are looking to grow your client base. In the Perrys case study you can see how it is possible to generate sales from a prospect list if you spend some time selecting those prospects that you want to mail.

- **Connect with networking referrals.** Direct mail is an effective way of introducing yourself to the referrals passed to you by your networking colleagues. A letter that focuses upon the benefits you offer, suggests a meeting and includes some genuine customer testimonial to boost your case could be the first step to securing new business.

- **Communicate with a targeted media list.** Persuading a journalist to acknowledge your press release, let alone publish it, is not always easy. Sending a concise accompanying letter, perhaps including an enticing lumpy element, stands a good chance of at least grabbing their attention. You can find out how Coco Loco did just this in Masterclass 7, and read the letter too.
- **Communicate with those people that subscribe to your blog or email newsletter.** Any person that has subscribed to your blog or email newsletter has demonstrated that they are interested in you. However, although this interest may have been demonstrated in an on-line manner, do not presume that all dialogue needs to be similarly restricted. Discern the level of interest by requesting your subscribers to provide a business or home addresses, explaining that you would like to send a mailshot promoting a service you think will appeal to them.

As you can see, with direct mail you can communicate effectively with many different target audiences. When targeting businesses, however, it is easy to forget that real people with their own tastes and preferences sit behind the business names. When these people receive your mailshot, they are going to compare your offering with the experiences they have as an individual consumer. So treat them as individuals, not simply a business name on a list.

Before embarking on your mailshot, ask yourself the following questions:

- Who am I targeting and why?
- What is my message?
- What case studies and testimonial can I use to strengthen my message?
- What facts and figures, before and after examples can I use to strengthen my message?
- Why should the reader consider my message? What's in it for them?
- Will an offer open the door to a dialogue?
- What are the deep underlying needs of each different group that I am targeting?
- Have those needs changed recently? Do I know my audience really well or should I undertake some research?

- What objections could the recipients have to my message and how should I address these in my mailshot?
- This audience is not using me. Could they be using a competitor or have other arrangements? Can I address this or at least recognise this in the mailshot?

I would also encourage you to complete your positioning statement before planning your first mailshot, so read the tips in Masterclass 2. This will provide you with up-to-date, good quality, benefit-driven content upon which to build your mailshot. Some of the questions above will be answered in your positioning statement.

How Will You Find Your Target Audiences?

If direct mail is being used to help grow your business, there may come a time when you need to buy or rent a mailing list in order to increase your client base. Use the following top tips to ensure that the data you select is of the right quality to deliver good hot prospects rather than a mountain of returned unopened envelopes.

- Ensure that the data provider is a member of the Direct Marketing Association, is registered with the List Warranty Register and complies with the Data Protection Act.
- Ask about their mailing accuracy guarantee. An exemplary provider of data will have an accuracy guarantee of 98%. What does this mean? It means that if more than 2% of the list comprise of "gone away" or "ceased trading" you will receive a refund for each rejected record above that 2% allowance. If the list provider does not provide any such guarantee it suggests that the list is not regularly cleaned.
- If you plan to contact the prospects on your list via the telephone, ensure the data is automatically checked against the Telephone Preference Service and Corporate Telephone Preference Service registers. If the data has been checked against these registers, you can confidently call the people on the list for up to 30 days after buying the data, knowing that they have not opted out of receiving cold telephone calls.

- If you rent a mailing list, ask how many times you can use it. You can usually rent a mailing list for a single use or for multiple or unlimited use over an agreed period of time. As Liz covers in Masterclass 10 too, you won't get away with unpaid additional uses if you've opted for one-time use only. In every mailing list there are "seed names," names used to monitor mailing list usage and uncover any deception.
- Clarify the level of information that you will receive for each prospect. Is a named contact included for each company and, if so, what is the job title for that name? For example, an accountant may want to reach the financial director in a large organisation and the managing director in a small business. What percentage of the list comes with a named contact?
- Give clear and detailed instructions about the types of businesses that you want to target and those that you would prefer to exclude. This is crucial. It's worth spending several hours refining your list so that you end up with only those prospects that you want to target. A couple of examples of specific requirements are:
  - "Owner-managed businesses, one to three director shareholders, between £300,000 and £1m annual turnover in the LS18, LS19 and LS20 postcode area."
  - "Commercial insurance brokers in the RH6 to RH19 postcodes with a minimum of 3 staff, no maximum."

Requirements such as these will result in a highly targeted prospect list. Vague requirements such as "Small businesses in Warwickshire" will result in a prospect list that includes many businesses that do not fit your criteria of ideal client.

Similarly, when it comes to excluding companies that you do not wish to target, it is again much better to be specific than vague. Specifying that you wish to:

- "Exclude all businesses with an annual turnover below £77,000 plus all takeaways, fish and chip shops, cafes, confectioners, tobacconists and newsagents, irrespective of turnover."

. . . will result in a far more accurate list than the one you will receive if you simply state that you want to:

- "Exclude all retail businesses and small businesses."

- Before committing to buying a list, ask the list provider to supply a written statement detailing the number of names, how they are segmented into different classifications and postcodes, and the terms of your rental or purchase agreement. Make sure that you know what you are buying. Ask them how they source their data, how often it is replenished and checked, and for their mailing accuracy guarantee.

You probably still want to know more about how to ensure your direct mail campaign is a success, so let me see if I can help by addressing the five questions I am most frequently asked about direct mail.

Five Direct Mail Questions and Answers

1. How Can I Ensure That My Mailshot Is Opened?

This is not as hard as you imagine. You simply need the envelope to grab the attention of the recipient. There are a number of ways in which you can go about doing this. A good quality white window envelope looks formal and professional and therefore generates curiosity. Conversely, an envelope in your corporate colours will often stand out from the rest of the mail delivered that day. Handwriting the name and address of the recipient will infer that a personal message is included inside, whereas enclosing your mailshot in a jiffy bag or coloured padded envelope will suggest a free gift of some kind. Add an item to your mailshot to make it "lumpy" and your recipient will immediately be intrigued. Coasters, pens, mouse mats, keyrings, fridge magnets, retro sweets, teabags, organic chocolate bars and product samples where appropriate are some of the items I have used in order to make a mailshot lumpy.

Ensure that any lumpy enclosure is pertinent to your brand and that it is aligned to the message within your letter. If you want your mailshot to bypass the gatekeeper or PA, which is especially important when targeting senior individuals, make sure that your envelope has "Confidential Addressee Only" written above the address details. If you're mailing people within striking distance of where you live or work, why not hand deliver your mailshot, with the words "By Hand" written neatly in the top right-hand corner of the envelope. That will definitely get it opened!

2. Do I Have to Follow up Everyone I Mail by Telephone for My Mailshot to Work?

In the real world it is not always possible to do this and, in fact, there may be times when a follow-up phone call is not needed anyway. One example of a call not being necessary is when you are using direct mail purely to keep in touch with your customers. Following up every time by phone could be regarded as intrusive.

In many cases, however, there is real value in making a call to a selected number of recipients in order to begin that all important two-way dialogue. So, when planning your mailshots, build in some time for follow-up calls, but make them only to those VIPs that warrant this personal approach.

A phone call is not the only way to follow up a mailshot and maintain momentum. You can follow up with another mailshot, with an email, with a LinkedIn invitation, by posting a message on Twitter or Facebook. I am often asked how frequently you can mailshot an individual before they become irritated by your overtures. There are no hard and fast rules. It depends upon the quality of your message and whether you are communicating information that the individual will really appreciate. One of my clients mails his customer base each month with details of a different offer, whereas another will mail their cold prospect list on a quarterly basis to coincide with the production of their high-quality newsletter.

3. What Response Can I Expect from My Mailshot?

This really is the $64,000 question. Every campaign is different. The level of response that you receive will vary depending on what you are asking the recipients to do and the relationship you have with them. For example, you could expect a fairly high response (say, 25%) when mailing your customer base with a survey, but repeat the exercise with cold prospects and this figure will drop considerably. If you ask your customers to respond to your mailing in order to receive a free upgrade, again you can expect a very high response. But mail them with an offer to buy new products or services and the response will be much lower. Rather than trying to predict the level of response and then potentially being disappointed, concentrate instead upon the costs of your mailshot and compare this with the value of new sales achieved as a result of the campaign. If we look at the example of Perrys Chartered Accountants (see Case Study No. 1), the response rate from their mailshot was 2%. This does not sound exceptional but, in reality, the fee income generated from those 20 new clients easily covered the costs of the mailshot. Also worth consideration is that Perrys retain their clients for many years. When the lifetime value of each client is calculated and contrasted with the one-off cost of the mailshot, the argument that the campaign was a great success was a very persuasive one indeed. Do bear in mind the lifetime value of a new client obtained through a direct mailshot when you evaluate the costs and benefits of a campaign.

4. What Can I Add to My Sales Letter to Make My Mailshot More Interesting?

In some situations a simple, hand-signed sales letter, written on good quality letterhead paper, is sufficient for its purpose and any additional enclosures would be inappropriate. This would be the case, for example, if writing to senior decision-makers. In other cases, however, it is true that enclosures can give a sales communication some added weight and interest. Examples of the type of enclosures that could be added to your sales letter include your latest newsletter, a press release, a voucher, a sheet of common questions and answers, a competition, some customer testimonials and a selection of customer case studies. The quality of your enclosures should be high and the content up-to-date. A label detailing your new contact details stuck onto a leaflet to cover your old contact details immediately conveys a sloppy impression. A newsletter that's obviously several months old will do the same. But one fantastic letter, with or without a lumpy item, could be all that is needed for your message to have real impact.

5. How Do I Go about Writing a Great Sales Letter?

Here are some easy-to-implement tips:

- Don't skimp on the weight and quality of the paper. Hold it in your hands. Does it look and feel professional?

- If you are enclosing your business card ensure that it matches the look and quality of your letterhead.
- If you can hand sign your letter, that's great; if not, aim for the best quality printed signature possible.
- Don't be put off writing a long sales letter. In tests, long sales letters tend to outperform short ones.
- Write in a conversational style. Read your letter out loud to hear how it sounds.
- Your introduction should spell out why you're writing to the recipient.
- Use the template at the end of this masterclass so that your letter is nicely laid out and therefore easy to read.
- As covered in many of the masterclasses in this book you're more likely to maintain the reader's interest if you use the words "you" and "your" throughout rather than "us" and "we."
- Refer to your positioning statement so that you can lavish your letter with benefits.
- Include positive customer testimonial but ensure it is recent and genuine.
- Consider asking questions to add variety to the letter.
- Can you make a great offer?
- Are you making it easy for the reader to get in touch with you? Don't assume everyone wants to email you. Offer choices.
- Pass your letter to a person who is unafraid to challenge you or offer constructive criticism.

The Sales Letter Template

Here are the components of a successful sales letter:

- **The Johnson box:** The Johnson Box refers to the few inches of space above the salutation. If you have something really special that you would like your letter to lead with, use this space to grab the reader's attention. You could use it to ask a question, as I did in the example of the BEL Signs letter (Case Study No.3), or to include some positive testimonial from a customer. Perhaps you could share a compelling fact or statistic about your product or service. If this was an advert, the Johnson box would be your attention grabbing headline. You don't need to use the Johnson box every time by any means, but if you have something to shout about it, it's a good space in which to do so.

- **Your salutation:** Dear Mrs Ferguson, Dear Mike, Dear Dr. Collins, Dear Householder – the salutation must be appropriate, accurate and, if possible, to a named person.
- **Your introduction:** A neat, short paragraph explaining in a friendly, conversational style the purpose of your letter. Review the introductions in the three letters included in the case studies at the end of this. Think to yourself "Why am I writing to this person?"
- **The heart of your letter:** Ideally this will consist of some bullet points or a few compelling paragraphs describing the benefits that your product or service can offer. When using bullet points, try to keep each one to a few lines of text. If this is not possible, revert instead to writing mini paragraphs. Bullet points stand out and will always be read over and above any other part of the letter. So make sure that they contain strong benefits that you know will appeal to the recipient. Again, study the case study letters to see how the main benefits were emphasised.
- **Your penultimate closing paragraph:** This provides an opportunity to reiterate your offer, to elaborate on the benefits covered in those bullet points, to promote the goodies on your website, to share a powerful statistic about your services, client retention rate, money saved etc. Your call to action can be presented here – "Visit our website" or "Pick up the phone and call us now!"
- **Your final sign off:** Continue your charm offensive. You are looking forward to hearing from the person and you're grateful they have taken the time to read your letter etc.
- **Your Postscript (PS):** This is located a couple of centimetres below your signature and title. It is not always necessary to include a postscript but it can be useful. Why not reiterate your offer or use the space for some genuine client feedback? Sharing a persuasive statistic or even a memorable quotation can also be effective.

Three Successful Direct Mail Case Studies

To show direct mail in action here are three client case studies. I have chosen these particular case studies because they represent three very different businesses that have used direct mail to good effect in different ways. Each letter focuses strongly on the benefits on offer, and provides a clear call to action. Study each one and consider how you can emulate the layout and content for your own business.

Case Study 1 – The Accountant

The business: Perrys is a firm of chartered accountants with seven branches throughout London and the South-East of England.

Why direct mail? Perrys had experienced disappointing results from their previous direct-mail programme. On close inspection this was largely attributable to the poor quality of the mailing list (28,000 cold prospects, small to medium sized businesses). The number of "gone away" and incorrect addresses arising from each direct mail campaign had climbed to an unacceptable 25%. However, Perrys remained convinced that direct mail was a tool that could be successful in increasing their client base by encouraging targeted businesses to consider changing accountants should they be dissatisfied with their current service.

The first campaign: B2B list specialists, Marketscan, were asked to build a brand new prospect list to a strict selection and exclusion criteria. The businesses selected needed to be of a certain size and type, and be within a close radius of a Perrys branch. The full name of the decision-maker was provided for over 80% of the targeted prospects on the list. The prospect list was run against Perrys' client list to ensure that any current clients were removed from it. The list size was 26,000.

The first mailshot comprised a letter and a Perrys calendar. Twenty prospects immediately responded and converted to customers. Furthermore, hundreds of other recipients contacted Perrys to request additional literature. Every branch reported "exceptional levels of meeting requests" from businesses that had been targeted within the mailshot. The list is now mailed every three months and is cleaned by Marketscan prior to mailing. This ensures that any businesses that are no longer operating are removed. The response level from all subsequent mailings has remained high.

Why was this mailing successful? There are two reasons; the quality of the data and the time spent on developing a genuine message that would appeal and have resonance with the recipient.

This is the letter that accompanied the calendar

Dear Mr Wellington,

Happy New Year!

The start of a new year inevitably brings with it the desire to make positive changes. And so in the spirit of improvement many of us struggle to the gym, embark on a weight loss regime and vow with a vengeance to curb all excesses. **But what about your business – have you made any resolutions to move your business forwards this year?** For example, are you contemplating moving from your existing accountant or, if that seems a bridge too far presently, are you interested in benchmarking the service levels and tax planning expertise that you're currently receiving with what we could offer you instead?

Are you at a crossroads? Do you have burning tax planning questions in connection with your business that are not being addressed by your accountant? If so please contact us for an informal meeting at no charge.

- **We can look at your accounts and identify areas for improvement.** There may be tax planning advantages and tax savings you're currently not taking advantage of.
- **You can tell us what you expect from your accountant** contrasting this with what you're receiving now and where you would like to see improvements.
- **You can get to know us, to understand our service ethos and discover the benefits of having a proactive**, highly experience accountant with an unswerving aim to minimise your tax liabilities *and* act as your best defence against the Revenue.
- **If at the end of this meeting it's clear that you won't benefit from our service** we will not hesitate in telling you so.

After this meeting . . .

You will receive a comprehensive summary of our recommendations and advice within 48 hours. This will include an itemisation of recommended services and the fixed fees.

Why Perrys?

Customers tell us we offer the best of both worlds – a local and proactive service (as you can see we have seven branches throughout London and the South-East) with the reassurance of being a long established and trusted brand. Customers benefit from our network of business and tax planning experts. *Our fees are exceptionally competitive* and our customers comprise businesses of all sizes hailing from all sectors.

Getting in touch

Contact the Perry's branch that's local to you to arrange your meeting. Not sure? Telephone xxxxxxxxxxxxxxxxx or email xxxxxxxxxxxxxxx.

I look forward to hearing from you,

(Continued)

Kind regards

Xxxxxxxxxxxxxx

"Change is the law of life. And those who look only to the past or present are certain to miss the future."

John F. Kennedy

What Can You Learn from This Case Study?

- It can be appropriate to acknowledge within your letter that you realise that your cold prospect is using the services of a competitor.
- It is important to explain fully the benefits of arranging a meeting with you.
- An inspirational quote can add impact and flair.
- It is vital that your cold prospect list is current and up to the job.

Case Study 2 – The PC Repair Specialist

The business: PC PAL is a PC repair franchise with over 25 franchisees operating throughout the UK.

Why direct mail? PC PAL's franchisor, Jat Mann, had built a very successful marketing model based on leafleting, local advertising and search engine optimisation of the PC PAL website. When the recession struck, however, this marketing strategy was reviewed, improved and expanded. Direct mail was one of the new tactics to be introduced.

The first campaign: The first mailshot comprised of a letter, a business card attached to the letter by paperclip, an attractive and professionally produced leaflet, and a yellow and black pen (PC PAL's brand colours). These were all enclosed in a bright yellow envelope. Rather than being mailed, this mailshot was hand-delivered by each franchisee. The target audience was the neighbours of recent customers. Whenever a PC PAL franchisee completed a computer repair for a customer, they spent a few minutes popping the mailshot through neighbours' letter boxes. The envelope was not blank however! On the front, in very neat handwriting were the words:

"A note from your local PC PAL engineer" with "By Hand" written in the top right-hand corner of the envelope.

On the back of the envelope was written "Why your neighbour loves PC PAL and why we hope you will too."

This was an extremely successful campaign. For the PC PAL franchisee, it took only a few minutes to drop the envelopes through the letter boxes of a number of neighbours. Leafleting had already been a successful channel for the franchisees, but this mailshot stood out further from the usual unsolicited leaflets by being bright, attractive and lumpy.

Here is the letter that accompanied the mailshot:

Why Replace Your Computer or Laptop When It Can Be Repaired or Upgraded for a Fraction of the Cost and, you Can Enjoy £8 off Your First Repair or, 12 Months Free Internet Antivirus?

Hello,

I would like to introduce our business PC PAL to you because we are your local, qualified and fully insured specialists. We are the experts when it comes to breathing life back into your faulty computer whether you have a laptop, a PC or an Apple Mac.

It's frustrating, isn't it, when your computer starts playing up, especially if you rely upon it for work or for staying in touch with friends and family? It can be tempting to think that a problem (especially if it's a recurring one or you keep on getting problems that appear unrelated) means it's time to stump up a small fortune for a new model. **Stop!**

Before you even think about replacing your faulty computer, contact us. We can probably repair or upgrade it for a fraction of the cost of a new model. Take a look at the genuine client case studies overleaf if you are sceptical!

We repair your computer in the comfort of your home or office too. What's more, we don't charge a call-out fee and we offer out-of-hours appointments at no extra charge. You get real peace of mind with PC PAL. *We are CRB vetted, Microsoft qualified, fully insured and uniformed professionals.*

Do you have a problem with your computer now that you'd like an expert opinion on?

Here's a small selection of the problems that can be successfully resolved for a fraction of the cost of a new computer:

(Continued)

- Errors messages in Windows
- Wi-Fi is on slow or it won't connect
- The computer is very noisy
- The computer won't start or is very slow
- The computer displays start up errors or keeps crashing or freezing

Don't lose faith in your trusty computer! There could be many years of efficient operating life in it yet. And you're doing your bit for the environment too. Contact us today and *don't forget you will benefit with £8 off your first repair or if you prefer, 12 months of free Internet antivirus*.

Yours sincerely

Franchisee name

On the back of the letter we included several customer case studies that illustrated the value of repairing as opposed to replacing.

What Can You Learn from This Case Study?

- Case studies on the back of a letter can be used to reinforce the message on the front.
- A hand delivered mailshot is an effective way of reaching a small but easy-to-access local audience.
- A lumpy envelope is always intriguing.

Case Study 3 – The Signs Manufacturer

The business: BEL Signs specialises in making signs, exhibition banners and displays, and vehicle wraparounds for businesses, clubs and charities.

Why direct mail? BEL Signs had fallen into the trap of many busy businesses – not keeping their customers updated with what they could offer them. BEL Signs decided to use direct mail to update their clients because, like the products they sell, it is a tactile and visual medium.

The first campaign: The opening line of the letter was inspired by a conversation that Peter Bedford, MD of BEL Signs, had with a customer who had asked him, "Peter, what do you do apart from signs?"

This became the leading headline of the letter. Peter's business card was attached to the letter by paperclip and that was the total sum of the mailshot – one letter; one business card. The introduction was based on the theory that honesty is the best policy and that charm is more effective than the hard sell. It was important that the company completed their positioning statement before the content of this letter could be finalised, but once this had been done and the letter was sent out, BEL Signs reported "an exceptional response" with many existing customers contacting them to request quotations for additional services or products.

Here is the letter, a long one at that!

"Peter, What Do You Do Apart from Signs?"

Dear Mark,

This was the question that a long-standing customer asked me at a networking event in Horsham last week. I must confess that it brought me up short. I realised that perhaps not all of our valued customers including yourself may be aware of the services we offer, which is why I'm dropping you a line. And, because BEL Signs are celebrating our 30th anniversary, we're adding something a little extra to any order you place of £100 or more.

In response to that question, we can offer you the following high-quality services from our manufacturing unit in Horsham. It's worth remembering too that we don't outsource any part of your order *so we can offer you a 100% quality assured guarantee and a very competitive price*.

- **Work clothing** – supplied by us and then embroidered to the highest standard with your business details. Polo shirts, jackets and fleeces, overalls, blouses, work shirts, trousers, high specification safety clothing and more.
- **Promotional clothing** – when you don't want to spend an arm and a leg at your show, exhibition or seminar but you do want to make your team a walking billboard for your brand. Our premium economy range is perfect; our embroidery superb.

(Continued)

- **Clothing for your club** – football, bowls, golf, cricket, tennis, darts and fitness. You name it. In the last 30 years we have kitted out more clubs and fitness centres than you could shake a stick at. We are the local specialists.
- **Personalised clothing for your special events** – hen nights, stag dos, anniversaries, business launches, birthdays, book launches, product promotions and more.

The good news is that you don't have to order hundreds of items to benefit from our great prices and legendary service! Whilst we supply and embroider thousands of items of clothing, we're just as happy with an order of 12 T-shirts. Ask for a quotation and why not call in to see samples today – just phone us beforehand. We can also offer you a complete in-house design service so you don't need ready-to-go artwork by any means.

What else can we help you with?

- **Exhibition banners** – from an inexpensive high impact pop-up banner at just £75 to an all-singing, all-dancing exhibition stand. Don't trust your brand to an anonymous business on the Internet when you can get Internet prices with a genuinely attentive and expert service from us. We can also supply all of the bits and pieces that go with your exhibition stand – acrylic leaflet and business card holders, mini table top pop-up banners, presentation folders screen printed with your details.
- **Vehicle wraparounds** – where the entire vehicle is used as an advert for your business. Our experience in this area is vast so talk to us first.
- **Crash repair signage** – a service that's in demand by many vehicle repair specialists. When the vehicle has been repaired we will repair or replace the signage.
- **Specials** – the projects that you can't put under any other heading! Recent examples include producing and screen printing panels for a manufacturing plant, printing the business name on engine components and, producing the stainless steel labels for bell pulls. If you have an off-the-wall requirement do talk to us.

And of course, as you know, we do signs! You may not be aware of the breadth of our signage service. So, rather than list these, here are a couple of examples. For Belmont Homes we've produced a 24-panel hoarding, provided stainless steel signs for their buildings, pop-up banners that promote their show apartments, provided all of their sale board signage plus their branded leather folders and pens. For another client with a requirement of 300 A Boards we guaranteed and completed their job in three days when a competitor was quoting ten.

Please do not hesitate to contact me or any member of my team to discuss your requirements.

Yours sincerely

Peter Bedford

Managing Director

PS: With your next order of £100 or more you'll receive a special commemorative anniversary mug filled to the brim with jelly beans.

What Can You Learn from This Case Study?

- An offer is always likely to be well received by your existing customers.
- Letting your customers know what you can offer them beyond their present arrangements with you is a valid reason for a letter.
- Cross-selling new products and services to existing customers is a cost-effective way of generating more business.
- Accurate customer records are essential. Consider whether yours needs to be updated before you begin mailing.

Masterclass Summary

- Direct mail is an excellent, low cost marketing tool that enables you to reach your target audiences on a one-to-one basis.
- If direct mail hasn't worked in the past, be prepared to revisit it with a new approach. Don't shoot the messenger!
- Spend time crafting your message. With a captivating and charming message you can grab the attention of your reader from the moment they open your envelope.
- Blend direct mail with other marketing activities.
- Social media is idea for making informal connections and preparing the ground before sending your mailshot.

- There is no viable alternative to a clean, legally compliant and up-to-date mailing list. Choose your list provider carefully. Brief them thoroughly.
- Clean your customer list before using it for direct mail.
- A nicely worded letter on good quality paper, business card attached is often all that's needed to have the right impact.
- Add a promotional gift to your mailshot so that it becomes lumpy, is intriguing and stands out from the envelopes that your recipient is used to receiving.
- Don't expect too much for too little. Mailing a cold prospect and hoping they will buy there and then could be overambitious.
- Facts, figures and genuine positive client testimonial will reinforce your benefit driven message.
- Use the back of your letter to spice up the content, add visuals, questions and answers, case studies, your latest press release, images from your website etc.

Masterclass 9
How to Take the Chill out of a Telephone Cold Call

In this masterclass you will learn:

- How to build a warm relationship with a cold prospect on the telephone.
- Why it pays to focus on meaningful conversations rather than sales.
- How to build rapport, confidently answer objections, make friends with the gatekeeper and build your brand on the telephone.

Telephone cold calling is renowned for dividing the opinions of small business owners. In the largest camp are those business owners that have tried it, had little, if any, success and are consequently very much against it as a marketing tactic. There is another group of businesses that have avoided cold calling because they can't imagine anything worse. And then there's the smallest group; the folk that have tried and persevered with telephone cold calling and, by doing so, have managed to make it work for them. For that reason this group of business owners become strong advocates of cold calling, and I belong to this group.

Over the years I have made thousands of telephone calls to cold prospects on behalf of my clients and have managed to secure significant amounts of new business. I have always viewed the cold call as a first step towards building a relationship with both warm and cold prospects. It is easy to dismiss cold calling as ineffective if you're viewing it purely as a channel for a one hit sale. If the aim is to persuade the person to buy from you in that very first call, then it is likely that many calls will end in failure. If it is viewed instead as a tool that will enable you to build an awareness and interest in what you offer, cold calling can offer real value. So, if you have dismissed telephone cold calling because you have been unsuccessful in the past, let me try to persuade you that with a little practice, perseverance and patience, the telephone can become a very effective medium for moving warm and cold prospects closer to the idea of buying from you.

Let's start by looking at five reasons why a person may struggle to obtain the desired results on the telephone when calling cold prospects.

1. **Selling by script.** It's hard to believe but many businesses still use a script when making telephone cold calls. Scripts make the caller sound mechanical and are a barrier to building a beneficial rapport with the potential customer. There is also the risk that if the caller is met with an objection or a question that necessitates leaving the script, the call goes to pieces. I am sure you have received these

types of calls yourself, and I hazard a guess that at the first opportunity you terminate them.

2. **The school of hard sell.** Callers that have only one objective in mind, that of clinching the deal in the very first conversation, will come across as pushy, impatient and even bullying. They believe that if they walk away from the conversation without a sale or a meeting the call has been a waste of time and they pursue it no further. Their technique is to start the call by asking a number of quick fire questions to ascertain a budget. If they believe that the prospect has the budget for whatever they are selling they will subject the person to a stream of sales patter during which it can be impossible to interrupt. These callers are very hard to shake off and it is often necessary to hang up to end the call. If they believe there is no budget for a sale however, they will quickly end the call to move onto the next prospect without any qualms. There is no attempt to build rapport or to make the call a more pleasant experience. The deal is all that matters.

3. **I don't know who you are but I want you to buy from me.** Identifying your target audience is just as important when cold calling as it is with other marketing activities. Calling a list of numbers without any knowledge of the people at the other end, whether they're likely to be interested in what you're offering is likely to render the vast majority of calls ineffective.

4. **Too timid to talk!** For some people the whole experience of making a cold call is too unpleasant for them to fully commit to the process. They grab the first opportunity to end the call having felt awkward and uncomfortable throughout. Very few calls will be successful and cold calling will happily be condemned as an inefficient activity, never to be tried again.

5. **You're calling people who have subscribed to the Telephone Preference Service (TPS).** Anyone that has subscribed to a TPS (see www.tpson-line.org.uk for more details) has actively requested that they do not receive cold calls. If you subsequently do make an unsolicited call to these people, they are unlikely to be receptive no matter how charming you are. If you're buying or renting prospect data, you must ensure that it complies with the TPS if you want to avoid the risk of a fine or a sharp response.

Let me reassure you that cold calling can be successful if the correct focus and application is given to it. However, expectations do need to be managed. No matter how focused and skilled you are as a caller, you will encounter many rejections from people not interested in what you have to offer and from people that simply do not take cold calls. Do not allow yourself to become despondent in the face of these rejections. Your aim is to generate an interest in what you offer amongst the minority of people open to what you have to say. In my experience, one successful call in which rapport is built with the prospect showing an interest in what I am offering, quickly banishes any feelings of gloom I may have after a series of ineffective calls.

Building Relationships with Cold Prospects

I have mentioned focus and commitment when making cold calls, but what is it exactly that you should be looking to achieve from that first call with a cold prospect?

- You're aiming to create an awareness of you and your business and so encourage your prospect to want to find out more about you.
- You want to generate an interest in what you are offering.
- You hope to address any questions or objections that may be raised.
- You want to encourage your prospect to evaluate what you offer in more detail.

If you were relying on email correspondence to achieve this same progress with a cold relationship it could take many weeks or months. And realistically, although developing the relationship with a cold prospect on your first call in the manner mentioned above could be termed as the perfect call, it could still be termed as a successful call even if only one of those objectives was accomplished. At a time when so many business people are glued to their computer screens, the telephone provides an opportunity to cut through the on-line noise and build a warm relationship through a two-way dialogue.

So What Does It Take to be Successful on the Telephone?

Before you embark on your cold calling campaign, it will help to have completed your positioning statement. From this statement you should compose a sheet of concise benefits and have these available to refer to during your telephone conversations.

Consider having the details of some case studies to hand to paint a picture of your experience and expertise with similar businesses. A few lines for each one should be enough to aid your memory during the call. Can you add any facts, figures or statistics that will add further weight to your message? Make your benefit sheet easy to read so that you can access the information in seconds. Tweak it to reflect your sector specific experience as you move from one target audience to another. Don't trust the details of your experience and expertise to memory. Commit them to paper. When in full flow on a call, it can be easy to forget an important benefit that could prove to be the defining point in the conversation.

The Power of Practice

The biggest challenge when making a cold call is to be concise enough to maintain the attention of your prospect, yet still take the opportunity to paint a compelling picture of what you offer. You want your prospect sufficiently enthused to want to learn more about you at a time when they've had to stop what they were doing to answer a call they were not expecting.

How can you be concise and yet descriptive when making those cold calls?

Firstly, find a quiet space. Then allow yourself just 60 seconds to answer each of the following questions. These questions cover the sort of information that you're likely to want to convey to a cold prospect during that first conversation. By practising to answer them concisely you'll be better prepared to speak articulately and without hesitation when making the calls for real. You will sound eloquent and confident.

- Can you tell me about your business?
- What kind of clients do you currently work with?
- How could you benefit my organisation?
- What kind of budget would we be looking at?
- What do your qualifications and accreditations mean?

- Why should I do business with you?
- How do you compare to competitors?
- How do you deliver added value to your clients?

When you start cold calling, make a list of the questions you are asked, especially those you find challenging to answer. You can then practise your answers to these new questions in readiness for future calls.

It will help if you can record your answers and listen to how you sound. Being compelling and succinct is vital in maintaining the interest and respect of the person you are calling.

Your Voice – a Vital Asset in Your Cold Calling Toolkit

On the telephone your voice is extremely important. The person at the other end can't see your animated facial expressions, your warm smile and the sincerity in your eyes. They only have your voice on which to base that first and lasting impression. For your voice to be an asset on the telephone, you must become self-aware. And this entails spending some time identifying your "irritation hooks" by listening to how you sound when on the phone.

Here are some of the more common ones:

- **Talking too loudly.** This can make a person impossible to listen to for more than a short while.
- **Talking too quietly.** Similarly frustrating for the listener, who won't necessarily ask the caller to speak up.
- **Talking too fast.** This can also irritate the listener and could sap any initial interest.
- **"Umm"-ing and "err"-ing.** The caller will come across as lacking in confidence and probably frustrate the listener.
- **Overusing certain words.** Overusing words such as "basically," "you know," "obviously" or ending every statement with "yeah?" is likely to focus attention on the repetition rather than the message.

- **Being too authoritative.** The caller runs the risk of sounding arrogant, high-handed and self-righteous.
- **Talking in a flat and monotone voice.** The caller projects a lack of enthusiasm and interest and is likely to bore the listener.

Because the listener needs to focus upon a caller's voice, quirks of speech can seem more obvious on the telephone than when speaking face-to-face. However, any "irritation hook" is likely to make it difficult to build rapport.

So, with this in mind, how do you then develop your very best telephone voice whilst staying true to your accent and your natural tone?

Here are some simple voice tips to help you on the telephone. Study the voice tips in Masterclass 11 too.

- **Include plenty of pauses** when speaking to give your prospect time to reflect on what's being said. These pauses are a sign of a confident assured person and should replace the usual "umm"-ing and "err"-ing or the repetition of irritating phrases as mentioned earlier.
- **Don't try to be jovial throughout the entire conversation.** This is likely to exhaust you and could well result in your prospect doubting your sincerity. Instead, emphasise keywords to convey your enthusiasm for what you are saying. "We recycle *95%* of all commercial waste *and* our client retention rate is *99%.*"
- **Try to make each sentence count.** Don't allow one sentence to merge into another; aim for each one to pack a punch. "We have delivered over 1000 telephone cold calling masterclasses to small businesses *just like yours.*"
- **Know when it's time to change your tone of voice.** If your prospect is telling you that times are hard, or is sharing a challenge they are facing, respond with empathy and warmth. Emphasising keywords during such a conversation would not be appropriate.
- **Ensure that your body language acts as a support to your voice.** Although the person you're speaking to cannot see you, your positive mannerisms and expressions will be projected through your voice. Some people like to stand

when making a cold call, others to be seated at a desk. However, if you become preoccupied by your mobile, are clicking your pen, surreptitiously trying to drink your coffee or slumping in your seat gazing out of the window, you are potentially sabotaging the call. Such distractions will definitely be reflected in your voice and your lack of concentration will be picked up at the other end of the line.

The Power of Preparation

Grabbing five minutes on the hoof in between meetings may be okay for the occasional telephone cold call but if you're serious about building relationships on the telephone then allocate time in your diary – ideally at least 90 minutes per session. The environment in which you call is important too. If your office is noisy you will need to find a quiet space so that you can bring your undivided concentration to every telephone call. You might love the buzz of a noisy office but your prospect will not welcome it.

Let's look at other ways in which you can prepare for a good cold call.

- **Do your homework on each cold prospect.** Five minutes spent looking at their website and any LinkedIn and social media profiles will enable you to build an accurate picture of the person you will be calling and their business. Any useful nuggets of information that you find will help you to develop a relationship and identify needs during the call.
- **Be prepared to take copious notes every time.** You are embarking on a journey with that first cold call, hopefully one that will eventually result in a new client. By recording the details of each conversation you will build a valuable dossier of information on your prospect, one that will enable you to reconnect each time you speak. Do not trust details to memory because you will forget them and repeating questions to your prospect in subsequent conversations will only irritate.
- **Plan before each call.** If you are focused before each telephone call, you'll come across as being professional, helpful and far removed from the usual

scripted telesales person. So before each call allow yourself a few minutes' time for preparation, and consider the following:

- Why am I calling this person?
- What am I hoping to achieve?
- What can I learn from my previous call?
- Why should they be interested in listening to me?
- What information am I hoping to glean from them?
- What objections could they raise?
- **Set realistic targets based on "meaningful conversations."** You can establish a target number of calls that you would like to complete in a session but be prepared to revise this target once you start calling. In fact, rather than setting a target for the number of calls to be made in a session, I would encourage you instead to aim for a certain number of "meaningful conversations," the conversations that you believe are most likely to progress to a sale. You may only manage to hold one or two calls of this type per session, or you may get several, but these are the calls that count. When you begin calling, record the number of "meaningful conversations" that you manage to hold in each calling session. You will then be able to set yourself realistic targets that motivate you rather than impractical targets that will only deflate you and provide a reason to stay away from the telephone. What constitutes a meaningful conversation? You will need to draw up your own checklist but here are some initial thoughts:

Meaningful conversation checklist

- You got through to the right person.
- They agreed to take your call.
- They asked you questions that demonstrated their interest.
- They raised objections that you successfully handled.
- The objections you could not answer were not deal breakers.
- You understood their needs.
- You were confident you could meet their needs.
- They wanted to move to the next stage of the decision-making process with you, e.g. they asked for more information/to arrange a meeting/to

169

schedule another call/to introduce you to another colleague/to be sent a quotation etc.

Negotiating Past the Gatekeeper

The term "gatekeeper" is commonly used to describe the PA or receptionist in an organisation whose job it is to appraise a caller before passing them through to the person they have asked to speak to. Whilst there are some gatekeepers that you will never manage to get past when making a cold call, there are many others who will be more than happy to connect you if they feel that your call is valid.

Here is a tried and tested gatekeeper introduction that I developed. It's called the "Partial Reveal," the idea behind it being that you only reveal as much as is needed at each stage of the conversation with the gatekeeper. There is little to be gained from steaming in at the start of the conversation with a full-blown pitch in the hope that you'll be put through straight away. Start with this polite introduction and if pressed, reveal why you're calling as follows:

You. *"Good morning. Could I speak with Mr Joe Blogs please?"*
G.K. *"Who is it?"*
You. *"It's (your full name) from (your company name)."*
G.K. *"Will he know what it is in connection with?"*

You (choose one of the following).

1. *"I hope so. We're currently working with many (a few lines about similar clients you are working with) and I need to discuss this with Joe."*
2. *"I hope so; I have been given Joe's name by (your contact) who has asked me to call him."*
3. *"I hope so. I am following through on a communication from last week. Thank you."*
4. *"I am sending Joe a communication and wanted to introduce myself very briefly before he receives it. Thank you."*

G.K. *"Putting you through."*
You. *"Thank you so much for your help, what is your name please?"*

If this approach does not work adopt this last resort tactic which plays upon the good nature of the gatekeeper as follows:

> *"I appreciate that you can't put me through to (name of the person or their title) but no one knows this company like you. What would you do in my position? How would you reach them?"*

Always ask for the gatekeeper's name. You may have to call several times to get through to your prospect so being on first name terms with the gatekeeper is important. The gatekeeper deserves your charm. They are often treated rather ungraciously by cold callers, so representing yourself to them in a warm, grateful and courteous way will make a positive first impression, and you may even gain an ally! If you are calling small businesses, bear in mind too that the gatekeeper may be related to the person you want to speak to and so could influence whether you get the business or not.

Making a Professional Introduction to Your Cold Prospect

Having safely negotiated the gatekeeper, you now have to make a favourable impression on the prospect you are going to speak with. Your introduction must be professional, concise and friendly and should make clear you're not a telesales caller. What follows is the introduction that I use when I am cold calling on behalf of Techmobility, a business that adapts vehicles for disabled motorists. The cold prospects are salespeople responsible for selling cars to disabled motorists in motor dealerships. The purpose of my call is to ascertain their present arrangements and to introduce Techmobility as an alternative or additional adaptation specialist.

> **S (salutation)** *"Good morning."*
> **I (introduction)** *"My name is Dee Blick from Techmobility."*
> **R (reason)** *"We adapt vehicles for disabled motorists and passengers under the Motability scheme and work with many Ford dealerships, but not yours presently. We are renowned for our discreet adaptations."*
> **P (permission)** *"I would just like to introduce myself to you briefly. Is now a good time to talk?"*

Use this example introduction and the S.I.R.P framework to compose your own introduction. Some of the people you're calling will accept your call simply because you have asked for permission to talk, others may ask you to call back at a more convenient time. Don't be disheartened if the majority of calls fall into the latter category. Try to arrange a specific day and time to call back and confirm this arrangement by email if possible.

Set the Scene at the Start of Your Conversation

Permission to talk granted, it's tempting to steam into a sales pitch. However, try not to rush ahead. Instead, explain to your prospect *what's going to happen next* in your conversation:

> *"Thank you. If I could just start by . . ."*

and, using the previous example of Techmobility,

> *". . . asking how you currently recommend adaptation specialists to your customers."*

or

> *". . . explaining a little about our business and how we currently work with Ford dealerships . . ."*

If given the opportunity to speak about your business, be concise, talk benefits and always conclude with a question to bring your prospect into the conversation. The time you spent planning the call should ensure that you're fully prepared for when your prospect ask the question: "Tell me more about what you do." The following example should provide some ideas on how to map out your response to this question. You can see that we emphasise how long the business has been established to build trust, and focus on the two key benefits, the mobile workshops and the customer care team.

> *"We've been established for over 20 years and have three fully qualified engineers working from mobile workshops. We will come to you; there is no need for you*

to take time out of your working day to bring vehicles to us for adaptation. We have a dedicated dealer customer care team that will provide you with regular updates on your customer's vehicle. Can I ask you, please, how many vehicles you adapt each year and what influences your choice of adaptation specialist?"

Be Prepared Beforehand with Your Questions

If you want to avoid a one-sided monologue, in which you say an awful lot but fail to build a dialogue with your prospect, you will need to ask questions throughout the conversation. Questions are vital in demonstrating that you really are interested in understanding your prospect's needs. Crucially, the answers will also help to steer you in the right direction. If you're not asking questions you can easily find yourself making recommendations based on what *you think* your prospect needs rather than what *they actually* need.

Make a list of those questions that you really do need answers to. When asking the questions, let your prospect know there is a benefit to them answering. Continuing with the example of Techmobility:

> *"**Can I ask,** is your current adaptation specialist able to handle all your adaptation requirements, **as I will then be able to** identify those services that we offer that your customers are not currently benefiting from?"*

Perhaps the most important question you can ask your cold prospect is the one towards the end of your conversation:

> *"Is there anything you would like to ask me that we have not covered in our conversation or that I have not answered to your satisfaction?"*

Don't assume that because you've discussed benefits, asked questions and built a dialogue that a meeting is a foregone conclusion. Your prospect may still have unanswered questions that could form a barrier to a meeting but may not necessarily ask them if not prompted by you.

If you are feeling confident that the conversation has been an extremely positive one, ask this bold but incisive question:

"We would love to do business with you and I'm confident now that we have spoken that you would benefit from working with us. What's standing in the way of this happening?"

We All Love a Listener

To be a good listener on the telephone requires self-discipline. We can become so caught up in our enthusiasm to talk that we forget the importance of listening. Make a conscious effort not to interrupt or speak over your prospect at any point in the conversation. Allow a few seconds to elapse after your prospect has finished speaking before starting to speak yourself. You can demonstrate that you have been listening by referring back to key points your prospect has made during the conversation.

Eight Tips for Building "Appropriate Business Rapport"

When you're at the first stage of building a relationship with a cold prospect, it can be tough building rapport. You don't want come across as being too formal, nor do you want to appear overly friendly and risk sounding a little insincere or presumptuous. Here are eight simple ways to build appropriate business rapport. Much of what follows has been covered earlier in the masterclass.

1. Research your cold prospect before you pick up the telephone.
2. Ask for permission to speak instead of launching straight in to the conversation.
3. Ask intelligent and relevant questions that are appropriate to your prospect and the reason for your call.
4. Employ a warm yet professional tone of voice.
5. Demonstrate that you are listening.
6. Find common ground. It always helps if you can identify a shared interest. Do you share a similar outlook on business or life? Do you have a mutual contact or play the same sport?
7. Pay sincere compliments. How do you feel when a person you meet for the first time pays you a sincere compliment? Pretty good, I suspect. Yet so few of us feel comfortable paying compliments. In every call try to find an opportunity to say

something complimentary. You could compliment their work ethos, their values, what they have achieved in their business, how they are presenting themselves during the conversation, how they are overcoming challenges or trading in difficult conditions. There is, of course, a fine line between passing on compliments and being obsequious. However, if you genuinely think something nice about the person you are speaking with, don't be afraid to say it. You are more likely to hold meaningful conversations simply because you made your prospect feel good about themselves.

8. Remember to be courteous throughout the call and to say *"thank you"* when appropriate. Recognise that this person you called out of the blue has given you their time, has listened to you and has answered your questions. Acknowledge this.

How to Handle Objections with Success and Confidence

I have much to thank Andrew for. Andrew was the training manager of a cleaning franchise that I rang in my early days of telephone cold calling. I was selling customer care training programmes and would struggle whenever I encountered an objection, especially if that objection came soon after I had asked for permission to talk. But, on this particular day, it was Andrew's response that gave me the opportunity to test a new approach, one that I have continued using ever since. After asking Andrew if "now is a convenient time to talk," he said:

"We already have a training provider for our customer service training that I am happy with, thank you."

To which I replied: (I have highlighted the important phrases):

"I can understand that. In fact some of our clients have more than one training provider. **At this stage** *I would simply welcome the opportunity to chat informally with you to see if we can identify any areas in which we could potentially add further value to your training programme.* **If at the end of the call** *you still feel the same, at least you'll know that you really are getting the most from your training provider and budget."*

Not only did Andrew agree to the conversation, he subsequently became a high-value client.

So what was it about this approach that worked so well?

- I empathised with Andrew's response rather than asking a volley of questions with the aim of trying to discredit his existing training provider.
- I made it clear that the call was not going to be a hard sell by emphasising at the beginning that I only wanted to chat informally with him.
- I explained to Andrew that there was a benefit in him continuing with the call by explaining that there could be the potential to add further value to his current training programme.

You can use this approach with some other common objections.

> *"Can't you just send me some literature?"*
> *"Yes I'm very happy to do that but **is it possible** to take a few moments of your time now to identify how **we could benefit you** with our XYZ products or services. We have experience of working with organisations that are **similar to yours** and have delivered some exceptional results."*
> *"We don't have a need for your services/products."*
> *"Could I just ask **out of curiosity** how you currently (insert the service you are selling e.g. train your staff)."*
> *"I'm not interested."*
> *"Can I ask why that is? **Many of my clients** said this to me when I initially called simply because the timing of my call was not convenient. Is there a better time for us to have a conversation?"*
> *"That seems expensive."*
> *"**Could I ask why** you think it seems expensive?"* (Rather than responding in a defensive manner and trying to justify your charges, find out why your prospect is thinking along these lines. Once you know the precise reasons why they think you're expensive, you can respond with confidence.)

Here are some tips on how to handle objections in general:

- **Don't interrupt.** Pause before responding.
- **Use your voice appropriately.** Don't become irritable or impatient even when the objection is clearly an irrational and unfounded one.
- **You don't have to respond immediately to every objection.** If your prospect is in full flow, let them talk. What you perceive to be an objection may simply

be your prospect mulling over your proposition, sharing what's going on in their mind. Wait patiently and address it further into the call. This will give you time to gather your thoughts and think about what to say. Write the objection down so you don't forget it.

- **Be honest.** If you can't satisfactorily handle an objection or challenge, admit to this and explain why. Your integrity will be appreciated and may stand you in good stead for later in the call. You are unlikely to be able to overcome every objection but not every objection will be a deal breaker.

Stay calm, focus on your breathing and remember to be courteous at all times. If you have spent time planning the call and have a list of previous objections, you shouldn't be taken by surprise on any call.

Close That Conversation with Confidence, Purpose and Flair

A short but focused telephone call can end successfully if your conversation has been a meaningful one. If your purpose when calling was to arrange a meeting, don't be reluctant to suggest one. Use this closing structure to help you.

> "I have really enjoyed our conversation today (name) and thank you for your time."
>
> "What I suggest based on **what we have discussed** is that we meet to take this further."
>
> "I can currently do XYZ dates in the morning up to 12.00. Which is most convenient for you?"
>
> "What I will do in the meantime is (send you a link to our website/email you the contact details of clients you can speak to about our services ahead of the meeting/email or post literature that summarises the benefits of our service/send you an invitation to connect on LinkedIn/follow you on Twitter etc.)."
>
> "Let me confirm the correct spelling of your name and take your email and postal address."

What If Your Cold Prospect does not Want to Meet?

Not every first meaningful conversation will culminate in your prospect agreeing to a meeting. You will quickly become disenchanted if your definition of a successful call is that it has to end with a meeting being arranged. It may take several telephone calls, interspersed with follow-up emails answering questions and confirming conversations, before a meeting is agreed to. The person you are calling has to know, like and trust you sufficiently to be open to doing business with you and the time this takes will vary depending on the character of the individual, the decision-making process and how the organisation appoints new providers. For some organisations, this process may take months; for others, days. Some days you will be very pleasantly surprised. You will have called a person at absolutely the right moment. They are looking to buy, you can provide what they need and there is nothing else to do but to secure the deal. At other times you will feel as though you have taken one step forward and two steps backwards, especially if a follow-up call is postponed, or your prospect leaves and you have to start again with someone else in the company. Allow for these setbacks and adjust your expectations. Don't set yourself up for disappointment.

The road to cold calling success is not always smooth but hopefully by following these tips your hot prospect pipeline will increase and your efforts will attract new business.

Masterclass Summary

- Ditch the script, the hard selling and the high-pressure techniques!
- What do you want to achieve from cold calling? Are your expectations realistic?
- Use your positioning statement to compose a succinct benefit sheet.
- Practise what you want to say, and the questions to ask, before picking up the phone.
- Research the social networking profiles of each person you're calling as well as looking at the company website.
- Scope out your capsule introduction so that your first words don't falter.
- Your voice will make or break your call. Is yours warm, professional, confident and friendly?
- Emphasise keywords, pause and listen.

- Make friends with the gatekeeper. They are always deserving of your courtesy and consideration.
- Take detailed notes of each conversation. They are fundamental when re-establishing contact in follow-up conversations and communications.
- Pay a compliment! Thank the person for listening and taking your call.
- Don't answer objections defensively. Empathise, think about what is being said then put your case forward.
- If all the signs are good and the person has a genuine need for what you are offering and is interested, close with confidence – ask for that meeting!

Masterclass 10
The Secrets of Successful Email Marketing

By Liz Barnes, FCIM Chartered Marketer and business to business (B2B) e-marketing expert

In this masterclass you will learn:

- Why email marketing is still one of the best tools for reaching business audiences.
- Tips about how to get your emails opened and responded to.
- Why you should invest in your database.
- Tips for renting B2B data.

I was delighted when Liz Barnes, a highly respected Chartered Marketer and Fellow of The Chartered Institute of Marketing, offered to share her e-marketing tips and expertise in my book. Liz has many years' experience running e-marketing campaigns for small and large businesses and is renowned for talking expert marketing common sense. I am sure you will find her advice and insights invaluable.

At the end of this masterclass I share a couple of emails from my own e-marketing campaigns that I hope you will find useful to use as templates when you commence writing your own emails.

Long Live Email Marketing!

Ten years ago, I embarked on email marketing seriously for many of my clients. We were delighted with the results. There have been many changes in the intervening period with improvements to the tools you can use to build your own campaigns. It's now pretty straightforward to build a full colour e-newsletter or sales email that looks good in everyone's inbox – with no knowledge of how to programme HTML code. This email broadcast software (as it's called) is also good at managing your email lists by automatically dealing with unsubscribe requests, or emails that bounce back. Because of these tools, email marketing has proliferated and our inboxes are groaning with all manner of emails trying to sell to us. But email marketing is still highly effective at getting your message across.

The rules governing data protection and email marketing differ depending on whether you're selling to consumers or to a business. Most of the tips in this masterclass apply to businesses that sell to other businesses and those that sell direct to customers, but where there are important differences in regulation, these are indicated and I have restricted those discussions to business-to-business email marketing, the area in which I specialise.

Why Use Database Marketing?

The more detailed information you have about a customer the better you can antici-pate their needs and forecast what they'll buy. If you have a small list of customers but are keen to acquire more, you may need to invest in data in order to build pros-pect lists you can then target and sell to.

- Good data enables you to achieve better, tighter targeting.
- Good data enables you to reduce your marketing costs. You are only contacting people most likely to buy.
- By analysing your database you can improve your products and services based on a clear understanding of your customers' needs.
- Database marketing can help you build relationships and encourage loyalty. You can keep in touch with customers and prospects.

Why Email Marketing?

Email marketing is still one of the most effective ways to generate leads and increase sales. Whilst our inboxes fill quickly – most of us are happy to remain opted-in to communications. We sometimes buy purely as a result of receiving an email because the time is right.

The many benefits of email marketing include:

- It's inexpensive. Even using a broadcast tool, each email costs a fraction of a penny to send.
- You can reach active, lapsed and potential customers.
- You can get your brand and product messages in front of high numbers of specified buyers.
- Email is personal – you can include the name of the recipient and/or other relevant data such as the name of their company, where they work, the last time they purchased.
- You can segment your audience on your database and send different messages to different groups. This is harder and more expensive with brochures and print runs.

- Your target audience is often happy to receive emails – they have either opted-in, or they will opt-out if they don't find them relevant.
- Advances in email broadcast software and database management systems enable you to manage the processes yourself.
- Email is versatile – you can create newsletters with several articles or send simple text-only reminders.
- You can include a range of different actions and track each one of them.
- It's quick to implement and you can see the results of your campaigns almost immediately.
- You're able to reach people at their desktop, mobile or tablet.

As with any marketing method it pays to consider why you want to use e-marketing and who you want to reach. Are you looking to:

- Remind customers about your existing services?
- Build your prospect pipeline and generate enquiries for your sales team?
- Encourage lapsed clients to consider buying again?
- Build on your clients' loyalty by keeping in touch with a regular newsletter?

To ensure you get good results from email marketing, you'll need to invest some time and some money. Budget for data management, for a professional design of your email template, for professional copywriting or editing and the costs of email sends if you're using a broadcast tool.

Target Audiences and Quality of Data

Relevance is vital in email marketing. Many of us are happy to receive emails for goods and services where the message is relevant – even if we're unlikely to buy there and then. Define your target audience carefully. Take time to clean your existing database and, if you're also renting data, specify it carefully so that the recipients are likely to find your emails relevant, even if they don't respond immediately.

Campaigns and Timing

I recommend that you plan your activity at least six months in advance. Your email campaigns should dovetail with the rest of your marketing activities as well as any planned product launches or follow-up sales activity. If you have a complex product or service that takes a while for it to be adopted by decision makers – you're likely to want to drip feed your email marketing, perhaps developing a theme and gradually providing more information over time. There's nothing set in stone about how frequently you should email your database but if your unsubscribe rate starts to increase, you may be emailing too frequently.

What Makes a Good Email Message?

Charming, well-written and relevant copy is at the heart of any email communication whether you're sending a promotional offer, a newsletter or a service update. So, in addition to my tips, make sure that you read the other copywriting tips included in this book before writing your emails.

- Address the person by their name (see data and personalisation).
- Talk to them as though you're in a conversation, focussing on their needs and challenges instead of overselling your company.
- When you've got their attention, explain how you can help. Most good sales emails are only two or three short paragraphs. Keep the main body of the email focused on one subject only.
- If you want to suggest other services or products or to highlight other features about your company, use a different area of the email for this. If you're using a graphical format you can use a separate panel or buttons for these messages.
- If you have segmented your database you can use this knowledge in the body of the email e.g. "*As a retailer in <<name of town>> you'll understand the impact of the proposed superstore . . .*"
- Newsletters are different to a standard email as you're likely to be writing about different subjects. Use a compelling title for each article with a short opening paragraph followed by "*Read more . . .*" The remainder of the article should be hosted on your website which is a good way to encourage readers to visit you on-line.
- If you're embarking on a newsletter for the first time, take time to plan the articles you'll include for the rest of the year. You probably need at least three short articles for a newsletter and the themes should be varied.

- Ensure that you don't just talk about your company. What motivates or worries your audience? Let your emails and newsletters demonstrate you understand your audience's needs.

Calls to Action

These are vital. Have at least one on every email. If you're using a graphical format, buttons work well but, on plain text emails, you can still use links or CAPS to show your customers how to take action, e.g.:

- Buy now
- Get a quote
- Request a call back
- Call us now
- Find out more (link to specific page on website)
- Ask a question by email (link to email)
- Free download (goes to a sign-up form first)

Graphical Format or Plain Text?

Find out which works best for your business.

You may decide to alternate between the two formats. Graphical format emails are good for raising awareness of your logo and for brand styling and may grab attention. Buttons work much better than hyperlink text for the "calls to action." This format is also more pleasing on the eye and images entice people. The downside is that many people switch the settings on their inbox so that the pictures don't download and therefore much of the benefit of a graphical email is lost. You're also reliant on using an email broadcast service (where you have to pay for each email send). These broadcast services do provide email template builders but can take time to master. You will need to test how the final email looks in different browsers (Outlook, Gmail, Thunderbird, mobile devices).

You might need to commission a designer and developer familiar with these tools to build a template that matches the style of your brand.

Be aware, too, that a significant number of emails are now read on a mobile device – a trend set to continue. Check your graphical format on a mobile. Consider increasing the font size and reducing the number of images.

One advantage of plain text emails is that they aren't immediately recognisable as a marketing or sales communication. Recipients often read the first line of the email before deleting it. As you will see with Dee's email text for Cocoa Loco at the end of this masterclass, if you have crafted a compelling first line your reader could well be encouraged to read on and discover what's in it for them.

Another interesting advantage of plain text emails is that you can do a mail merge (e.g. from Microsoft Word attached to a spread sheet of contacts) and send it out via Microsoft Outlook. This means that you won't be paying "per recipient" as you do when using a broadcast service. The advantage of this method is that the deliverability is usually better because emails sent via a broadcast service can get blocked by firewalls. Your plain text email also looks as though it has been sent by a known contact. The disadvantage is that you don't get any measures of who opened your email and it may take a time to master mail merging. You will also get many "undeliverables" (bounce backs) which need to be managed. If you do use plain text emails you must show people how to unsubscribe. You will also need to check with your ISP their terms for sending several emails in one go. Usually you won't be able to send more than 500 in an hour (rules vary) – so you may need to use a batch process for sending.

One of my clients (a training company) wanted to reach its 5000 database to cross-sell their one day training courses. They changed from sending graphical format emails to plain text via Outlook with astonishing results. Whereas previously they had been getting a 30% open rate but only 2–3 bookings per course, with plain text this increased to 8–12 bookings per course. We arrived at the conclusion that this was attributable to a higher deliverability rate and that the email read as a concise and appealing letter.

Improving Open Rates

If you want to improve your open rates you must be relevant. This entails having a good database, ideally of people who have opted-in to receiving emails from you.

For B2C marketing and some B2B marketing, you will need the recipients' permission to email them (opt-in) – see the section on permission. If the main message of your email including your opening line is not relevant to the audience you are targeting you are exposing yourself to the risk of the message being deleted immediately.

As well as being relevant you can improve open rates by:

- Making the subject line obvious – don't try to be clever or intriguing.
- Ensuring that the "From" should ideally be a named person.
- Personalising the email with first name or title and second name.
- Considering other ways of personalising such as mentioning the company name, their industry or geographic location.
- Doing a small test with two different subject lines to see which gets the most opens.

Unsubscribes and Bounce Backs

Email broadcast service providers will automatically handle your unsubscribes and bounce backs by not mailing these recipients again, taking a record for each campaign. However, it's important you go back to your original data source (CRM system or database) and flag those who have unsubscribed so that you don't inadvertently email these folk again. If you send messages to people who have unsubscribed you're committing an offence and could be liable for a hefty fine.

Once an email address has bounced back three times it's safe to assume it's no longer valid so you may want to flag this in your original database. Data does deteriorate. It's estimated that around 33% of B2B email addresses are no longer valid after a year. If you're operating at more than a 25% bounce back, your data might be too old and in need of a clean-up. There's a danger you could get blacklisted as a spammer.

Sharing – Forward to a Friend and Social Media Links

Great email campaigns are shared through forwarding to a friend or via social media. With the training provider mentioned previously, 50% of the delegates booking a place only found out about the training from being forwarded the email by a friend. Email broadcast tools provide a "forward to a friend" link as well as other social media buttons. I would also recommend that you have "Follow us on LinkedIn or Twitter" or "Like our Facebook page" to encourage engagement.

Permission Marketing

You need to comply with the Data Protection Act (1998) and supplementary regulations of the Privacy & Electronic Communication Regulations 2003 and amendments of 2011 on how to gain permission to email within the law. These regulations look daunting as their focus is on B2C email communication. For B2B email marketing you need to refer to the Information Commissioner's Office *Guidance for Marketers on the Privacy and Electronic Communications (EC Directive) Regulations 2003* which clarifies your obligations. The first part of this document gives regulations advice for B2C email marketing and there are some useful tips about best practice. The specifics regarding B2B are found towards the end of the document.

Your obligations in B2B electronic communications are as follows.

- You must not conceal your identity when you send, or instigate the sending of, a marketing message by electronic mail to anyone (including corporate subscribers).
- You must provide a valid address to which the recipient (including corporate subscribers) can send an opt-out request.

Visit the Information Commissioner's website www.ico.gov.uk and, if you feel unsure, take advice from a lawyer before embarking on your e-marketing campaign.

Remember, you're more likely to get responses from people that have opted in to receiving your communications because they have shown an active interest in being kept in touch.

Here are my top tips for business mailings.

- When a person makes an enquiry, follow up with an email which includes an option to "opt-in" to receiving a newsletter or further information about your business.

- Ask subscribers who have been on a list for more than 12 months if they want to continue receiving emails from you.
- Offer different ways for people to register with you (see Acquiring Data) and give them the option to opt-in to receiving further information.
- A two-stage opt-in process is considered best practice i.e. initially ticking a box to confirm they want to receive information. This takes them to an additional screen or an email is sent asking them to confirm their email address and verify their opt-in choices.
- Opting-out is an alternative route which you will often see (*tick here if you want to opt out of receiving our company updates*) but is a little less robust although still legitimate for business to business email marketing.
- If you're emailing cold leads from a prospect list you've rented from a data provider, it's a good idea to include opt-in choices. This is because as soon as prospects opt-in, you have the right to contact them at any time and don't have to cease emailing them once you've reached the expiry date of your license.

Be aware that many email broadcast service providers are US companies where the regulations for businesses emailing other businesses differ from UK email service providers. Many have quite strict terms and conditions, stricter than current UK legislation. If you break their terms and conditions they may close your account and you may be blacklisted. For this reason, I only use UK-based email service providers.

How Do I Get a Good Database?

Now that you've read some compelling reasons in favour of having a database and engaging with email marketing, you need a good database.

I have introduced many clients to database management tools (sometimes called CRM or Customer Relationship Management systems) and whilst there may be a few weeks on a steep learning curve – the results have been tremendous. One client increased their student numbers by 20% because they were able to follow up enquiries more efficiently (by email) than other colleges and they continued to remind enquirers about course start dates and other training. Another client took great care to transfer paper-based records onto their database. This enabled them to conduct important market research amongst past students and their parents. These research outcomes enabled them to reposition themselves successfully as a top provider of professional business training in London.

There are two main ways to build a database:

1. Your own data that you have gathered including current customers, past customers and prospective customers. You may also wish to include data from your address books. Please be aware there are rules governing how you store and use data in the Data Protection Act 1998.
2. Through renting a list from a data supplier.

Acquiring Data

The best possible database is one you've grown yourself from enquirers and customers. These people have shown an active interest in your company and are more likely to be favourable towards you. There are various ways to encourage your customers or enquirers to provide you with their contact details including:

- An enquiry or "contact us" form on your website.
- A brochure request form.
- A newsletter sign-up.
- An application for a trial or a cut-down version.
- Downloads from your website e.g. a "how to" guide or a user manual (sign-up required).
- Entry form for a special offer e.g. free postage, free gift, 20% off first order.
- Registration for warranty, guarantee or servicing options.
- Order forms and order confirmation.
- Invoices and despatch details.
- Recommend a friend or referral schemes where you incentivise your customer.
- Collecting business cards at personal meetings and networking.

- Collecting data at PR events or exhibitions via business cards, competitions, brochure request forms.
- Customer feedback – customers are often happy to provide their contact details on questionnaires. Remember to explain how you're going to use this data.

Contact or sign-up forms

The golden rule? Keep them as simple as you can for the task in hand. So, for a newsletter sign-up, you could ask for *First Name*, *Last Name* and *Email Address*. You may also want to add a field for *Company* and perhaps *Job Title*. However, the more fields, the less likely people are to complete the forms.

The secret is to capture more data gradually as your prospect or client moves through the steps in the buying process.

For example, they might first sign up for your newsletter by completing the 3 key fields above. Why not try following up with an exclusive "how-to guide" which is only available to newsletter subscribers? This time they need to provide *Company Name* and *Job Title*. And then finally, you could follow up again with a 20% off the first order where address and phone number are needed in order to download the voucher.

You may also have a "contact us" form on your website. Make this simple to complete with basic details so you can make that initial contact. For example, you can make the *Email Address* field compulsory but the *Phone Number* and *Address* fields optional. It's good practice to ask how people would prefer to be contacted.

Privacy Policy and Terms & Conditions

When you're capturing data in this way, it's important you have a statement of how you will use the data. This is usually in the form of a link to your privacy policy on-line but you may also want people to confirm they have read and understood your terms and conditions which could include information on how you will use their data. Whilst it's not essential in the UK to request businesses to opt-in to receiving business to business mailings, it's still good practice to do so. You may want to give some options e.g.:

- sign up to our newsletter
- sign up to our email bulletins
- sign up to our offers or updates on products/services

If you're reaching consumer markets (B2C), there are much stricter regulations as discussed in the section on permission marketing.

Storing and Accessing Data

If your customer database is large and growing, you may have discovered the frustrations of storing customer information on Excel spreadsheets.

If you're sending regular, personalised communications, either email or printed, then sooner or later you're likely to need a good system for data storage and retrieval. There are many database tools available. You may already have Microsoft Access if you have a business version of Microsoft Office. However, if you want to record details of your latest interaction with a customer and segment your database according to specific criteria, consider a Customer Relationship Management (CRM) system. You'll want to weigh up the pros and cons of using a cloud-based option where the data and system is hosted on-line, or a local desktop system which is installed on each computer.

The advantage of the cloud CRM option is that your team can access your database and update customer records when they are on-line, irrespective of where they are working.

The main reason why small businesses elect for a CRM system is because it can organise information on a customer by customer basis for each of the following functions:

- sales pipeline/leads/orders
- customer service
- marketing communications

We call this a "single view of the customer" which means that everyone in the organisation in sales, customer service and marketing has access to the same information about the customer in the one place. Locally installed CRM systems may also be less costly in the longer term.

Organising Data Management

Small businesses can be awash with data and it's often stored in different places; phone contacts, address books, invoicing or quoting systems and social media. Everyone within the business will have different contact lists which may of course overlap. Using a centralised database such as a CRM system can help put all these names and numbers under the one roof in the right order. Make sure that everyone using your CRM system understands how they should input the data and which fields are crucial. Why not assign someone as "database champion," responsible for keeping everything updated and in good order?

Type of data you can capture (variables)

I've helped many clients set up their marketing database from scratch and we've found it invaluable to spend time thinking about the data they want to capture and how it will be used. There's a natural tendency to build something complex, to find that you can only complete 20% of the fields. A flexible CRM system, which allows you to add fields when needed or delete fields you never use, is a good idea. I use Salesforce.com for many clients, with its relatively easy drag-and-drop control functions.

There may be some really important variables that are relevant to your industry – but don't get carried away in trying to gather too much data. It's not always easy to elicit this information from customers because:

- They don't want to give away too much personal information especially if they can't see the relevance of it.
- It makes enquiry forms too long.
- If you're buying or renting data, you may find that the level of detail isn't available or you have to pay extra for every variable you request.

Useful Fields in a Database

This list is not exhaustive but it should get you thinking about what information you would like to capture.

B2C

- First name, last name, title (Mr, Mrs, Miss etc.), email address, postal address, landline and mobile number, Instant Message ID, social media ID, Skype ID.
- Demographic information e.g. gender, age group, number of children, employment status, home ownership, household income, family stage, occupation, nationality, social class.
- Note that the Data Protection Act (DPA) 1998 requires you to have specific permissions to hold certain data e.g. sexual orientation and ethnicity.

B2B

- Type of organisation, industry/sector (Standard Industry Classification (SIC) code), ownership status (public, limited company, partnership, sole trader) geographic location, £ turnover, number of employees, age of company, annual revenue.
- Name of contact i.e. first name, last name, title (Mr, Mrs, Miss etc.), email address, company address (billing and mailing), switchboard, direct line, mobile, website, Instant Message ID, social media ID, Skype ID.
- Job title, Reports to, Assistant.

Usage

- Heavy/medium or light user.
- Product/service sold and repertoire purchased.
- Value and volume of order.
- How frequently they buy.
- When they buy (e.g. time of week, month, year).

Sales and marketing

- Sales cycle: prospect, enquirer, quote supplied, current customers, lapsed customer, closed/lost customer.
- Type of contact: prospect, customer, supplier, partner, agency, competitor.
- Opted out, opted in (to whichever type of communication).
- Newsletter subscriber.
- How did they hear about you? (often called lead source).
- Source of data (and expiry date if purchased).

Renting or Buying Data

Ideally you would work from your own large database of customers and enquirers but this isn't always possible. You may be considering renting or buying data to reach more prospective customers.

It's not easy to buy high quality data where the ownership of data passes to the purchaser for perpetual unlimited use. Beware of suppliers who offer you seemingly brilliant deals. Before working with me, one of my clients bought 50,000 records for around £500 for a perpetual licence. Once I started working with the list, I realised that the supplier had simply taken a mailing list and artificially formed email addresses from the first name, last name and domain name of the website URL. The bounce-back rate was horrific and they were in danger of being blacklisted as spammers.

Data is usually rented for a given licence period – often 12 months.

Here is some advice about buying data for B2B companies:

1. Use reputable data suppliers. The Direct Marketing Association accredits list providers. Get recommendations from colleagues, compare quotes and use data brokers too.
2. You get what you pay for. Data providers sometimes offer special deals (particularly at Christmas) but may choose to downgrade the data for these deals, missing important information that you need such as first names or telephone numbers.

3. Specify your data requirements first and then use a broker to help you understand the different options: www.Marketingfile.com provides a very good service for this. But be aware of the additional price you're paying for this background service.

4. Ask how many records the data supplier can find according to your specification (this is called a "count"). Some lists are bigger than others and you might be able to refine and target better if you have a bigger list to draw upon.

5. Always ask the data supplier to tell you the source of their data, how they gained permission.

6. Don't over or under specify i.e. if you're never going to do a full direct mail campaign, you don't need a full postal address but you may want to buy postcode, county or city data so that you have a good idea for geographic targeting.

7. You may want some fields for future use e.g. industry type or size of company. Ask if you can get this information free within the deal or at a reduced rate once you've agreed the rest of the specification.

8. It's always better to buy "named contacts" i.e. each record comes with a name. These days you want first name and last name (and preferably title) because most emails are personalised e.g. "Dear Liz."

9. You can specify that you don't want any generic email addresses (e.g. info@company.com) although if you have a named contact this may not matter.

10. Use suppression files i.e. send your existing data to the list provider so you are not in danger of buying duplicates of what you already have.

11. You should also ensure the data is screened against files for deceased and goneaways. If you're likely to use the data for mailing or follow up by telephone you should ask the provider to screen against the Mailing Preference Service and the Telephone Preference Services.

12. For business to business emailing, you shouldn't use personal email addresses such as Hotmail, Gmail and Yahoo as this is deemed as mailing consumers and you need specific opt-in permissions to do this.

13. If you're emailing businesses you should not send emails to sole traders or employees of non-LLP partnerships unless they have opted in to receiving emails. This is because the Data Commissioner rules that technically you're emailing individuals (not part of a registered organisation) and so it is

considered as mailing consumers. Ask your data provider to ensure these groups are excluded from your purchase.

14. Check your licence arrangements carefully. How many times can you use this list? Is it as many sends as you like within 12 months, or 12 sends in just one month?

15. Don't abuse the terms of your licence because data suppliers can levy heavy fines. They use their own "seed" email addresses within the list they provide to check your number of sends.

16. Ask for a sample of records before you buy and check you have all the fields you want and that the formatting looks OK.

Data Quality – Your Database

Data deteriorates more quickly than you think so budget to refresh your own data, ideally annually.

Data entry is an important part of data quality so establish clear data entry rules for everyone who uses your database. I've seen poor practices including all uppercase or all lowercase typing simply because it's easier and quicker to input. Address fields and postcodes should always be in the same format. It's important that the data entry process isn't too onerous, so don't have too many fields and don't make too many compulsory. Encourage those entering data to be proud of what they're doing, explaining the importance of accurate data in building relationships with prospects and customers.

If your data is old it may be unclean and incomplete so consider paying to have it cleaned and to remove any known undeliverables (email addresses which bounce back), duplicates and poorly formed email addresses. Many companies undertake data cleansing and there are some surprisingly cheap services on-line e.g. Email Movers. Some companies also provide an "appending" service where you can ask for fields to be added to your data e.g. first name or postcode or even email address. Restrictions apply for using appended records for email marketing to consumers – and it can be costly – so get a quote first. However, if you own your business data the cost of appending vital details can be low relative to the cost of renting that data each year.

Measuring Performance

Measuring the impact of your email marketing is easy. Look at:

- Analytics provided by your email service provider e.g. open rates, click through rates, pages visited, forwards, replies, bounce backs, unsubscribes, deliverability.
- Website analytics (number of visitors to specified pages on the days of the email campaign and how long they spent on these pages).
- Enquiries by phone, email or via a contact form.
- Referrals (forwards), source of referrals and value of the referrals.

Be methodical about recording these measurements. It's surprising what you can learn from looking back over several campaigns. In analysing one client's results we found that graphical format emails only worked slightly better than plain text but that sending emails early in the morning or late at night did not work as well as during the day up to 4pm.

Thanks to Liz for such practical, useful and expert tips.

I would like to conclude this masterclass by sharing two successful emails I created for two very different clients. One, Cocoa Loco, makes organic chocolate products; the other, ISM, designs and manufactures security systems for organisations on a global scale. For Cocoa Loco we used a text-only email with the underlined text being a link to the relevant web page.

For ISM we used an HTML newsletter with links on each case study to the ISM website.

How could you emulate these approaches to promote your own business using email?

Cocoa Loco Valentine's Day Campaign

Our audience was Cocoa Loco customers that had willingly opted in to receiving monthly emails from Cocoa Loco. This email was sent two weeks prior to Valentine's Day, February 14th.

Hugs and kisses guaranteed on Feb 14

Dear (name of customer)

As a lover of our divine handmade and fair-trade organic chocolate, if you're looking for an extra big hug and a huge sloppy kiss on Valentine's Day, pop over to our website. You'll find the most perfect melt-your-heart-and-melt-in-your-mouth range of Valentine's gifts, each one lovingly crafted by hand at our HQ, the Chocolate Barn using only organic and fair-trade ingredients.

We've got something for any sweetheart including yours – the most special sweetheart in the world!

Hearts and flowers slab – a gorgeous and decadent slab, adorned with daisies and hearts, measuring 30cm by 20cm beautifully packaged (all recyclable packaging of course) and just xxxx

Champagne truffles – the heart of each truffle is laced with champagne. It is then enveloped in creamy milk chocolate, dunked in chocolate and tumbled in rich chocolate flakes. 12 truffles beautifully boxed for just xxxx

Milk and pink hearts – 12 chunky milk chocolate and real raspberry chocolate hearts with a little love message. Just xxxx

Heart shaped brownies – 12 gorgeous, rich and utterly sinful dark chocolate brownies each one hand cut into a beautiful heart shape. Just xxxx

Place your order today for guaranteed hugs and kisses!

If you want your loved one to have their romantic and scrumptious chocolate goodies in time for Valentine's Day you must place your order on-line by XXXXX date and you will receive an extra discount of 5% off your order. And don't hesitate to call us on XXXXXXXXXX for a chat.

Kind regards,

Sarah Payne

Founder

Cocoa Loco

ISM (Integrated Security Management)

This was the first graphical email newsletter sent to ISM's database which comprised largely of visitors to their exhibition stands opting in to receiving email newsletters from them. It was sent within a few weeks of the new ISM website launching.

Welcome to the new ISM monthly newsletter. Once a month we will deliver a dose of news, case studies and interesting security statistics to your inbox – with no fluff or filler and never more than once a month.

The brand new ISM website has been a hotspot for thousands of visitors worldwide since it launched in January. With exciting and informative video content, a technical library, new client case studies and hot topics plus the latest on the critically acclaimed patent protected Genesys 2, it's worth a visit.

Discover how the London Borough of Hammersmith and Fulham ticked their "green credentials" box *and* reduced their operating costs when tasked with improving the concierge systems for 5 estates. How did ISM's Genesys Security Control Room Management System and Ultimate intercom and door entry system eliminate the need for any construction work?

Why did the contractors working on a high security integrated project for The Office of Public Works in Ireland specify Genesys 2 to integrate CCTV, access control, intruder, fire and intercoms? What was the connection with the pioneering Siemens SigNET intruder detection alarm system?

An astonishing statistic

The Growth Partnership Company Frost & Sullivan anticipate that the market generated revenues from PSIM systems of $142.9 million in 2011 are likely to have increased to $2.79 billion by 2021.

Just how many purchasers of security systems believe that security is a grudge purchase? 10%, 90% or 40%?

You can see how the purpose of Cocoa Loco's email was simply to generate sales from existing customers, whereas for ISM the purpose of their email was to keep in touch with potential high value prospects, keeping the ISM name front of mind by informing them of projects that showcased their competence and abilities.

Masterclass Summary

- You can still get great results with targeted and well-written email marketing but you must clarify why you want to use email marketing.
- Relevance is vital, so craft different messages for your different target audiences and keep your database up to date and clean so you are only emailing people who want to hear from you.
- The best database comprises of those who have opted-in to receive your emails so actively look for ways to acquire their contact details and gain their permission for you to email them.
- Legislation governs the use of email marketing, so ensure that you understand the rules before embarking on your campaigns.
- Think about whether you want to send graphical format emails or plain text emails. Mix the two formats, test one against another.
- If you want to supplement your own database with rented data, adhere to the legal obligations and take your time to specify your data requirements, getting quotes from different suppliers.
- A CRM (Customer Relationship Management) system could be really beneficial for you. Nowadays, they are much less costly and much easier to set up.
- Test, measure and improve. A great benefit of email marketing is that you can get good statistics about how it is working, particularly when using email broadcast software.
- The same good practice rules for copywriting apply to your emails. Use "you" and "your" when possible; have an engaging tone and write with your reader front of mind.

Masterclass 11
How to be a Confident and Engaging Public Speaker

In this masterclass you will learn:

- How to become a confident, compelling and charismatic public speaker.
- The many business benefits that public speaking offers.
- How to plan, rehearse and deliver a first rate presentation.

I must admit to some hesitation about calling this chapter of the book a "Master-class." The tips that I have included here are based purely on my own personal experience. There are probably a number of world-renowned techniques and systems that are useful in helping a person become an accomplished public speaker, but I'm afraid you won't find them in this book. Instead I will be providing you with details of the approach that I take to public speaking, an approach that has evolved from my first nerve-ridden experience 15 years ago of asking one question at a PTA meeting in front of about 10 people, to speaking in front of 200 business women at The British Library and thoroughly enjoying myself.

It was after speaking at The British Library, with nothing between me and my audience other than a few notes nearby and a clip-on microphone, that it dawned on me just how far I had come in the last 15 years. Somehow I had managed to progress from being petrified at the very thought of public speaking to being an accomplished and confident performer, able to command fees for some of my speaking engagements, and having the skills and know-how to be able to train my clients in how to be successful at public speaking themselves. So in this masterclass I would like to share some of the tips that have helped me to make that leap. Whether you have never spoken in public before but recognise that it's a skill you really should have in your armoury, or you already speak regularly but are aware that your performance could be a little more polished, you should find something in here to help you.

Why Consider Public Speaking?

Public speaking demands much from you, not least an ongoing struggle to overcome your nerves. But there are many benefits to be had from putting yourself through it, including:

- It helps to reinforce or build your expert status, setting you apart from competitors that have neither your confidence nor ability to stand up in public and share their expertise.

- It builds your confidence, improves your self-esteem.
- It becomes a source of new and exciting business opportunities. When you make a conscious decision to stand up and speak, you become a focus of attention and, as such, attract many business propositions.
- It's the ultimate PR tool – it's free, and it makes you very visible!
- It can help in building your profile: locally, nationally and possibly even internationally.
- It enhances your presentation skills, and this can only help when you are networking, pitching for business or speaking on the telephone to prospects and clients.

And yet many of us shudder at the thought of public speaking. At the back of our minds is the worry that we will either go blank through nerves, humiliate ourselves in some awful public way, or that what we have to share will not be sufficiently interesting to engage an audience. If this is you, do not worry. It was certainly me 15 years ago. But if you are passionate about what you do, are unwavering in your commitment to deliver an exceptional service to your clients and are willing to learn some presentation tips and techniques, you will surely be able to take your place in the spotlight.

The speakers that we tend to admire are those that stand on the stage and make it look so easy. They speak from the heart, have few if any notes and build a strong connection with their audience. Their seemingly effortless presentations are, in fact, the result of many hours of practice; their message has been carefully crafted, their body language well rehearsed. They probably suffer from nerves like the rest of us, but they have found ways to control or even suppress them. There is no reason why you cannot follow in the footsteps of these successful speakers if you are prepared step out of your comfort zone and go for it.

Step One: Your Starting Point – Self-Belief!

Whilst it's understandable to have limiting and negative feelings about your ability to speak in public, these feelings are not going to serve you well if left unchallenged.

Introduce your negative chatterbox to a positive and uplifting voice. This does not mean that the negative thoughts will go away, but each time one pops into your mind, counter it with a positive and affirming statement. Here are some of the positive things I say to my negative chatterbox:

"I am an accomplished and confident public speaker."
"I am really looking forward to sharing my marketing knowledge with my audience."
"I am so looking forward to meeting this audience."
"It's going to be a fantastic event because I am so well-prepared."
"People have to do far worse things than stand up in front of an audience."
"I am so lucky to have been given this opportunity to speak. My competitors would love to be in my position now!"
"I will be fantastic!"
"I am unstoppable!"

You can concentrate too much on why you shouldn't get up on that stage when, in fact, there are far more reasons why the opposite is true. Write down your empowering slogans and refer to them when a negative thought pops in your mind. Imagine these negative thoughts are on a television screen. Diminish each one with an imaginary remote control until it becomes a tiny dot.

Step Two: Building Your Magnetic Stage Presence

When delivering your presentation, make sure that you command the space available in order to attract and maintain the interest of the audience from start to finish. Look upon your presentation as a theatrical performance with you as the leading character. You want to appear in control of your surroundings, to exude confidence, to own your space. Here's how you can achieve this.

Make Your Voice the Sweetest Sound to Your Audience's Ears

How often have you attended a talk and switched off from the presenter either because their voice was so quiet you struggled to keep up with their message or you became bored with their subdued delivery? Or maybe you have taken a dislike to a speaker because they were so loud that it became off-putting and you found it impossible to warm to them. Conversely, you may encounter speakers that have no impact on you whatsoever. They neither irritate nor impress. You can hear them perfectly well but their style is lifeless and consequently they fall into the category of "forgettable."

Your voice is an incredibly powerful tool. Use it to its full ability.

- Start by projecting your voice when you're in the shower, car or garden, when walking in the countryside or when you're alone in the office. Practise speaking in different tones: loudly; quietly; enthusiastically; dramatically etc. Become connected to the variations in the sound of your own voice, and use them whenever you can.
- Find a book that you really like and select some favourite passages. Read each passage out loud. Pause between sentences. Emphasise keywords, some with a humorous tone, and others in a dramatic manner. Repeat this exercise several times. Imagine that you are an actor and these are your lines. Record some of these readings and play them back. What do you sound like? Ask a friend or relative for feedback. Make notes. What do you like about your voice? What have you learned about your voice? What improvements would you like to make before you start public speaking? This is a fun exercise and one you will learn from. It will instil in you the confidence that comes from knowing that you can use your voice as an instrument when you are presenting.
- Make a point of attending as many presentations as you can to critique the presenters, taking notes that you can refer back to. What do you particularly like about a speaker's voice? How do they use their voice to bring their presentation to life and to maintain the attention of the audience? What can you learn from them? What would you avoid? How is the audience reacting to the speaker? Use these experiences for more voice practice, more recording and evaluation.
- Study the presenters on the television shopping channels. (I learnt many tips on how to present my voice from listening to and watching the presenters on

the shopping channel, QVC.) Or listen to how radio presenters place emphasis on different words and vary their pitch in order to ensure their delivery is lively and engaging. With only their voice to hold a listener's interest, they must be entertaining and convey their personality solely through their control of the spoken word.

- Practise using a microphone then listening to what your voice sounds like through it. At some events you will need a microphone, so become used to holding one and moving with it in your hand. Use a hairbrush or something similar to practise at home.

Your Body Language – Confident, Warm and Welcoming

We can all recognise poor body language in a presenter: hands in pockets, pacing rapidly up and down the stage, arms permanently folded, standing rooted to the spot, jangling keys or fiddling with a pen. And, unfortunately, the best content and the finest speaking voice can be rendered ineffective by poor body language. Body language is an important means of communication and should be seen as the supporting act for your content and delivery. It needs to be natural, but expressive. Start by being aware of your body language habits.

Allow yourself five minutes to deliver an unrehearsed presentation on one of the following topics, standing in front of a full length mirror.

- If I ruled the world I would . . .
- The memory I most cherish is . . .
- If I had one wish I would . . .
- Success in business is . . .
- What I most admire about myself is . . .
- If I won the lottery I would . . .

Focus on your body language when delivering this presentation. Now, repeat this away from the mirror but video yourself so you can analyse your body language properly. Do you look comfortable, confident and welcoming? What can you improve and what must you eliminate? Is your body language supporting your presentation or detracting from it? Do you repeat a particular movement several times during your talk? (My husband, for example, had a nervous habit of repeatedly pulling up his shirt sleeves whenever he had to speak in front of an audience – something he wasn't aware of until he was photographed while speaking. Every photo showed him either pulling up one sleeve or the other. He always wore short-sleeved shirts from then on!)

Now repeat the exercise, this time using these body language tips.

- Imagine your audience is in front of you and you have just taken to the stage. Look to the middle of your imaginary audience then to the left, back to the middle and to the right all the time radiating a smile that includes your eyes. You will need to repeat this throughout your talk if you are aiming to connect with all of your audience.
- Using your arms, imagine you are demonstrating the shape of a large circle to your audience. Then, after doing so, drop your arms to your side, their natural resting place.
- Now imagine that you are describing a beautiful landscape to your audience, one that you really love. Use your hands, arms and head to describe the scene but, instead of using your voice, describe the scene in your mind.
- Time now to be aware of your legs. Feel the ground beneath your feet. Don't let your feet be stuck together otherwise you will look rigid. Practise moving around taking a few steps to your left, then to your right, then moving forwards and backwards a little. When you are presenting you will need to earmark an area in which you can move around comfortably. Whilst your audience does not want to see you stuck on one spot looking into the distance, they will not appreciate you moving around the room at such a pace that you become impossible to focus on and challenging to hear.

By practising, recording and evaluating your body language, you will begin to develop a real stage presence. After a little while you will intuitively know which physical style of expression suits you best – a style with which you are always comfortable and one that complements and enhances your presentation.

Looking the Part

When presenting to an audience, your overall look and image has to support your presentation and convey that you are an expert in your field, a person worth listening to. For these reasons, you should always look smarter than your audience. When you take to the stage, your audience will form an immediate impression of you based on what you look like. If you don't look the part then what you have to say when you open your mouth will be filtered through that initial negative impression. It's important that you feel confident about your appearance because this will have an impact on your performance, and I don't recommend that you wear something that you do not feel comfortable in as a person. However, do spend some time thinking about the outfit you will wear and ensure that as a minimum, you look clean and well groomed.

- If you are unsure about the image that you want to convey but are serious about developing as a public speaker, it may be a good idea to invest in the services of a style adviser or image consultant.
- Build a small capsule wardrobe for your speaking engagements comprising of clothes you feel confident in, that you look smart in and that enhance your skin colour, body shape and hair.
- Pay attention to what you smell like. It is likely that many of the audience will be keen to ask you questions after your talk, and want to find out more about what you do. Overdoing the perfume or aftershave or answering them with bad breath is only going to put them off.
- Don't forget your footwear! You will be appraised from head to toe. Scruffy or scuffed shoes and scratched heels give a shoddy impression.
- Your hands will be on show too so make sure your nails are neat and unbitten and your hands are clean.

You will find an extra layer of confidence from knowing that you are going to look good up on that stage.

Step Three: Your Audience

While listening to you, you want your audience to believe that:

1. **You are as sharp as a tack.** You know your stuff. You are an expert.
2. **They are benefiting from listening to you.** You are not *promoting* your business; you are sharing tips, best practice and information that can really help them.
3. **You care.** Your audience wants to feel and believe that you genuinely want to help and inspire them.

If you are tempted to write your presentation without first gaining an understanding of the profile of your audience, or their expectations and the length of time they presume you will be speaking for, you run the risk of delivering a presentation that nobody wants to listen to.

- Ask the organisers why they have invited you to talk. You have to meet their expectations as well as those of your audience.
- Ask the organisers to provide you with as much information as possible about your audience. What level of knowledge are they likely to have on your proposed subject matter? What would they most want to gain from listening to you?
- What has worked well at past events and what has not? What subject matter and style of presentation was well received and what did not go down so well? Any advice you can gain in this area can only help you in planning your presentation.
- Will the audience be looking for an inspiring story, a selection of tips, or just some general guidance?
- Will you be speaking on your own or as part of a programme with other speakers? Who are the other speakers? What are they talking about? It's useful to know this to avoid the risk of replicating or conflicting with their content.
- How long do you have to speak? Will you be expected to offer a question and answer session within this time too?
- With the answers to these questions, you can move with confidence to the next stage, developing your theme and writing your presentation.

Step Four: Developing Your Theme

You won't be able to cover everything there is to know about your subject matter in your speaking slot, and nor should you want to. If you try to cram as much information as possible into your speech, you could end up irritating or baffling your audience. Consider what information and messages you would like to impart to your audience bearing in mind the time you will be speaking for. Be prepared to scale down your content if upon review you realise that you're trying to cover too much. It's far better to cover a few topics clearly than to risk confusion by rushing through more material than your time comfortably allows. Many business people are happy to come away from a talk with one or two nuggets of information. Concentrate on providing quality content rather than a huge amount of content.

Be clear yourself about the central theme of your talk and what you would like your audience to take away from it. For example, I recently delivered a keynote speech at the Electrical Contractors Association conference. I found out beforehand that my audience comprised of electrical contractors, each with around ten employees. The advice given to me by the organisers was that these contractors believed that marketing was a baffling and daunting subject and could see little value in it. They preferred to market their business through word-of-mouth recommendations. I therefore focused my 60 minute talk on:

- Initially explaining that marketing was not just about advertising or networking but had a much deeper meaning and one that all small businesses should embrace. To help do this I shared my favourite definition of marketing: that it is a philosophy of business that places the customer and the prospect at the centre of the universe. My purpose in doing this was to make the audience aware that the business of acquiring and retaining customers is the business of marketing.
- I outlined the mistakes that small businesses often make with their marketing, including relying solely on the power of recommendation from existing customers, so that members of the audience could identify with some of the mistakes and recognise they were not alone.

- I explained that marketing is not something for small businesses to be afraid of and that even if a small business is able to employ only the basic principles, this is often enough. I expanded by giving five marketing tips that I was confident the audience would understand and could easily apply to their business. This took the lion's share of my talk (40 minutes).
- For the last five minutes of my talk I performed a light-hearted marketing exercise, acting it out with a member of the audience so that my talk could end on a humorous and hopefully memorable note.

Throughout my talk I used case studies to explain how other professional trades had benefited from marketing, so that the audience members could identify with what I was saying and understand how the tips were applicable to them too. I avoided jargon and explained everything in a simple and easy-to-understand fashion. I stayed on after my talk to answer questions.

What can you learn from the way in which I planned and structured this talk? Hopefully, you can see how beneficial it is to start with an overall theme for your talk and then, once happy with this, to move onto planning it out in bite-sized segments. The time spent planning your talk is never wasted, so don't be happy with sketching out your ideas and leaving it at that. Go into the detail, the nitty-gritty. If you have to make several changes and tweaks to your talk, that's a good sign! It shows that you really care about delivering top class content to your audience.

Step Five: Writing Your Talk

For a person to be successful at public speaking, great content is of equal importance to a powerful stage presence. So, let's look at some of the considerations when sitting down to write a great speech:

1. **Write with no purpose other than to deliver exceptional content to your audience.** Forget any notion about selling your services or sneaking in promotional plugs about your business. You are not there to deliver a pitch; you are there to deliver real value for the audience. This attitude will ensure that your audience

will listen with interest throughout your speech. Trying to sell to them is a sure-fire way to turn them off.

2. **Keep your talk simple.** Bearing in mind the time you have available, consider including some tips and illustrating these tips with a case study or compelling fact. Often you will find that the parts of your talk your audience remembers and appreciates most are those in which you illustrate a point with a story, fact or statistic.

3. **If you are not sharing tips, can you tell a story that will underpin and strengthen your central message?** For example, for an IT specialist, speaking about the importance of businesses backing up their computer records off-line and explaining the technicalities of doing so may not be sufficient to engage an audience fully. If, instead, the speaker illustrates their message with some genuine and interesting client case studies, the audience are likely to buy into the information while being entertained at the same time.

4. **View your speech as being made up of three parts.** The first part is your introduction during which you need to establish your credentials as a speaker on this subject in order to gain the respect of your audience quickly. You thank the organisers for inviting you and the audience for turning up to listen to you. You explain briefly what you are going to cover in your talk and how your audience will benefit and let them know how long you will be talking for. It's also a good idea to let the audience know if you are providing a handout because this may influence their decision to take notes. If you don't want to be interrupted with questions, make this clear at the outset too. Having run through the less exciting aspects of your talk, you may now want to indicate that your talk itself is about to start by providing a memorable quote, fact or statistic relevant to your topic. Allow about 5 minutes for your introduction in a 30 minute talk.

The second part of your talk is your subject matter; what you have been asked to deliver. This should encompass the lion's share of your talk. As mentioned earlier, focus on telling real stories, using case studies, sharing tips and connecting what you are saying with the needs of your audience.

The third part of your talk is your close. Allow five minutes at the end for your closing remarks. Thank the audience once again for their time and attention and expressing your desire that they have gained something of benefit from what you have said. You may want to summarise some of the points of your talk, but this is not always necessary if you have been doing so throughout. If there is time for questions, invite these now if you have not been accepting them during your talk. Alternatively you may prefer to announce that you are staying on afterwards and would be happy to answer questions on a one-to-one basis. If you are not able to stay, provide your contact details so that people can get in touch with you after the event.

Write your speech in long hand but don't settle on this as the final draft. It will take several edits before being whipped into a shape that will wow your audience. Having arrived at this stage, it's time to practise your delivery. Don't lose sight of the purpose of your speech. Write this down and keep referring back to it when writing to help ensure that you don't deviate from it.

Step Six: Practice Makes Poised, Professional and Perfect

Your speech reads very well on paper, but it must now make that transition into a warm and enlightening verbal presentation. Read it out loud several times from beginning to end, remembering to practise your body language and voice at the same time. At this stage you are likely to be making some fine tweaks – what reads well on paper does not always sound natural when translated into speech. When you have practised delivering the final version of your speech several times, reduce it to bullet points on numbered cue cards. You don't want to stand in front of an audience with quivering sheets of paper, nor do you want to be at a lectern with your speech in long hand. Trying to read your speech word for word will make you sound stilted and scripted. Cue cards completed, it's time to practise again. Memorise your introduction and the introductory line to each new point, story or case study. By spending time on preparation and rehearsals, your confidence will grow. Soon your cue cards will be there merely to prompt you rather than act as an essential crutch. When you see a speaker on a stage with just a few notes, sounding supremely confident, it is usually because they have invested many hours in practising beforehand and are pretty comfortable with what they are going to say and how they are going to say it.

Step Seven: Checking out the Venue

The more you can find out about the venue you are speaking at, the better. If you can visit it before your speech, do so. But, if you can't, find out the following from the organisers:

1. Will you be provided with a microphone and, if so, will it be hand-held or clip-on? It's always worth asking for a microphone even if you don't have to use it on the day. A packed room will absorb speaker sound alarmingly. If you are to be using a hand-held microphone you will need to practise holding your cue cards in one hand with your microphone in the other.
2. Will the audience be seated at tables or in rows? This will help you when you're visualising delivering your talk.
3. Where will you be delivering your talk? On stage or standing in front of the audience with just a few feet separating you? Again, it will help your preparation beforehand if you know the set-up.
4. Will you be provided with a lectern? If not, request a small table for your notes and some water because your mouth may get a little dry during your talk.
5. If you are using a PowerPoint presentation, will you be expected to bring your laptop to the venue or can you provide your presentation on a memory stick? It is worth having a back-up plan in case a technical glitch results in your PowerPoint slides not being shown. If you're using the slides as prompts for your speech, for example, having a matching set of cue cards would mean that you are still able to present. I have attended talks at which the speakers have been completely thrown by the IT equipment being faulty and, in each case, the speeches did not go ahead.
6. If you are going to use a flip chart, find out if the venue can provide you with a flip chart stand. Prepare your flip chart ahead of the talk ensuring you don't cram so much on each sheet that it becomes unreadable. Some speakers prefer to use a flip chart rather than cue cards to help them remember the key points of their talk. When using the flip chart do not speak with your back to the audience whilst turning the sheets over. Turn each sheet in silence, stand back for a few seconds, face your audience and resume your talk. Practise using a flip chart in this way before your live presentation. You don't want to appear clumsy or feel flustered as you fumble with the sheets.

If the venue is not within a reasonable travelling distance, consider staying overnight so that you are fresh and alert the next morning with some time for last-minute rehearsals. The last thing you want is to turn up late and flustered because you were delayed by traffic.

Step Eight: Delivering Your Speech

The day has finally arrived! You are well rehearsed and feel confident about your ability to deliver. There will be butterflies in your tummy but you are ready to claim your place in the spotlight and shine. Here are some tips on how to calm your nerves before delivering an incredible presentation:

1. Arrive early at the venue to immerse yourself in the atmosphere and to become familiar with the unfamiliar. If possible, bring a friend or colleague with you so that you're not alone. If you are given the opportunity to network with the delegates beforehand, take it. You'll feel much better delivering to an audience in which there are people that you have already built a connection with.

2. Brief the organisers on how you would like to be introduced. If a long-winded narrative about your skills and abilities is likely to make you feel nervous before you take to the stage, let them know this and provide them with some concise facts about your background, membership of professional associations and anything that connects you with the audience. Think about what qualifies you to stand in front of the audience and share your expertise, and make sure this is communicated either by the organisers in their introduction, or by yourself if you are not being formally introduced.

3. It's natural to feel nervous in the build-up to taking to the stage. Don't be worried if your heart beats faster than usual. It's perfectly normal and shows that you care about your presentation. Slow your breathing. Inhale then exhale slowly counting from 0 to 6 between breaths. When a flicker of nerves, fear or panic enters your head, greet it with one of your positive slogans, diminish the negative chatterbox to a tiny spot and bring the focus back to your breathing.

4. Smile at everyone that you see before walking to the stage and smile to yourself so that your body releases positive, feel-good endorphins.

5. When you are called to the stage, stand up slowly, smile and walk purposefully towards the area from where you are going to deliver your presentation.

6. When you get to your spot, give yourself a few seconds to become composed. Feel the ground beneath your feet, turn on your warmest smile and start to take in all of your audience so that everyone sees your smile. Don't worry if your heart is still beating fast. Once you move into your presentation, you'll become so focused on your content and delivery that your heart will resume its normal beat.

7. As you move through your presentation, if your mouth becomes dry, simply pause for a few moments, take a sip of water and smile. You don't have to say anything to your audience. What seems like a lifetime to you is just a few seconds to your audience and it gives them an opportunity to reflect on your previous point. Pausing also gives you the air of being a confident and assured presenter.

8. Remember to keep looking around the room, catching the eyes for a few seconds of a particular member of the audience before moving to another, then taking in the whole audience. This helps provide the impression that you are talking to the audience as individuals, rather than as a group. Don't allow yourself to be distracted by someone yawning, fiddling with their phone or even walking out when you are talking. These minor distractions happen to all speakers and are to be expected. Move your gaze from that person and keep focussing on your content and delivery.

9. If your mind goes blank it really is not the end of the world. There are some simple things you can do to regain your composure. Firstly, be reassured that most speakers have blank spots in their presentation, when the next thing they are about to say momentarily escapes them. Your mind will usually recover from these minor blips in a few seconds, especially if your cue cards are to hand or you can look at your flip chart to get your bearings. But if your mind goes blank completely and you don't have a clue about what you're going to say next, buy yourself some time with a little audience interaction! Ask your audience if they can provide some feedback on what you have just said, or opt for a show of

hands on the point you have just made if this is appropriate. This gives you time to compose your thoughts, locate the right cue card or flip chart sheet and reconnect with your presentation.

10. If, as you move through your presentation, you become aware that your body language is a little formal or you are talking a little quickly, just correct yourself and continue.

11. If you are using flip chart sheets or PowerPoint slides, explain to the audience what you're about to reveal before doing so. For example: "Let's now look at the seven deadly sins of small business marketing, one at a time." Allow the audience a few seconds to absorb the information you have just revealed before continuing with your presentation. Also, avoid the temptation to look at the slides while talking. Always address the audience. If you need to point something out on a slide, do so, and then turn back to the audience to continue your talk.

12. If you are interrupted during your talk by a member of the audience, despite making it clear that you will only take questions or comments at the end, explain firmly: "That's an interesting question/comment/view but I'd like to answer it at the end of my talk/afterwards." As the speaker, you're in charge. Allowing yourself to be distracted by comments and questions could seriously sidetrack you and jeopardise your presentation. You may have made an individual happy by answering their questions but you won't be popular with the organisers or the rest of the audience if you short-change them on your promised content or overrun your allocated slot.

Stage Nine: Reflecting on Your Performance

It is human nature that as you reflect on your talk, you will be rather critical of your performance. Whilst there will be elements of your presentation and delivery that you can improve upon, the likelihood is that you have much to congratulate yourself for. Rein in the self-criticism, be kind to yourself and give yourself a big pat on the back. You have done something that the vast majority of folk shrink away from. If the audience has been asked to provide feedback, ask the organisers if you can look at their comments so that you can improve your future performances and use the positive testimonial in your marketing communications.

And Finally

If you really get bitten by the public speaking bug and find yourself becoming a sought-after speaker, be sure to publicise your availability for speaking engagements on your website, including testimonial from organisers and delegates. Let web visitors know when and where they can see you speaking and include a list of the subjects you speak about so that an organiser can see at a glance why you're the perfect fit for their needs.

Masterclass Summary

- Public speaking is the ultimate PR tool. It's free, and enhances your expert status and reputation with clients, prospects and people of influence.
- Control your negative chatterbox with positive and affirming statements.
- Your voice is a powerful tool. Rehearse your full voice range.
- Attend many presentations, observing the presenters, taking notes of what works, what doesn't, what to emulate, what to avoid.
- Stand in front of a mirror and practise your stagecraft.
- Have a capsule wardrobe; items of clothing you look and feel good in.
- Gather information from the organisers about the event and the audience. What will go down well?
- When planning your talk, focus on some salient and interesting points underpinned by case studies, memorable facts and figures.
- Write your talk in full, read it aloud several times and transfer to cue cards.
- Memorise your introduction and the introductory lines for each point.
- Arrive early, check out the venue and where you will be talking.
- Visualise yourself delivering the performance of your life.
- When you take to the stage, accept your heart will flutter. Pause, smile, have a sip of water, find your feet.

- If you lose your thread, it's no big deal. Ask a question, gather your composure and smile again.
- Afterwards reflect on your performance, what went well and identify improvements.
- Always pat yourself on the back.
- If you get bitten by the public speaking bug, promote your availability on-line and in print, with glowing testimonials.

Masterclass 12
How to Build Your Expert Status

In this masterclass you will learn:

- Whether you are already a genuine expert but are yet to acknowledge this.
- How to build your expert status and the many benefits of doing so.
- How to use your expert status to generate additional income streams.

Inside many business people sits an expert. For some people their expertise is quite narrow – they have extensive knowledge of a particular piece of legislation, for example. For others, their expertise may be broader and they know huge amounts about a particular product or service, or even sector.

Expertise is not limited by profession or dependent upon academic qualifications. Although some experts are recognised for their technical skills gained through study and research, others are respected for their knowledge attained through experience and practice. One individual can be an expert on baking, another, an expert on bedbugs.

What Defines an Expert?

Experts are those people that we look to for sound and helpful advice, for profound insights, clarity and guidance.

- A genuine expert has a deep-seated ambition to share their expertise to the benefit of others. Whether they are being paid to do so or are giving their advice for free, they nurture a strong desire to help.
- A genuine expert is not content to settle for the knowledge, skills and expertise that they have already attained and that has led to their acknowledged expert status. They are hungry to learn more and to share this new knowledge once they have made sense of it. They are usually at the cutting edge of their particular topic, aware of new thinking, upcoming products etc.
- A genuine expert has a track record of results with customers which endorses their expertise and skills. They are happy to offer their insights and experience and, if you decide not to work with them, they're satisfied that they've helped you in some small way on your journey.

- The genuine experts are those people that command attention. They are invited to speak at seminars and exhibitions; their opinions are sought by journalists and bloggers; they're asked to contribute to articles. They are regarded by their peers and their target audiences as being a trusted and reliable source of relevant information and outstanding expertise.

There are many benefits to being considered an expert:

- When times are tough, your expert status means that you are less likely to feel the pinch of recession to the same extent as your competitors. In good times you are likely to be turning work away. Being a credible, in-demand expert goes hand in hand with building a successful business.
- Many experts repurpose their knowledge and expertise into new products and services, so developing additional income streams. The cupcake maker writes a cookbook and runs bespoke cookery classes. The business consultant runs seminars and conferences, confident that their status as an expert will translate into bookings. The social media trainer writes e-books, develops podcasts and webinars and develops an on-line membership club.
- Being an expert means that you are regularly given first refusal to work on attractive and exciting business opportunities, and this can often entail working with other experts too.
- In a sea of competitors, an expert can expect to attract a greater share of business without having to fight too hard to obtain it. Your expert status draws people to you rather than to your competitors.

Are You Reluctant to See Yourself as an Expert?

One fear that holds many of us back from acknowledging ourselves as an expert and recognising that we have something of value to share is the fear that that there is somebody "out there" who knows more than we do. How can we therefore proclaim ourselves an expert? Put these limiting beliefs and fears to one side and focus instead on the knowledge and experience that you are able to share. There is room for many experts!

There's also a tendency to downgrade our knowledge, defining it as mere common sense. In fact, what can now seem to be common sense to us may in fact be the result of many years of experience, study and dedication. It is anything but common sense to the people keen to learn from us.

Another common concern is that there may be an expert in your field already who covers a similar territory to yourself. Again, don't be put off by this. In the small-business community, for example, you will often find many experts within the same field, each one holding a position of respect and authority and with their own following of supporters and advocates.

You may be thinking, "This is not appropriate for me or for where I am in my business currently." However, although building your expert status may not seem to be a priority for you right now, that doesn't mean to say that a little further down the line you won't want to benefit from the advantages that such status can provide. So please allow yourself the time to work through the following process. You never know, you may find that you're a bona fide expert already and just haven't acknowledged this or benefited from it.

Building Your Expert Status

Many of the masterclasses in this book will help you to build and cultivate your expert status as you put the tips into practice. For example, by building your business through targeted marketing you help to build your expert status within those targeted sectors at the same time. By investing time in understanding and researching your audiences you will accumulate significant knowledge and experience in that particular sector. By honing your skills as a public speaker you will become a focus of positive attention.

The steps that follow are designed to encourage you to think about what it may take for you to become a recognised expert, how you can promote your expert status and, ultimately, how you can benefit from being considered an expert. Capture your initial thoughts as you work through each section. At a later stage it will be worthwhile revisiting these notes and expanding them in greater detail.

Your goal at the end of this masterclass should be to create your personal expert master plan.

Step One: Why would you want to be considered an expert?

There are a number of reasons. Here are just a few:

- To create new business opportunities.
- To differentiate from competitors.
- To make a sale easier by shortening the decision-making process.
- To help retain customers.
- To acquire new, bigger and more profitable customers than your current customer base.
- To increase the likelihood of your new products or services being successful.
- To build a local/national/international reputation.
- To charge more for what you do.
- To help recession-proof your business.
- To take your business into the next league.
- To make you feel good about yourself – self-fulfilment!

Step Two: Credibility and integrity. What can you bring to the table to establish yourself as an expert?

This is an opportunity for you to perform a stock take of . . . you! What have you achieved to date in your career? Your positioning statement should help you here. Any unsung assets could be crucial in building your expert status. Consider the following:

- Your specific expertise.
- Your specific experience.
- Your techniques and skills.
- The results and positive outcomes you have achieved for clients.
- Your qualifications, training, accreditations, membership of prestigious bodies.
- Your programme of continuous professional development.
- Your awards and accreditations.

Step Three: Are there any gaps in your expert status, and how can you fill them?

Having audited your skills and experience, you may have arrived at the conclusion that there is more work to be done in building your knowledge and expertise in an ongoing process.

- Learning – what do you need to learn and how/when will you accomplish it? Should you consider joining a professional body or undertaking any formal learning programmes?
- Should you attend seminars, training events and conferences on a regular basis, making a commitment to attend a certain number each year?
- Could you join discussion groups with your peers on social media platforms? Should you be contributing to forums organised by your professional body or membership association?
- Are there any books that you would benefit from reading? What papers, blogs and journals could you subscribe to?
- Are there opportunities for you to gain new qualifications or accreditations?

Step Four: Your different audiences. Who would you like to make aware of your expert status?

It's important that your target audiences are aware that in their midst they have you as a genuine expert to listen to, refer to, learn from and do business with. You don't want to waste time in targeting everyone with your expertise – only those you want to build a relationship with. These will include:

- Some or all of your customers.
- Charities and groups you would like to work with (corporate social responsibility).
- Some or all of your lapsed customers.
- The new audiences you have defined in Masterclass 3.
- Introducers and referrers that could lead you to new customers.
- Strategic partners.
- Specific editors and journalists.

- Specific local and national publications, in print and on-line.
- Suppliers to your business.
- Peers that are less experienced than you and can consequently learn from you.

Step Five: Through which channels should you promote your expert status?

In order to be recognised as an expert you need a platform upon which to demonstrate your skills and expertise, so consider the following:

- Are there any on-line and printed papers, journals and magazines that you could potentially contribute to?
- Blogging – could you benefit by publishing a regular blog and responding to blog posts that are read on other sites by your audiences, sharing your expertise and knowledge? Could you write guest posts for other bloggers?
- Podcasts and webinars – can you run your own, or volunteer to be the expert on others?
- Do you need to review your social media strategy and make more of a conscious effort to share tips and useful information with your followers?
- Public speaking – are there opportunities for you to speak at the specialist conferences and events attended by your target audience? Are there local exhibitions or networking groups you could speak at?

Step Six: What marketing communications are needed to reinforce your expert status?

Are your marketing communications amply revealing your expert status? For example:

- Your website. Does your website content include enough information about your knowledge, skills, experience, training and qualifications to convey you as an expert? Could you revise your "About us" page by adding your biography? (Take a look at mine at the front of this book to guide you.) Do you need to add the logos from the membership associations and professional bodies you belong to? Should you include a "Press" page on your website so that journalists know you are available for expert commentary? Do you need to include or update the client testimonials on your website?

- Your blog. How up to date is your blog? Is it a bit of an afterthought? Are you taking it seriously enough? Are you using the opportunity that a blog provides to share your expertise, or is it a bit frivolous? What part do you want your blog to play in building your expert status?
- Your sales literature. When you read through your sales literature, is it obvious you are an expert or do you focus solely on describing what you offer? Is there an opportunity to provide prospects and customers with a précis of your experience and how, as an expert, you can deliver added value?

Step Seven: How can you create new income streams from your expert status in addition to what you freely give away?

Consider these questions carefully. You may find that your expert status opens the door to many new income generating opportunities over a period of time.

- Could you organise seminars, conferences, exhibitions and masterclasses?
- Could you run training events or adult education evening courses?
- Could you develop a membership club?
- Could you charge for some of the material you write?
- Do you have experience as a public speaker? Could you charge for some of the events you speak at?
- Could you develop mentoring and coaching sessions?
- Could you communicate your expertise in a series of short "How to" books in print, audio, video, on-line etc.?

Becoming an expert is definitely achievable but needs to be worked at. It requires dedication, consistency, and endless enthusiasm. But, if you love what you do, it's most definitely worth the effort and not just because you find yourself with a much healthier bank balance. Ask most experts what they love about being recognised as an authority in their field and they will tell you that helping others is, without doubt, the best reward of all.

Masterclass Summary

- Being recognised and respected as an expert does not necessitate having a string of qualifications! Your experience and expertise could be more than enough.
- Genuine experts share for the benefit of others, are keen to learn more and have a great track record of success.
- Don't let self-limiting beliefs hold you back from recognising yourself as an expert.
- Don't dismiss your knowledge, skills and experience as mere common sense.
- There can be many experts from the same field sitting alongside one another. There's room for you!
- Being considered a genuine expert has many benefits. You sell more, retain more customers and find it easier to withstand tough trading conditions.
- Perform a "stock take" of your many assets. Are you already an expert but failing to recognise this?
- Identify gaps in your learning and experience. Genuine experts are always looking for opportunities to learn more.
- Identify those audiences to which you want to communicate your expert status and consider how you will reach them.
- Change your communications to reflect your expert status.
- You can generate additional revenue streams as an expert, so don't be content to sit with what you are offering now. Explore!

Masterclass 13
How to Wow Your Customers with Genuine Customer Care

In this masterclass you will learn:

- **How to deliver sensational customer service on a shoestring budget.**
- **The importance of delivering small extra touches on a consistent basis.**
- **How to turn a complaining customer into a raving fan.**

I had a distinctly underwhelming experience when dealing with a small business recently. It confirmed to me as a marketer and consumer that so many small businesses unwittingly get it wrong when they sign up a new customer by simply delivering the minimum and little else.

Let me elaborate. I ordered two nutritional supplement products from this small business. It was my first purchase and the products were not cheap. They arrived within three working days, which was great. However, when I opened the box I found that it contained the two products and nothing else. No covering letter from the small business owner expressing his delight at welcoming me as a new customer and letting me know that he was available to answer any questions I may have about the products. There was no thank you card, no catalogue or leaflet promoting other products I might be interested in purchasing. He had my email address yet didn't use it as an opportunity to send a nice message checking that the goods had arrived and I was happy with them.

Perhaps you think I'm being a little unreasonable. After all, I received what I ordered and within the timescales promised. And, you're right, as a consumer I can't really complain about the efficiency of the transaction. As a marketer, however, I can't help but feel that this business owner has missed a massive trick. By treating me purely as a transaction, by shipping the goods smoothly before moving onto the next order, he has forgotten that behind each purchase is a real human being; someone who with a little nurturing could evolve into a loyal and long standing customer. As things stand, however, I may buy the nutritional supplements again if I am pleased with them, but will I buy them from the same small business owner? Maybe not.

As a small business owner, your biggest challenge lies not in servicing your customers, but acquiring them in the first place. So it makes sense that when you do get a new customer, you do your utmost to retain them. If your customers are not treated well they will be quick to take their business elsewhere.

Let's look at some of the reasons why a customer may feel dissatisfied with the service offered to them.

- They feel neglected, unloved and unappreciated.
- They complained about one aspect of their purchase but did not feel that this complaint was handled satisfactorily.
- They had a bad experience but said nothing and just moved on.
- They were happy with the product or service but felt that the after-sales service was unreliable and inconsistent.
- The business increased its prices but didn't manage the price increase sensitively and tactfully with their existing customers. Understandably some were alienated by this.
- The expectations of the customer were not managed at the outset. This resulted in a discrepancy between what the customer thought they were buying and what they actually received.
- They encountered some abruptness or a lack of attention from members of the business team.
- The staff were unable to service the customer to the standard required, perhaps through lack of training.
- Although the initial sale was successful, no effort was made by the business to keep in touch afterwards. Consequently they were forgotten by the customer and subsequent purchases were made elsewhere.
- The sales team overpromised or misled in order to clinch the sale and ultimately this led to disappointment.

It is unrealistic to expect every customer to remain loyal to your business even if the service they received from you was of a high quality. Their decision to buy may be based on price alone and so they are always on the hunt for the cheapest deal. It may be that their needs change and your business is no longer able to meet their requirements. I work with many small businesses that concentrate on delivering the most attentive and considerate customer care but they also recognise that this does not insulate them against the loss of a customer. However, if you can build your business on the basis of delivering high quality and attentive service to all your customers, and you can maintain or even improve this as your business grows, you will build loyalty from a core of customers that is hard to shake.

Two views of the perfect sale:

1. **An efficient and trouble-free transaction.**
2. **An opportunity for a new relationship.**

If you have received an adequate and businesslike service when buying a product or service, there's every chance that the business you dealt with takes the view that the perfect sale is something that is delivered quickly, efficiently and without fuss.

-   They recruit customers primarily for a single sale.
-   They focus on product features.
-   Their customer contact is moderate.
-   They believe that quality is the responsibility of production.
-   The purpose of communication is to sell hard and persuade to buy.

For some purchases, this approach is absolutely fine. When buying a cheap pen for example, we would probably pop into the shop nearest to us that sells pens. We would expect only minimal customer care; the speed and ease of the purchase being the major consideration. We would walk out of the shop happy with the transaction and should we need to buy a pen another time, we would again simply walk into the shop nearest to us at that time. For more weighty purchases, however, this approach is not so appropriate. The businesses we are drawn to when making a considered purchase and that we choose to use time and time again are those that embrace the idea that a sale presents an opportunity to build a relationship with the customer and that this relationship is built through great customer care.

Businesses try to achieve this through:

-   Focusing on retaining customers.
-   A bias towards product benefits and delivering solutions to customer needs.
-   Viewing the delivery of exceptional customer service as absolutely vital.
-   Rich and frequent customer contact.

- Making customer satisfaction the responsibility of every member of the team.
- Ensuring that their customer communications are informative, targeted and address customer needs.

For these businesses, the customer is the most important person in the company and every employee recognises this and engages with customers accordingly. The customer is not regarded simply as a profit-generating unit to be processed as efficiently as possible.

Let's look at what a customer is likely to want from your business:

- **Reliability** – they want to count on you to deliver a high standard of customer service consistently.
- **Credibility** – they want to be sure you are trustworthy.
- **Knowledge** – they want to be confident you'll always make the effort to understand their needs thoroughly.
- **Responsiveness** – they expect you to be swift to respond to questions, requests and complaints.
- **Competence** – they want to be sure that you have a high level of skill and knowledge.
- **Politeness** – they want to be treated by you and your staff in a courteous, friendly and welcoming manner at all times.

In order to build enduring customer relationships that meet these expectations, consider the following:

1. **Make a list of the channels through which you communicate with your customers.** These may include email, social media, your website, telephone, printed letters and face-to-face encounters. Now, analyse the quality of the service you are delivering to customers through each channel and at each stage of their journey with you. Consider any improvements you can make. Involve your customers by asking for feedback. One of my clients discovered that the quality of the emails being sent by members of his team in response to customer queries varied dramatically. Some of the team would provide a thorough, accurate and

well-written response, addressing the specific points raised by the customer, whilst others were sending poorly composed emails comprising of just a few lines and that ignored many of the key points. The poor quality emails required the customers to contact my client again, this time complaining because their questions had been handled in what they viewed as a cursory and indifferent manner. As a result an urgent staff training programme was undertaken.

2. **After analysing your different customer touch points, create templates for your written correspondence, and frameworks for telephone calls (not scripts) accompanied by training notes for your team to use when communicating to customers.** Whilst they will need some autonomy to make changes in order to respond fully to a customer's request, by working from high quality documents and with notes to assist them, the quality of each customer interaction will improve. Review these communications regularly as new scenarios are experienced. Also, consider whether there are additional communication channels that you can take advantage of. On-line videos explaining how your product or service works, for example, may not be something you've considered before but could be a help for your customers and your team.

3. **Establish processes so that your team know how a customer should be treated in scenarios that require an efficient, methodical and organised approach to their requests.** A help desk to which customers phone in and email requests would become a chaotic and unreliable service if each member of staff was given the autonomy to decide how a customer's request should be responded to rather than having processes and guidelines to follow. By establishing and documenting best practice processes, you build confidence and trust with your customers and efficiency in your business.

4. **Explain in detail to customers how they can contact you, when they can contact you and who they can talk to when they have a problem.** Let them know your expected response times too. Make sure that you respond to a customer complaint or request for help as quickly as you do when a customer wants to buy from you.

5. **Keep the human touch.** Don't let technology or automation come between you and your customers or it will act as a barrier that inhibits conversation.

6. **Ask your customers how they would prefer to be contacted whenever you need to get in touch with them.** Don't assume that every customer is happy to

receive a text or an email just because it's more time efficient for you. Some will appreciate a telephone call; some may even prefer a letter.

7. **Manage the expectations of your customers at the buying stage.** Let them know what they will be getting for what they are paying. This will hopefully prevent any misunderstanding that could lead to dissatisfaction further down the line. Forty per cent of complaints are the result of customers receiving inadequate or incorrect information about what they were buying and what was included in the price. With this is mind, it's worth making a specific effort to ensure that your customers are aware of exactly what you are offering them. This may necessitate sending an email or letter explaining exactly what is included in your price, listing any added value supplements that you're building in at no charge and, importantly, detailing those extras that will result in an additional expenditure. My graphic designer, Louise Lucas of The Colour Suite, is very good at this. She provides every customer with a thorough, written quotation that includes her design fee and the number of customer requested changes to her design that are included within that fee. Clients understand that if they decide to make more than the specified number of changes to her design, her original fee will increase accordingly. Louise also explains how long the quotation is valid for, how she will present her designs, and provides details of the additional services that she includes but does not charge for. As clients are aware from the start that requesting several sets of changes will incur an additional fee, it also encourages them to deliver a clear and specific brief at the outset.

8. **Consider creating a customer care charter.** When you have a small customer base and you are the only person responsible for looking after them, it's easy to lavish attention and care on each customer all the time. But as your business grows, you will need to ensure that your customer care standards are adopted by the new members of your team, without exception. A customer care charter can help you to achieve this. When VB-Airsuspension grew their business in the UK to include a nationwide network of dealers responsible for fitting and servicing their air suspension, the MD, Oliver Drinkwater, recognised the need for a customer care charter. He wanted to ensure that every dealer would service every VB-Airsuspension client to the high standards he had established when he founded his business. Oliver did not impose the charter on the dealers

as this may have been met with some resistance. Instead he secured their commitment to it by making clear the reasons behind wanting to introduce it. He explained that, whilst dealers were generally adhering to these standards already, it had become necessary with the growth in the dealer network to ensure that the high standards were adopted consistently and without exception. The service standards were therefore formalised in a two-page document and included:

- **The response times to which a dealer should adhere when responding to a service request.** (The aim is to ensure that all service requests are dealt with to the same timescales by every dealer and without being subject to the personal preferences of any dealer.)
- **The clothing the dealer has to wear when servicing the vehicle.** (This helps each dealer to project a professional image and to be recognised as a VB-Airsuspension dealer by wearing VB-Airsuspension branded clothing.)
- **The dealer needs to ensure the customer is happy with the repair or service before signing the paperwork.** (This helps reduce the risk of additional work being necessary due to the initial repair or service not being to the customer's satisfaction.)
- **The dealer is to replace any components they have used from their stock by ordering them the next working day after the repair or service has been completed.** (This helps ensure that the next customer's service or repair is not delayed because the part required to complete the job is unavailable.)

A customer care charter is only as good as the people that are entrusted to implement it. Make sure your team realises its importance. This is vital if your customer care charter is not only for internal use, but is something that your customers have access to as well. Periodically, check that is it being adhered to by your team. Engage in some mystery shopping and make follow-up calls to a selection of customers to check whether they have received the service promised to them in your charter.

9. **Consider ways in which you can delight your customers and increase their loyalty to your business without adding to their bill.** Here are a few examples of how some local businesses have made this work:
   - **My hairdresser, Vincent Di Lena, opened a cafe below his hairdressing salon a few years ago, serving freshly brewed coffee and snacks.** Every hair

salon customer is offered free unlimited drinks from the cafe whilst having their hair styled; a real treat.

· **Our accountant, Gareth Bridgland, naturally charges for his expertise and for preparing our accounts.** General telephone conversations or email correspondence throughout the year are not charged for.

· **Creative Vision Promotions provide free samples of promotional gifts to customers and prospects.**

Think about the extra gestures you could offer without suffering financially and that would be appreciated by your customers.

10. **Don't promise a customer something you'll be hard pushed to deliver.** How many times have you been told by a business they will call you back at a certain time and then the call fails to materialise? Customers have to know that they can trust you if they're to remain loyal and recommend you. Before you make a commitment to a customer, make sure it's one that you can keep. If getting back to a customer within the hour is unrealistic, promise to call back within two hours. If you are constantly apologising because you did not meet your commitments, customers will feel neglected and these feelings of disappointment will lead to them being ripe for defection.

11. **Ask for regular feedback from your customers, not just with an annual survey.** Consider a "How did we do?" card sent in the post, a telephone call after their last transaction to find out how happy they were with your service, an email asking if they will spend a few minutes evaluating their experience as your customer. You might want to find out:

· **What they appreciated about the service they have just received.**

· **What they would change about the service they have just received.**

· **If they would be willing to provide some positive or constructive feedback on you or a member of your team.**

· **How they rate your service overall.** Be specific. You could ask your customer to comment on your response times to questions and complaints, how they are greeted on the phone and face-to-face. Do they rate you as knowledgeable and helpful? Are you providing good value for money?

12. **Maintain contact with your lapsed customers.** Try to discover why they no longer buy from you and what their arrangements are now. Will they consider

using you again? What improvements will you make in the light of any constructive or negative feedback?

13. **Treat your employees well.** The quality of the customer service you deliver is contingent on the commitment and skill of the employees providing it. If your idea of training a new recruit is to let them learn on the job, or you think that developing your people means handing them a book on customer service, you're not showing your employees that you care about them or that you care about the service they deliver. Invest time in training your new employees away from your customers before allowing them to act as your frontline brand ambassadors. And refresher courses for existing employees are worth introducing too. Optimum Kitchen Appliance Superstores, established a training scheme requiring each store manager to run a 60-minute training session every Monday with the sales and customer service team. A year-long training programme was established and each manager received instruction in how to be an effective trainer. The training delivered to the team included telephone skills, building rapport with customers, handling complaints and the importance of listening to customers' needs. This education has not only equipped each team member with new and improved skills, it has made them focus on the importance of customer service as part of the selling process.

When you're confident that your employees can deliver excellent customer service, allow them some leeway. Encourage them to be resourceful, to find alternative solutions if they feel that a standard approach is not going to be appropriate in a specific customer situation. Customers appreciate it when they can see that an employee is going beyond the call of duty to help them. They feel valued and respected.

14. **Instil in your employees the importance of being polite and respectful with customers in both face-to-face encounters and in writing.** Saying "please" to a customer when asking a question and "thank you" when a customer has taken the time to be helpful or patient costs nothing but has such a positive impact. Beginning an email to a client with, "Dear Mrs Bloggs, thank you for taking the time to write to us" is friendly and polite and so much better than the perfunctory "Dear Mrs Bloggs, in response to your email . . ." Another reason to create those high quality communication templates!

15. **Recognise that exceptional customer service starts with you.** Regardless of what you feel inside about an awkward or challenging customer, you must ensure that you are always courteous and respectful when talking about your customers to your employees. They have to believe you really do mean it when you are talking to them about the importance of customer service. Moaning about a customer with your employees in earshot or, worse still, directly to them, sends out the wrong signal entirely. You do not want customers to become the butt of jokes and sarcasm rather than being seen as the people that are paying the wages. I was brought into a business to deliver customer service training after it had become evident from customer feedback that the customer service was sub-standard. It transpired that the service manager was regularly openly critical and disrespectful of customers that were unhappy with the service they were receiving. Over a period of time his attitude had rubbed off on his young team with dire consequences. It can be hard to undo this negative behaviour, so make sure you are a genuine champion of customer care.

16. **If you are using social media channels such as Facebook and Twitter, there's every chance that some of your customers will find you on these sites and will engage in a friendly, open dialogue with you.** Others will ask you questions, some will voice complaints. Make sure that you monitor your social networking presence several times throughout the day so that you can respond to any customer requests or comments quickly. If you don't respond at the weekend, let customers know this. If a customer is not happy, send a nice message asking them to contact you, or let them know that you will be in contact with them. Take the problem off-line. Don't play out a disagreement or write a series of responses to an unhappy customer in full view of your followers. You can also use social media to promote your clients occasionally. Let your followers know about a client's special event, their special offer, or write something nice about a client's business. This works especially well if your client is on the same social networking site too.

17. **Keep your customers close to you by ensuring they are updated with news of any changes and improvements in your business before anyone else hears.** Don't let your customers stumble upon the fact that you've changed your logo or your business name, that you have introduced a new product or service to your range, that your terms and conditions have been altered or that you've

increased your prices. Take the time to drop your customers a line. If you're doing something as important as increasing your prices, a brief email may not be the most appropriate way of communicating this. Although hiding behind an email may seem preferable to picking up the phone or explaining to a customer face-to-face, you may fail to communicate the valid reasons for a price rise and consequently end up alienating a good customer. A face-to-face encounter is more likely to secure their understanding. By keeping customers informed of what's happening in your business you're letting them know they are important to you.

Dealing with Complaints

In order to understand how best to deal with customer complaints, let's first consider what is likely to be going through the mind of an unhappy customer before they decide whether to bother complaining or not:

- They might not believe me.
- I bet they won't listen to me.
- This is going to be a real pain to resolve.
- This is going to be unpleasant and I might get angry.
- This is really inconvenient; the last thing I want when I'm so busy.
- They'll try and fob me off.
- I hate complaining.

It's little wonder that so many aggrieved customers decide not to complain but simply take their custom elsewhere leaving the business owner none the wiser. Those customers that do complain but are not dealt with to their satisfaction are then only too happy to voice their dissatisfaction to anyone in earshot. But the happy customer, the one whose complaint was listened to and resolved in such a way that it met or even exceeded their expectations, turns into a powerful ambassador for the business. They don't just talk about the product or service they have bought; they extol the virtues of the great customer service they have received too. With social media providing customers with a powerful voice and a very wide reach, it has never been more important to approach complaints in a sensitive, attentive and caring way. Here are some tips that will help you to accomplish this.

- Look upon each complaint as an opportunity to identify and to correct problems within your business, the silent saboteurs. By getting to the root of a complaint you may discover that there are areas in which essential changes and improvements need to be made but that have previously gone unnoticed. Are your salespeople over-promising so you are unknowingly under-delivering as a result? Are your sales communications or your website lacking in clarity and detail? Are your manuals, technical specifications or product brochures missing important information? Are some members of your team lacking in product training and so failing in their duty to explain the details of your product or service accurately and clearly? If you look upon a complaint as something to be dealt with swiftly in order to get a customer off your back, you could be missing a good opportunity to improve the service you provide and reduce the number of complaints you will receive in the future.

- Always allow your customer the benefit of the doubt when making a complaint. You may occasionally encounter a customer that is a habitual complainer with no real grounds for dissatisfaction, but this type of customer is thankfully very rare. The vast majority of customers that complain do so because they really believe they have been treated badly. And although such complaints can sometimes be hurtful, try to greet them without cynicism or distrust.

- If a complaint arrives via email, your website or your social networking page, acknowledge it as soon as possible but ask for a contact telephone number so that you can establish a two-way dialogue. A volley of written messages sent back and forth could well prolong an unsatisfactory situation and exacerbate the problem.

- Listen to your customer without interrupting them. Although it is tempting to butt in with explanations and answers whilst your customer is talking, especially if it becomes clear at an early stage that you are clearly not to blame, bide your time. Take notes, gather facts and let your customer talk. Don't ask them to calm down if it's clear from their tone of voice they are angry. This will make them even more irate. What an unhappy customer wants above everything else is to be listened to; for their voice to be heard.

- Empathise with your customer. This is not an admission of guilt on your part, but it shows that you care and that you want to resolve the problem. Let them know that you understand how they feel and that your priority now is to resolve their complaint. Stand in their shoes. They may have taken time off work to call you and the problem giving rise to their complaint may have really inconvenienced them.

- Aim for a solution that will restore your customer's faith in your business and that will make them happy again. Explain to your customer what you are going to do to resolve their complaint, when you are going to do it and who else will be involved. How does your proposed solution sound to them? Very rarely will you hear a customer complaining that you asked too many questions to get to the root of their problem and determine a solution.

- What if your customer has got it completely wrong? It is a black-and-white situation and you're not to blame. Explain to the customer in a calm and considerate way that they have misunderstood the situation without apportioning any blame to them. Can you make a goodwill gesture to your customer so that they hold you in high esteem once they have realised you were not at fault? Ask if there is anything you can do to prevent the situation from happening again. Just because the reason for the complaint was not your fault does not mean that you can't learn from it and take preventative steps to avoid any future misunderstanding. By taking this line you are also helping your customer save face. They may realise after all that they were at fault but they won't necessarily want you pointing this out to them!

- If you have to take several steps to redress your customer's complaint, keep them informed of your progress. Regular updates by telephone or email, a private and friendly message on Twitter or Facebook will be reassuring and will let your customer know that you have not forgotten them.

- If you have to pass the complaint to a member of your team, explain your notes in detail and brief them in person or over the telephone. Make sure they are clear on the role they are expected to play and any timescales they must adhere to.

- When your customer's complaint has been resolved, contact them by telephone. Are they happy with how their complaint was handled? Can they suggest any improvements in your complaint handling process? How do they rate the service you provided? I recently purchased a Christmas wreath with a hurricane lamp and scented candle in its centre from the shopping channel, QVC. It sounded exquisite when the presenters were describing it but on arrival it was a real disappointment with a number of faults. When I rang to complain, the customer service team at QVC were very apologetic and told me that the product would be collected from my home, at no charge, and gave me the date for collection. They reimbursed me before the product was collected without me having to ask for a refund, and rang a few days before the collection was due to remind me. They contacted me after the wreath was collected to ensure I was happy with the service I had received. I rated them 10 out of 10 because I had been delighted with their attentive service and their genuine desire to reassure me and apologise for the poor product. A complaining customer could well become your very best advocate so don't hesitate to make that final call to check all's well.

Finishing on a High with the "WOW" Model of Customer Service

A mediocre standard of customer service is no longer acceptable in today's world. You are unlikely to retain loyal customers unless your service is of the highest quality. Hopefully, this masterclass will have shown that you can deliver a fantastic customer service without spending over the odds. Use this simple but effective "WOW" model to make your customers fall in love with you even more!

Aim to delight your clients with one little extra . . .

- 1 moment of real thoughtfulness
- 1 extra minute of your time
- 1 extra check just to ensure everything's okay

The Impact of that One Little Extra can Lead to Customers Saying "WOW! . . .

. . . that's what I call an amazing service."
. . . that is lovely, thank you."
. . . I did not expect that."
. . . that is so thoughtful of you!"
. . . that's such a weight off my mind!"

The best little extras meet the following criteria:

- They're instantly noticed and valued by your customers.
- They're quick and easy to implement.
- They cost little or nothing and so don't make a dent in your budget.
- They're implemented consistently, not just when you're in a generous frame of mind or when you have the time.
- They always put a smile on your customer's face.

So spend a moment now to answer the following questions:

- What WOWs are you delivering now?
- What WOWs could you deliver in the future?
- Do you have the WOW mentality?
- Does everyone in your team have the WOW mentality?
- Who will deliver the WOWS in your team?
- How will you put WOWS on your agenda?
- How will you ensure WOWs remain on your agenda?
- How will you measure the impact of your WOWS?

Masterclass Summary

- Delivering an adequate or businesslike service to customers is no longer good enough.
- Delivering high quality customer service consistently is at the heart of retaining your customers and turning them into advocates.
- Look upon your customer as the most important person in your business universe.
- Customers need to believe and feel that you are reliable, credible, knowledgeable, courteous and responsive.
- List all your customer communication channels and identify the improvements necessary to take your customer service to a whole new level.
- Do you need to organise customer service training for your staff?

- Create high-quality communication templates and telephone call frameworks accompanied by training notes.
- Let customers know how they can contact you, and when.
- Manage customer expectations from the very start by ensuring that the information they receive is detailed, accurate and relevant.
- A customer care charter could help you to maintain your high standards as your business grows.
- Asking for regular customer feedback will help you to pinpoint and resolve any substandard aspects of your service.
- Nurtured and appreciated employees always deliver the best customer service, so be nice to yours.
- If you use social media check your pages on a daily basis.
- Customer complaints can often highlight what's going wrong in your business that you were previously unaware of.
- Give a complaining customer the benefit of the doubt; listen intently and aim for a solution that will restore their faith in your business.
- What extra little touches can you add to delight your customers further still?

Masterclass 14
Why You Should be Falling in Love with LinkedIn!

In this masterclass you will learn:

- **How to use LinkedIn to build awareness of you and your business.**
- **How to make positive and meaningful connections with people.**
- **How to use LinkedIn to contact hard-to-reach people.**

Although I have had a LinkedIn profile for many years, I am far from an expert on how best to use the tool. I do, however, recognise the important role it can play in marketing ourselves, and in turn our businesses. Consequently, it very much deserves its place as a masterclass within this book, and to sidestep my own inexperience with LinkedIn I have turned to the expertise of two businesswomen, Liz Barnes FCIM and Nicky Kriel. Both women are not only very active on LinkedIn; they also train small businesses in how to get the most from using it. For the purposes of this masterclass I have posed twelve of the most commonly asked LinkedIn questions to Liz and Nicky, each of them answering independently. I have then listed the five LinkedIn tips that I have found most useful as a small business owner.

1. How does LinkedIn differ from other social networking tools such as Twitter and Facebook? Is it a social networking tool?

Liz: LinkedIn is most definitely a social networking tool with its stated mission being "to connect the world's professionals to enable them to be more productive and successful". However, whereas Facebook could be viewed as the on-line equivalent of meeting friends for coffee and Twitter as enabling the type of short conversations that take place at the school gates or on a commuter train, LinkedIn is more akin to a business networking meeting.

Because LinkedIn is a professional network, the profile of users tends to be a bit older than other networks: 79% of users are over 35 years old, with the average age being 44.2 years (Pingdom Aug 2012). People are hanging out on LinkedIn because they want to meet and learn from other professionals, find jobs/contracts/opportunities and make connections. They are not particularly interested in small talk – they use Twitter or Facebook for that.

Nicky: LinkedIn differs from other social media platforms in the following ways:

- **Formality.** Facebook and Twitter are more casual and chatty whereas LinkedIn is always in business mode. It's not to say that people aren't friendly, but people act as if they are wearing a suit and tie.
- **Your information is all in one place.** LinkedIn allows you to show all your expertise in one place. It is easy to find out everything you need to know about another LinkedIn member without doing any other research. Twitter only allows you 140 characters and a link to your website. It is unlikely that people will research for business information on a Facebook profile.
- **Longevity.** LinkedIn beats transient Twitter and Facebook hands down for the length of time content can be accessed for.
- **Search function.** LinkedIn is, in effect, a giant database and the advanced search function allows you to search your connections and other people on LinkedIn with ease.

2. Is LinkedIn just for (business to business) B2B selling or do businesses that sell direct to consumers also benefit?

Liz: LinkedIn is the heartland for B2B on-line networking; the opportunities for B2C businesses are more limited. However, one important way in which both B2B and B2C companies can benefit from using LinkedIn is by creating a company profile that describes the range of products and services that they offer with information about their employees and their company contact details. Visitors to the company profile page will be able to learn about the business and the image that it presents, whether viewing it from the standpoint of another business or as a customer.

Nicky: We have to get away from the notion of B2B and B2C when we talk about social media and start thinking P2P (people to people). People do business with people they know, like and trust. LinkedIn's main strength is within its profiles. LinkedIn's groups allow you to get to know people on a more personal level through sharing opinions, information and advice. Each person on LinkedIn is both a business person and a consumer. If you treat people with respect and are helpful and knowledgeable, connecting people together whenever possible, you will do well on LinkedIn. LinkedIn is about networking rather than trying to sell to people.

3. How many times a week should I go onto LinkedIn?

Liz: It is estimated that approximately 68% of users access LinkedIn at least once per week with 36% accessing it daily. It does depend which market you are in, what you are trying to achieve and how many connections you have. One of my clients specialises in HR consultancy and training. Word-of-mouth and business networking has always been crucial for their business. LinkedIn has enabled them to have a much wider geographic reach than standard business networking meetings would have allowed. Consultants regularly join discussions within their Groups and repost interesting articles they've read or provide links to their own blogs and factsheets. Daily visits and sometimes several times a day have become normal for them – and LinkedIn has yielded some great conversations, contracts and job opportunities as a reward for their effort. The key is regularity and relevance. It is better to keep up steady activity, perhaps two or three times per week and undertake a variety of actions e.g. connecting, "liking" updates, commenting in Groups, endorsing others, adding your own posts, rather than a spate of activity during a short period of time and then nothing for weeks. It is demonstrating competence and professionalism consistently that will get you noticed.

Nicky: There is no absolute figure, but I would suggest that if you want to see real results using LinkedIn, just fifteen minutes a day (Monday to Friday) will make a big difference. It's not the length of time you spend on LinkedIn, but what you do with your time.

Every activity you do on LinkedIn will appear in your connections news feed. These activities include posting updates, updating your profile and adding connections. A very simple way to update your LinkedIn profile is by sharing great content that you read on-line. Most blog posts will have a LinkedIn button that enables you to share the article on LinkedIn or directly to one of your LinkedIn groups. So you can update your profile without even visiting LinkedIn.

Groups are a very powerful feature of LinkedIn, so it is worth investing some time each week to visit a few targeted groups and add to the discussion there.

4. Should I show all the different jobs that I've had over the years?

Liz: The simple answer to this question is "probably not," but let's look at this in a bit more detail.

If you are a young person keen to find your first or second full-time role, you probably want to show evidence of work experience whether this was part-time or volunteer work. However, you don't need to wax lyrical about routine Saturday jobs and you could consider grouping part-time positions whilst you were at school for example into one heading.

As your experience increases, you will want to reference those jobs or roles which have been significant in your development. Again, some people take career breaks or elect to take alternative roles when the children are young, so you may want to group these differently. But it isn't a formal job application, so don't feel that you need to account for every week of your working life. As we get older, it is likely that our early jobs may not be so relevant and it may therefore be more appropriate to provide just your last three or four positions. LinkedIn's job format doesn't lend itself so well to freelance or contractor roles so it is advisable to include the top five skills you want to be known in the top three job roles that you list.

Nicky: I think it is important to add all your full time positions on your LinkedIn Profile as long as they don't reflect badly on you. The reason for doing this is that LinkedIn has a very powerful search function and it will recommend people to connect with you based on your previous positions. When you reconnect with people from your past you don't have to sell yourself to them, they know you already. Many of these people will be in a different position from when you last had contact with them and will have a network of people who possibly might do business with you. When LinkedIn suggests people from your past it is a great opportunity to catch up with them, find out what they are up to and whether you can help them. You never know where reuniting with a past work colleague can lead.

Including your past job roles helps people to gain a rounded image of your experience. I would suggest that when you write about your past experiences, you write in such a way that they are as relevant to your current position as possible. Help people to see how your past makes you the right person for them to work with now.

5. What's the best thing to put in my "summary"?

Liz: It is interesting how LinkedIn summaries have changed even relatively recently – becoming more authentic and a little more relaxed. Referring back to the previous point, what do you want to be known for and what do people consistently say you are good at? How do other people describe you? What's your sector expertise and your subject expertise? Think about how you contribute in your role as well as describing something about your personality. I recommend that you write in the first person, "I am a . . . ," and don't overpopulate your summary with buzz words. Each year, LinkedIn publishes the most overused words in profiles. In 2012 these were "creative, motivated, multinational, responsible, experimental, effective, specialised, and analytical."

Nicky: In your summary you want to let people know who you are, who you help and how you can help them. The person reading it should know immediately whether you are the right person for them or which type of business you would be suited to. Think of your summary as a short story with an introduction, a middle in which you elaborate on how you help people and a conclusion with a call to action.

You don't want it to be an essay, but make sure you include the different ways you work as a business. Remember to write for your potential customer. It is not about you, but the benefits you offer your customers.

6. Should I bother to set up a Company Page with services/products etc.?

Liz: Company Pages operate like a mini website within LinkedIn and users love them because they don't have to leave the site to check your company out. LinkedIn requires a named person within an organisation to be the Company Page Administrator. They must have a personal LinkedIn profile and a company email address with the registered company domain name. An administrator can then set up other administrators if they so require. The standard LinkedIn company profile provides space to include a summary about your company including contact details and a banner image. You can add other pages for products/services and include You Tube videos and promotions. You are able to post details of any job vacancies that you are advertising and those staff that have individual LinkedIn profiles will automatically be included in the list of employees on the Company Pages if they specify the company as their current employer. Do check, however, that they use the same format of the company name in their job specification otherwise the connection will not be made.

Company administrators can post "company updates" to increase your visibility, announce news, promotions and job vacancies. Individuals who choose to "follow" companies will be alerted to these updates.

Nicky: I think that it depends on the size of your business and the resources you have available to keep your company page up to date. Company Pages have limited functionality at the moment, but I suspect that this may change. If you have the resources then it is worth having a Company Page for people to find out more about your business, but make sure your branding is consistent with your website and that it's kept up to date.

7. Should I "connect" with people I've never met?

Liz: I know some professionals who believe it is the only way to build their network and others who refuse point blank to do so – and there are some in between who may make the odd exception. If you really don't know someone who asks to connect with you, be careful before accepting the invitation as it could be from a competitor or from someone simply looking to build a database from which they can spam you. I would always check out their credentials first and perhaps ask a shared connection to provide a bit more information about them. But I'm not sure it is any more dangerous than speed networking (in person) and it can bring benefits, particularly if a person is looking for a very specific skill set which you can offer. Indeed, one of my clients won a fabulous long-term contract with a major company by connecting with someone he had never met but who was looking for his expertise and had found his blog posts and discussion threads most informative.

Nicky: It is always more important to build a quality network than it is to focus on quantity. You will become associated with the people you connect with on LinkedIn. Saying that, imagine if you went to a networking meeting and didn't talk to anyone you hadn't met previously. You would be missing out on great opportunities. Many of the great business opportunities on LinkedIn will come from people you don't know at this moment in time. Be open but take time to read people's LinkedIn profile before deciding whether you want to accept their invitation. The more connected you are, the more likely you are to turn up in search results. Just a word of warning: there are a group of people who will have LION in their headline. LION stands for LinkedIn Open Networkers. These people are just collecting numbers and aim to connect with as many people as possible. They are unlikely to know or care about their connections.

8. How do I decide which Groups to join?

Liz: Groups are a great place to hang out with like-minded colleagues – sharing ideas, discussing topical issues and learning from one another. You can search the Groups Directory and once you have joined a few, LinkedIn will suggest others. Start with the area of expertise closest to your skills and then branch out. I suggest that you join just a few to begin with and try to engage with discussions when you can. Each group provides statistics which shows the seniority of the group members, their geographic location (country and/or major town), job function and industry. I have chosen to join groups with a stronger local contingent with the expectation that I might meet some of the other members. You won't be able to review the members' list until after you've joined the group however, you may decide to select groups based on who in your network belongs to those groups. You can review the "profile" of any group's membership by looking at Group Statistics. Another way to consider which groups to join is to review the profile of someone you admire or want to be connected to – and see which groups they belong to. You could then check out the profile of that group in the Group Statistics to confirm that it is relevant and appropriate for you to join. Once you have joined you will be able to contact group members directly (unless they had adjusted their personal settings to prevent this).

Nicky: You can join up to 50 groups and I would recommend you join groups freely to see what they are like. Make sure that you change the email notifications for the groups you join to receive digest emails once a week otherwise your inbox will become filled up with daily emails. You can't be an active member in all these groups, but it allows you to expand your network. You can chat to people in shared groups without being connected to them on LinkedIn. You want to be regularly active in two to five groups. Choose groups where you can make a difference; ideally you want to be spending time with potential customers rather than your peers. You want to choose a group that is active and has discussions each week but not one that has thousands of members. Be a big fish in the ponds you choose. Avoid groups that are full of members promoting themselves and don't be one of them. Whichever group you choose, become a valuable member by offering advice, contributing to discussions and adding great value content.

9. **I have now built up a good number of contacts – how can I translate this into new business without coming across as pushy or desperate?**

Liz: An important thing you can do is to engage with people individually when the opportunity arises, e.g. if they post something you are interested in you can start a discussion or provide help if they have a query. Secondly, you'll probably want to engage in discussions within groups – people can get to see how you operate and what you know. It is OK to provide links to your own website/blog but this must be done in a way which is promoting discussion – not blatant self-promotion.

Remember the analogy of a business networking lunch . . . we all avoid the egotist who stands in the centre of the room crowing about himself and not listening to, or showing any interest in, anyone else. The idea is to share, discuss, give and be helpful – you will be rewarded.

Nicky: You are on LinkedIn to build relationships not to collect numbers and you will only build relationships by engaging with people. It is a good idea to make contact with a few of your connections in a personal way each week. Just because they are a LinkedIn connection doesn't mean you have to stay on LinkedIn to contact them. Try picking up the phone or arranging to meet them for coffee. Find out if there is anything you can do for them first.

10. Is there any advantage in upgrading from the Basic LinkedIn account to one of the paid-for versions?

Liz: Yes, because you can get LinkedIn to make introductions on your behalf and the search functionality is much better. These paid accounts also enable you to write notes on some contacts so it is acting as a contact database (no more writing on the back of business cards).

However, I would recommend that you start with the free version and become fully acquainted with the tool first to ensure that you understand how you are going to use it for relationship management and marketing activities.

Nicky: There are advantages, but most people under-utilise the free version of LinkedIn, so I would not recommend the paid version to most small business unless they are recruiting or they have a specific goal in mind. The free version of LinkedIn can be used very powerfully to grow your business through learning to use advanced search and Groups properly.

11. What are the biggest mistakes you see people make on LinkedIn?

Liz: One of the biggest turn-offs is too much self-promotion. After a while it just becomes noise and we skip past posts from those people that consistently promote their business.

Another problem is incomplete profiles that include no photo and perhaps no contact details. You may want to connect with them but you cannot be sure they are the right person.

I also find some discussions get very heated and political and I'm not sure it is doing anyone any favours. Yes, a few points might be scored but generally there are no real winners.

Nicky: One of the biggest mistakes is having an incomplete profile. If someone is searching for your name on a search engine, one of the top searches will be your LinkedIn profile. An incomplete profile looks unprofessional and is a missed opportunity. It is unlikely that even people who know you well will know all your work experiences and skills that you offer. Your LinkedIn profile is your on-line curriculum vitae. You would bore someone silly at a networking meeting if you had to rattle off everything you could do. If someone is interested in you, they will want to find out a bit more about you and your LinkedIn profile is a great way to show your expertise.

12. How do you use LinkedIn?

Liz: I use it as a rich address book which helps me keep up to date with my contacts in real time. I love to send personalised messages when I can, and follow my contacts' roles and interests whilst also seeking out other like-minded professionals to collaborate with.

I've also been delighted with the connections I've made by promoting my workshops – but I realise I need to be careful not to overdo that.

I now don't belong to any other "forums" outside LinkedIn as I can find a specialist on LikedIn really easily and I've benefited so much from reviewing and joining in discussions within groups. The most fun bit is encouraging my clients to use LinkedIn and then hearing how they've made new contacts which have led directly to new business, development opportunities and sales.

Nicky: My main objective on LinkedIn is for potential customers to find me and have enough information within my profile for them to want to contact me. With this in mind, I make sure my profile is optimised for search and that my summary is the best representation of what I do. LinkedIn now allows you to add videos and links into your profile so it is worth revisiting and tweaking your profile at least every few months.

I also like to keep "top of mind" with people I'm connected to, so I make sure that I update my LinkedIn status with interesting articles I have read throughout the week.

LinkedIn Today is a great source of useful content for me to share on other social media networks and it allows me to keep up to date with my industry news.

Most of the groups that I have been active in have led to friendships outside LinkedIn and I have connected to group members on Facebook, Twitter, Google+, and subscribed to their YouTube channels. These people have become more than connections.

LinkedIn has been a great source of business from people that I haven't met in real life.

Thanks to Liz and Nicky for their advice.

To conclude, here are five of my favourite LinkedIn tips.

1. **The best way to request LinkedIn connections.** Over time, as part of the process of building your LinkedIn network, you will issue and receive numerous connection requests. Connecting with someone is a simple procedure. You spot someone you would like to link to with, click "Connect," choose how you know that person . . . and then fall at the first hurdle by firing off the standard, impersonal message:

"I'd like to add you to my professional network on LinkedIn."

The likelihood is that your invitation will then sit amongst the many others bearing the same message – it may be accepted, or it may never be answered. The invitation message is too bland to trigger a keen response. If you really want that person to connect with you, spend a few minutes composing a personal and relevant invitation message – even if you don't know the person at all.

An invitation that includes a message reflecting your current relationship with the person you want to connect with, no matter how tenuous is hard to ignore. It shows that you are serious about connecting with that person and have taken the time to speak to them directly and personally. This is particularly important if you do not know the person but see them as being a potentially useful connection in the future.

Spend a moment browsing their profile, looking for common ground. You may have worked at the same company in the past, work in the same field, or simply have another LinkedIn connection in common. You may be an admirer of their work or have heard good things about them from others that you are connected with.

A message such as:

"Hi Jack, I see you run a bookkeeping practice in Coventry. I am an accountant in London but spent much of my youth living in the Coventry area. It would be great to connect to see whether we could do business together some time in the future."

. . . is more likely to be positively received by Jack than if he received the standard LinkedIn invitation from somebody that he had not previously heard of. He may respond by asking what part of Coventry you spent time in, and you are on the way to developing a relationship.

Similarly, a message such as:

"Hi David, I have heard great things about you from (name of person) and so would be delighted if you would link up with me."

. . . is likely to be warmly received simply because you are being genuinely nice to that person.

So before clicking "Send Invitation" the next time you find someone you would like to connect with, spend a minute or two composing a personal message. It will make a significant difference to how your invitation is viewed.

2. **Use LinkedIn to bypass zealous gatekeepers and personal assistants.** One of my clients, the MD of a training company, was finding it impossible to bypass the PA of a businesswoman she wanted to meet with. She knew that if she could just speak with the lady it would in all likelihood progress to a meeting. They shared much common ground, had similar business backgrounds and the business had a genuine need for my client's services. However this lady's PA was proving immovable and would not entertain emails or phone calls. And so, one Saturday afternoon, my client sent a charming LinkedIn invitation to the businesswoman in question, explaining that she knew how busy the lady was but that she also knew from the research she had carried out that they shared similar values and common ground and that they might both benefit from having an initial exploratory chat. The paragraph concluded with my client asking if it would be possible to have a brief conversation on the telephone. Within a few

hours the businesswoman responded, accepted the invitation and suggested a time for my client to call her on her mobile. Think about the best time to send your invitation to connect. It may be that the evenings and weekends are a good time to grab the attention of the person you want to contact and you may have a direct route to them.

3. **Consider amending your "headline."** When people find you in a LinkedIn search, they will see a little box containing your name, your photo and your headline. Your headline is a brief description of what you do and defaults to your current job title. So currently your headline may simply be "Accountant at Perrys." However, it is possible to change this headline to something more descriptive. You may wish your headline to say something like, "Chartered Accountant at Perrys, specialising in tax savings for the small business," for example, or maybe you would prefer it to say "A proactive and highly experienced accountant at Perrys, focused entirely on providing the best possible service for my clients." The choice is yours but this option provides the opportunity to describe you as something a bit punchier than "Accountant at Perrys."

To amend your headline, hover the cursor above "Profile" at the top of your LinkedIn page and select "Edit Profile" from the dropdown menu. This will take you to your edit profile page from which you will be able to select the option "Edit" against your name. This will take you to a page on which you will be able to amend your headline to be something more descriptive of yourself or your skills.

4. **Use LinkedIn in to enhance your off-line marketing campaigns.** When I was chatting to Ben Locker about LinkedIn, and how he used it, he shared a nice example with me. Ben approached 30 people on LinkedIn to whom he planned to promote the copywriting services of his agency by sending a personal letter. He sent a charming LinkedIn message to each one, alerting them to the fact that they would be receiving his mailshot within a few days. This early notification approach worked really well, something that Ben discovered when making the telephone follow-up calls. He used LinkedIn to generate awareness and interest in his business so that when his letter arrived it was not treated as

unsolicited mail and ignored but as an expected piece of correspondence that deserved attention. Similarly, Ashley Law Mid Sussex Independent Financial Advisors used a LinkedIn discussion group for accountants to alert the members to a free retirement planning seminar they were running. Of the 20 attendees at the event, 5 belonged to this discussion group. LinkedIn can be effective in warming up cold prospects but always be conscious about not overdoing the sales talk.

5. **Ask your trusted connections to introduce you to their connections.** One of my clients, Nicola Sales, of YourRecruit, wanted to be introduced to one of my LinkedIn connections, the head of a financial institution. Nicola had tried in vain to connect with him via a personal invitation and so emailed me to ask if I would introduce her to him. I was happy to do that, and endorsed Nicola heartily in my message to my contact. Within just 60 minutes of receiving my message he had responded to Nicola inviting her to contact him. If you're struggling to make a connection, check whether one of your existing connections is connected to your target. If your connection knows you well and respects the service you provide they should be only too pleased to perform the introduction. Be prepared to reciprocate too.

Masterclass Summary

- LinkedIn is a social networking tool but not one to use in the same way as Twitter or Facebook.
- Don't look upon LinkedIn as a tool primarily for businesses selling to other businesses. Think of it as an opportunity to engage on a person to person basis.
- Be active on LinkedIn – endorsing others, sharing in groups, liking updates and sending personal invitations to connect.
- Your LinkedIn profile should be up to date. It appears in on-line research results and so plays an important part in building your on-line reputation.
- Your summary should be friendly, letting people know who you are, how you can help them and how they can find you.

- Make sure that the network you are building is based on quality and you're not just collecting contacts for the sake of numbers.
- LinkedIn groups can be useful in building your knowledge and promoting your expert status.
- Bland and impersonal connection requests may be overlooked. Find common ground, be charming: send a personal message.
- Use LinkedIn to get past the gatekeeper and consider sending your charming connection requests outside normal working hours.
- Use LinkedIn to enhance your targeted marketing campaigns and promote your seminars/events etc. But don't oversell.
- Ask your trusted connections to introduce you to some of their connections on LinkedIn.

Twitter

Masterclass 15
How to be Terrific
on Twitter

In this masterclass you will learn:

- How Twitter can help you to grow your business.
- How to be sociable, businesslike and popular on Twitter.
- How to grow your following by avoiding the mistakes some people make on Twitter.

I realised the incredible power of Twitter as a marketing tool when I received a phone call from a business owner wanting to work with me. When I asked how he'd heard of me, he explained that one of the people he was following had re-tweeted one of my tweets in which I shared that my previous book was still top of the Amazon small business marketing book charts. He read the tweet, followed the Amazon link, purchased my book and after reading the first chapter decided he wanted to work with me. *All from just one tweet!*

Now, whilst I am not a Twitter expert, I've managed to get some amazing results from Twitter. I have connected and corresponded with many of my readers, have been booked for several public speaking events and have found some fantastic experts that I have subsequently worked with and that have spoken at my events – on top of gaining new clients. Twitter has been influential in building my status as a small business marketing expert and has enabled me to reach talented and interesting people with whom I would never have connected otherwise.

So, in this masterclass, I want to share my personal Twitter tips for business success, including some aspects of Twitter etiquette.

If you're not already on Twitter, how do you know if it's for you?

I don't believe that every small business owner should be "tweeting." In fact, for some small businesses it could be a complete waste of time. If a business's target audience, potential clients, existing clients or introducers do not subscribe to Twitter in meaningful quantities or the product or service being offered by the business is unsuitable, it is unlikely that the tool will be an effective marketing tactic. For example, one of my clients designs high-level security systems for financial institutions. Because of the highly confidential nature of their work and the fact that their clients cannot be named, posting messages on Twitter would be a pointless exercise for them.

Before deciding whether Twitter is an appropriate marketing activity for your own business, spend some time familiarising yourself with the tool. Look into whether any of your existing clients are already using it. Are there any prospects that you would like to do business with amongst the registered users? How about any influencers you would like to reach, suppliers you're working with, or any of your competitors?

If you discover that some of your clients or competitors already use the tool, take note of:

- Who is tweeting?
- What are they tweeting about and how often?
- Who are they talking to?
- Who is talking about them? (Using the search bar on Twitter you can find tweets that reference them. Place a hash tag before their business name to see if they are at the centre of any discussions.)
- What relationships are they forming?
- Who are they following and who's following them?

Within a few hours you should know whether Twitter is an appropriate tool for you and your business. If your competitors are regularly tweeting interesting information and tips to their followers and engaging in worthwhile conversations with them, you may feel that you're failing to properly represent your business by not becoming involved yourself. Or perhaps you'll find that your competitors are active on Twitter but not using it to its full potential, instead simply posting repetitive tweets promoting their services. In these circumstances you have the chance to establish yourself on Twitter and to outshine your competitors. If your clients are already regular users, joining Twitter yourself will provide the opportunity to build even stronger relationships with them by keeping in touch on a more informal basis.

Even if neither clients nor competitors seem to be active on Twitter, don't decide to dismiss the value of the tool until you've searched for people that inspire you and that you can learn from. Twitter is an excellent resource for broadening your skills and knowledge. There are many people happy to share their thoughts and expertise on Twitter. It also provides an opportunity to keep in touch with networking colleagues and business people from your community. Communicating with them outside your usual encounters could be helpful in keeping you on their radar for when a great business opportunity arises.

Social Media, Not Selling Media

Twitter is without doubt a fantastic and free marketing tool if you use it intelligently. It provides a quick and easy mechanism for making people aware of the products or services that you offer. But Twitter should not be viewed purely as an advertising vehicle. It is a social media channel and if you simply pump out messages promoting your products or services, you will fail to attract many followers and could even end up being blocked by other users. To use the tool effectively you really need to embrace the rationale behind Twitter. Join in with conversations; share your own expertise and promote the expertise and resources of others. Twitter provides the means to build relationships and this important aspect of marketing your business should not be overlooked.

Making Twitter Work for You

Make full use of your Twitter biography

Twitter allows you 140 characters to convey just how interesting you are. Use every character! And remember to regularly review your biography and to keep it up to date. Did you know that your Twitter biography appears in Google searches and that Twitter will recommend you to other people based on the words in your biography? Do you really want something as trivial as "I love frothy coffee" and nothing else to appear as your biography when you have this opportunity to include instead some punchy business keywords? People often make the initial decision to follow someone based on the information that they supply in their biography and the way in which it is presented. If your biography is stuffed with hash tags, includes only frivolous material or is poorly written, it's unlikely that you will come across as someone worth interacting with.

View your Twitter biography as your on-line elevator statement. Use everyday language and try to keep it current. For instance, I update my own Twitter biography whenever a new five-star review is posted on Amazon about one of my books. Choose a clear and smiling image of yourself as your avatar. This picture and an interesting biography will help attract the type of followers you're looking for.

Here are two good examples of effective Twitter biographies. (I am sure they will have changed by the time this book is published, but hopefully you can see how well they use those 140 characters.)

Nicky Kriel @nickykriel

Social Media Coach & Trainer, Master NLP Practitioner, Speaker, mother, friend & Toastmaster. Social Media strategy for SMEs. Visit my blog for useful tips

Robert Clay @marketingwizdom

INTJ Entrepreneur; strategist; author; speaker and business mentor to aspiring market leaders. Digital native and foodie into cars, design, Apple and skiing

Be present on Twitter

Although the vast majority of Twitter messages are posted as they are written, there is also the facility to schedule messages to be posted at specific times using tools such as *Buffer* (www.bufferapp.com). This automation can be particularly beneficial if you're aiming to attract followers in other time zones or if you simply want your messages to be posted at regular intervals without needing to be signed onto Twitter to do so.

You should still aim to log in to Twitter on a daily basis, however. Responding to messages plays an important part in developing relationships with your followers, and doing so several days after a message was sent will portray you as indifferent and slack. By logging into Twitter only every few days, you also run the risk of missing out on conversations and discussions to which you could genuinely add value and so present yourself in a very positive light. If you want your followers to get to know, like and trust you, you need to maintain a consistent and credible

Twitter presence. Although my own working days vary quite dramatically I do try to ensure that I check Twitter several times a day. If you can, try to find your own daily routine so that you do not view your time on Twitter as a chore: 15–20 minutes spread over your day should be sufficient.

Follow interesting and knowledgeable people

Twitter is as much about learning from others as it is about sharing your own expertise and generating awareness of what you offer. Seek out the experts, mentors, coaches, business people and inspirational folk that you already know or would like to know. It is highly likely that they will be a user of Twitter and will be posting fresh, relevant and interesting content that you will enjoy reading.

Share your expertise generously

Twitter provides an amazing opportunity to build your expert status by sharing your wisdom, experience and expertise. Using the tips in Masterclass 12 to guide you, draw up a list of the topics on which you can write in order to be viewed as an expert. Can you share two or three tips every day? Being recognized as a trusted expert will certainly help you to increase the number of followers and, of course, the more followers that you have, the more people that will be reading your messages. One point worth noting is that if you want your expert tweets to be re-tweeted in full, restrict them to 120–130 characters.

Ensure that your tweets can be read easily

Don't rush when composing each message and check it before posting. Tweets that contain text-speak or spelling mistakes should be avoided if you want to maintain a positive reputation with your followers. It only takes a few minutes to compose a tweet, so spend a moment reading it back and making any necessary adjustments so that you post a clear and concise message rather than a hurried and clumsily assembled muttering. Remember that most Twitter users are being presented with numerous tweets every day and therefore only spend a few moments scanning through them for anything of interest. Any tweets that are unclear or not easy to read will be dismissed without a second thought. So read your tweet through the eyes of the reader. Don't try to cram in too many words and, in doing so, resort to text-speak or strange abbreviations. Don't write your tweet IN CAPITALS or post one containing obvius speling mistakse (I recently unfollowed one Twitter user purely because they wrote many of their tweets in capitals and I found them to be irritating and jarring). Compose your tweets as though you are addressing an individual. Research has shown that "you" and "your" are words that are noticed in a tweet. "How are you today and what are your plans?" is more likely to receive a response than "How are we all today and what are we doing?"

Be careful what you tweet

Imagine that your most valuable client or a hot prospect is standing over your shoulder when you are writing. Will they like what they see? It is all too easy to post a tweet in haste, to share a dodgy joke, to respond angrily to someone or to agree with a controversial opinion. But doing so without due consideration may come back to haunt you. If you have clients and competitors following you and you're looking to build a great reputation on Twitter, try to avoid becoming entangled in controversy or argument. And certainly don't tweet under the influence of alcohol!

Respond to your @messages

Do this especially when being asked for help. As you build your following on Twitter through sharing your expertise, you can expect to receive tweets from other users keen to ask questions. Share your wisdom freely. Respond to these tweets promptly with a thoughtful answer and don't be afraid to suggest talking on the telephone or moving the dialogue to email if the 140 character limit becomes too restrictive.

Re-tweeting messages

When you do this, add a few words explaining why. It will be appreciated by the person who composed the tweet and your followers will understand why you believe the message is also relevant to them.

Promoting your products and services on Twitter

By all means promote yourself, but don't overdo it. Aim for an approximate ratio of two tweets in which you self-promote, to eight tweets in which you are responding to tweets, sharing your expertise, joining conversations, starting discussions etc. Then, when you do promote your business you'll find that some followers will be interested in finding out more because they have grown to know and trust you through your series of non-promotional tweets. I often use the privacy of a personal direct message when I want a follower to know about my marketing Boot Camps and why I think they would benefit from attending one. By doing so, I can make my message truly bespoke to the needs of my follower and, at the same time, avoid contacting all my followers with a promotional message that may not be appropriate for the vast majority.

The Holy Grail – How to Get Your Tweets Re-Tweeted

It's tempting to judge your effectiveness on Twitter by the volume of tweets you are composing. But this is not the true benchmark of your performance. One easy-to-measure yardstick that can be used to determine the impact and the popularity that your tweets are having is how many of them are re-tweeted. A re-tweet is when one or more of your followers, or indeed any person on Twitter, decides that your tweet merits sending on to their own followers. If you want your reach on Twitter to spread and to become known as an opinion leader in your field, having your tweets re-tweeted to hundreds or thousands of people is a great way of achieving this.

How to gain a re-tweet

There are a number of ways to encourage re-tweets but, fundamentally, it depends upon the content of your messages. If your tweets are educational, relevant, witty or inspiring and you have already developed a strong reputation amongst your followers, the likelihood of having your tweets re-tweeted is increased. Here are some further suggestions:

- **Useful nuggets of information and expertise are always welcomed**. It may take a little while initially for people to view you as an expert and not just someone else trying to sell something but, once you've established a regular pattern of posting informative tweets, your followers should soon recognize them as being of value and will pass them on to their own followers. But don't overdo it. If you concentrate purely on sharing a stream of top tips you will risk coming across as one dimensional.

- **Encourage the re-tweeting of your messages by re-tweeting those of others.** The saying, "What you give is what you get" is so true.

- **Become accustomed to responding to tweets** that you enjoy, find useful or find just plain amusing. In doing so you're drawing positive attention to yourself and when one of your tweets appears in a follower's timeline, they will be happy to re-tweet it because they already hold you in a favourable light.

- **Tweet about something topical that sits within your area of expertise**. For example, a baker could share an opinion about a cookery programme on the television, a musician about *The X Factor*, a personal fitness trainer about the Olympics and so on. If the debate is already happening on Twitter, the fact that you're sharing your opinion as an expert with a connection to the topic means that you're more likely to have these tweets re-tweeted.

- **When you promote your latest blog,** don't just share a link with a few bland covering words, let your followers know the benefits of reading your blog and of re-tweeting it to their followers. "*7 ways you can build a powerful Twitter profile – my latest blog*" has more impact than "*My latest blog on Twitter profiles.*" The tweet promoting your blog should read like the headline of an advert. Make sure the link is in the middle of your tweet. Did you know that over 55% of the tweets that are re-tweeted include a link?

- **Include the name of a follower that you would like to re-tweet your message in your actual tweet.** Add a few nice words promoting them. If there's a positive, obvious connection between your message and your named follower, they may well re-tweet your message to their followers. For example, if I wanted social media marketing expert, Nicky Kriel, to re-tweet a message to her followers in which I was promoting one of my workshops, then I could tweet: "Thrilled that LinkedIn guru @nickykriel is attending my Copywriting Boot Camp in June. Find out more about it here xxxxxxx" in the hope that Nicky would re-tweet my post to her own followers.

- **Share an inspirational quote or saying**, but also share why you like it or how it's helped you.

- **Ask a question:** *"What's your top tip to build your following on Twitter? Please tweet back."* You should receive a lot of answers and some followers will re-tweet your question to their own followers.
- **Thank every person that re-tweets your tweets.** Twitter is not just a means of communicating "one to many," it also enables "one to one" dialogue. A personal message, no matter how short, goes a long way towards building on-line rapport. Don't just thank a follower with an open message, send a direct message too if it really matters.
- **Make it easy for people to re-tweet your tweets**. Use fewer than 130 characters and restrict your message to one tweet. If your message is spread over several tweets the chances of it being re-tweeted diminish.
- **Brazenly ask for a re-tweet.** Adding the words "Please re-tweet" or "Please RT" has been proven to increase the likelihood of your message being re-tweeted. However, don't overdo this call to action because it may irritate your followers if every other tweet contains this request. Asking for a re-tweet works particularly well if you're looking for a new supplier or are asking a question rather than requesting one purely to promote your services.

Why Are You "Unfollowed" on Twitter?

It can be disconcerting to discover that, while trying to build your Twitter following, some of your existing followers have been unfollowing you. But don't rush to the conclusion that nobody loves you, as there could be a number of reasons why you're unfollowed on Twitter, such as:

1. A person followed you hoping you would follow them back. When you didn't, they simply unfollowed you.
2. Some people have some rather unscrupulous Twitter strategies! They choose to follow you (and many others too) on the expectation that you will follow them back. When you do follow them back they immediately unfollow you and hope that you don't notice this! Their aim is to appear important to the world by having many followers but following very few people themselves.

3. You were followed by a "bot" – an automated account programmed to collect as many followers as possible. When you don't follow back, the bot automatically unfollows you. When you do follow back, it still unfollows you, but usually a few days later. (My husband was particularly proud that within a few hours of creating his own Twitter profile he was being followed by "Horny Hottie." He was very disappointed when I explained that he had probably not been personally selected as being of interest to Ms Hottie, and that this user was probably a "bot". Sure enough, two days later he had been unfollowed.)

4. A person followed you on the basis of the content in one of the tweets you posted. If your subsequent tweets differed completely in their nature and tone from that tweet, they unfollowed you because you didn't deliver what they were hoping for. Don't worry about losing these followers – you can't please everybody.

5. You're not tweeting enough. Most folk on Twitter will periodically review their list of followers. If you haven't tweeted in the last month some will unfollow you because you're insufficiently active and are not providing sufficient reason for them to continue following you.

6. You're tweeting too much! You may irritate your followers if you flood their timeline with several tweets over a short period of time. Don't post too many tweets in a short period of time; spread them out over the day.

7. Your tweets have become broadcasts, full of information and links. Consequently you are seen as a rather one dimensional information centre. Remember that you're on a social networking site and so try to vary your tweets in order to maintain the interest of your followers.

8. You're not responding to the messages sent to you by your followers or are not responding within a reasonable time. This can give the impression that you are uninterested in those people trying to interact with you.

9. Your tweets amount to attempts to sell your products or services, and nothing more. A follower may therefore conclude that there is no value in following you.

10. You have been sharing jokes or humorous comments that are a little bit dodgy. This may upset some people.

11. Your tweets comprise mainly of a series of hash tags linked to individual words. This does not make for interesting or easy reading.

12. Your tweets are littered with spelling mistakes or are written in txt speak. This could be because you are rushing each tweet before publishing it or trying to cram too much into those precious 140 characters. The result is that you create charmless and unreadable messages.
13. Spend a few minutes thinking about why you choose to unfollow someone on Twitter. It could be that you're being unfollowed for these reasons too!

If you're concerned that you're losing too many followers, review your last 20 tweets. Do any of the descriptions above apply to them?

The Misuse of Direct Messaging

There are some pretty common practices within Twitter that are best avoided due to the irritation they can cause other users and many of these revolve around the use of direct messaging. Direct messaging is a feature within Twitter that enables you to send a message or update to just one person rather than to all your followers. It is also possible to automate direct messages and to arrange for all new followers to receive a direct message from you once they choose to follow you. However, if you decide to use this function, do so wisely. Receiving an automated direct message simply saying "Thank you for choosing to connect and I look forward to reading your tweets" is bland and impersonal but, equally, it is unlikely to cause offence. Welcoming a new follower with an automated direct message encouraging them to "Like" your Facebook page, however, will probably cause annoyance. If you want to encourage your followers to do this, send an occasional open message explaining what they will find on your Facebook page and why they should check it out. But let them get to know you on Twitter first before you even consider promoting your presence on other social networking sites. They have not followed you on Twitter with the purpose of "Liking" you on Facebook!

Similarly, thanking a new follower with an automated direct message encouraging the follower to buy from you or sign up to your blog is again pretty charmless and irritating. I'm sure that you would not walk up to a stranger at a networking event and ask them to "Like" your Facebook page, sign up to your blog, or buy something from you right away. Yet this is in effect what you are doing on Twitter if you send out automated messages of this sort.

Another way in which direct messaging can be wrongly used is to issue a statement or ask a question that is so generic it is in no way personal to the recipient. A direct message is likely to be given more attention than a general update, but if its content is impersonal and irrelevant to the recipient, the reaction is likely to be a poor one. I have even received direct messages from small business marketers suggesting that I may need their services, despite being a small business marketer myself. This lack of awareness and recognition of the relationship I share with them has often resulted in me choosing to unfollow them. The direct message feature within Twitter is a useful and valuable one, but make sure that you use it only to send personal messages and not as another means of automated self-promotion.

What Can I Tweet About?

This is the question I am asked most by people wanting to become engaged with Twitter. Many small businesses start out on Twitter with the best of intentions and then fizzle out after a few weeks because they've run out of things to say. Because Twitter is a social networking platform, you don't have to make every tweet about business. In fact, if you do, you risk boring people. I know I have mentioned this before but it does bear repeating: *people like to buy from people they know, like and trust*. Twitter provides you with a medium to help potential clients to get to know and, hopefully, like and trust you. By tweeting about some of the social aspects of your life, you are presenting yourself as a person to your followers. So don't shy away from sharing your personality, just remember to balance the number of social tweets with the business related ones. Here's a selection of suggested topics to get you started:

1. The weather!
2. A programme you've enjoyed on the television.
3. Food – have you just discovered a new recipe, or enjoyed a meal at your favourite restaurant? People on Twitter love talking about food!

4. What you're doing right now – have you just finished reading a great book, held a fantastic client meeting, or signed up a new client? Share it. Bear in mind that, whilst good news is always well received on Twitter, a heavy supply of bad news is not welcomed so readily.

5. Share your new blog or someone else's blog that you really like. Comment on a topical news piece or article. Share a newsletter, explaining why your followers will find it interesting.

6. Post something trivial that your followers may identify with. "Enjoying a coffee and some thinking time after a full-on day!" "On a crowded train people-watching. How about you?"

7. Promote your business in a non-businesslike way. Twitter is fantastic at spreading positive PR – if you have a lovely picture showing you receiving an award or have just received a great of piece of client testimonial, share it. Ask followers to share their good news when you do this too.

8. Share pictures of you, where you are, what you're doing. Often when I'm on my travels I will post a picture of the scenery if it is particularly attractive or unusual. I will also post pictures of me at my book signings and re-tweet pictures that my readers sometimes send me of them holding one of my books.

9. Helpful tweets always go down well, especially with local followers, such as alerting people to travel disruptions or weather warnings.

10. Use the hash tags to find discussions that you can contribute to.

11. Be lovely! Send congratulatory tweets to people that are tweeting about their successes.

Twitter provides the opportunity to build a worthwhile reputation, so think carefully about what you tweet. Make sure that your voice is welcomed and that your followers really want to hear from you.

How to Grow Your Followers and be Successful on Twitter

The tips you've read so far are designed to help you to become more effective on Twitter. If you'd like to kick start your Twitter activity, or fear that your current activity is failing to have the impact you hoped for, try following this 30-Minutes-a-Day Twitter exercise plan for four weeks.

Every day . . .

- Post two expert tips.
- Respond to two tweets that you find interesting or useful, explaining why.
- Re-tweet two tweets you think your followers would appreciate.
- Respond to all your @messages and direct messages.
- Post a business tweet – "what I'm doing now, where I am."
- Post a social tweet and twice a week add a nice photo.
- Find three interesting people to follow. Send each one a tweet explaining why you have chosen to follow them.
- Ask a question.
- Send a personal direct thank-you message to each new follower.

At the end of the four weeks, evaluate your performance. Have you gained sufficient new followers to make continuing with Twitter worthwhile? Have people been re-tweeting your expert tips, answering your questions and engaging with you?

Useful Twitter Tools

Here are some free Twitter tools that I have found useful.

- **Justunfollow** – justunfollow.com – shows you who has unfollowed you so you can make the decision to stay with them or unfollow! (You can also use the free version of manageflitter.com)
- **Tweetdeck** – tweetdeck.com – organises your tweets and messages into columns so you can read them easily, shortens your URLs and lets you add your Twitter lists to columns. (I use Tweetdeck. Hootsuite is popular too.)
- **Retweetrank** – retweetrank.com – shows you the percentage and number of your tweets that are re-tweeted on a monthly basis.

- **Tweroid** – tweroid.com – a great tool that analyses your followers and suggests the best times for you to tweet.
- **Twitpic** – twitpic.com – lets you share your videos and photos.
- And, if you want to find interesting people to follow, check out twellow.com.

I would like to conclude this masterclass with some fantastic Twitter tips from Robert Clay who I am sure by the time this book is published will have well in excess of 100,000 followers, something he has achieved without any spamming or automation as he explains here. I "met" Robert on Twitter and can confirm that he always answers messages personally and, by sharing really good content, he has built a very loyal following.

> I started using Twitter when it first became prominent in 2008, mainly to see what all the talk was about. I experimented with it, liked it, and gradually figured out how to gain maximum value from it.
>
> I now use it as a news source, to add to my knowledge, to maintain cutting edge awareness in my area of expertise and to discover, learn from and engage with people globally who share similar interests. I also use it as a publishing tool to share knowledge and information I come across which I believe will be useful to anyone involved in running or marketing a business.
>
> My strategies for using Twitter include:
>
> 1. Discovering, connecting and interacting with many of the world's top thought leaders on subjects that interest me, and keeping abreast of the latest thinking and trends in those areas.
> 2. Building an engaged following by sharing high-quality content that is designed to add value to my target client group.
> 3. Sharing links to my own articles drives significant traffic to my blog/website, and builds a self-selecting audience many of whom elect to receive regular emails, articles and newsletters, which often leads to interactions and eventually business.
> 4. Sharing links to other people's high-quality articles and attributing the articles to them, which not only helps them to build their own traffic and subscribers, but also creates goodwill and allows me to build relationships with some amazing people who would otherwise be all but impossible to reach.
>
> Following initial contact on Twitter, I've now met and built excellent relationships with recognised authorities in many fields. These are people I would endorse in an

instant and who, in turn, would likely endorse me and what I do, should I ever need them to. This, in time, will become a priceless asset that supports my own strategy of building a business that grows almost entirely by word of mouth.

I also regularly interact with people who I haven't yet met, and build trusted relationships with them. They could be authorities in their field, prospective clients, or just people with whom I enjoy interacting. Building such relationships makes it easy, when appropriate, to have a sales conversation.

Because I've built up a large following and also share high quality content 15–25 times every day, people assume that I'm constantly glued to Twitter. They'd be wrong. I spend maybe ten minutes on Twitter most days reading and responding to incoming messages. It does not take over my life.

A lot of people use Twitter services that create automatic responses to messages they receive; or put out automated welcome messages to new followers; or automatically follow back people who follow them. I do none of these things as the messages tend to be impersonal and meaningless . . . and I consider them to be spam.

But I do use technology to automate content sharing. At the start of each day, or when I get a few spare minutes, I either use Twitter lists to follow what a small, carefully selected group of around 100 trusted contacts are saying on Twitter, or use Google Reader to bring together a multitude of sources in one place, eliminating the need to trawl the web.

From either place I add articles of interest to "Pocket" for reading later. Pocket is a cloud-based service that captures articles with a single click and presents them beautifully on almost any smartphone, tablet, PC or laptop. It also makes it easy to share articles to many other services including Twitter, Facebook, LinkedIn, Evernote and Buffer.

To share articles I normally add them to my Buffer account with a single click from Pocket or a web browser. By simply topping up your Buffer account with fresh content when you get a few spare minutes you can maintain a consistent 24/7/365 social media presence.

People often want to know how I've built such a large following. It's not hard or complex. I constantly look for great content to share. I find it using Twitter or Google Reader, as mentioned above . . . and share it using Buffer. People frequently share those links in turn with their followers, a couple of thousand usually decide to follow me each month . . . and the numbers just build up over time.

When people respond to something I've shared or mention me for the first time, I generally check out their Twitter profile and website to get a sense of who they are. If their message merits a response (e.g. it doesn't just say "thank you for following"), I always respond in person, as soon as I can. This often leads to ongoing interactions which, in turn, lead to valuable business opportunities based on the level of mutual trust that builds up over time.

If you were to read my last 20 tweets, depending on the time of day, they'd most likely be a combination of links I've shared, interactions with people I'm following or who've responded to something I've shared or said.

So how do you build your following and extend your reach and influence on Twitter? Here are some tips:

- Above all look for interesting people to follow, but be very selective.
- Don't automatically follow back just because someone follows you. Only follow people that genuinely add value, if you value your time and sanity.
- Use Twitter lists to group together people, organisations, or media that tweet about topics that interest you. You can follow and interact with those people in a much more focused and time-efficient manner.
- Define your target market precisely and write articles or blog posts specifically for them. Share links to those posts on Twitter (I share each post about once a month) and share other great content you find.
- Use tools like Google Reader, Buffer and Bit.ly (which shortens links automatically and provides useful stats).
- Instead of using the normal Twitter website for interacting with people, I recommend you use a dedicated Twitter application like Tweetbot (for iPhones, iPads and Macs) or Hootsuite. You'll be able to accomplish a lot more in a fraction of the time.

Thanks to Robert for such excellent tips and I do hope that this masterclass has inspired you to tweet, knowing that in doing so you're not simply following the herd, but are using a social networking tool that can really benefit your business.

Masterclass Summary

- If you're new to Twitter or rejoining after a period of inactivity get your bearings by searching for prospects, competitors and potential introducers.
- Twitter is social media not selling media. If you concentrate purely on selling you will alienate people.
- Use every character of your Twitter biography to let people know who you are and what you do. It's your mini elevator statement.

- Scheduling tweets enables you to portray a regular and consistent presence on Twitter without actually accessing the tool; but you also need to be available to respond to tweets, listen and share.
- Find your own tweeting routine. It can be five minutes here and there or a dedicated time slot, but try to tweet every day.
- Use Twitter to build your expert status. Share tips freely.
- Tweets full of text talk and spelling mistakes are off-putting and portray you in a bad light.
- Spend a minute or two composing and checking each tweet.
- Don't tweet in anger, get drawn into controversial debates or use expletives.
- You can promote your business but only in between sharing, listening, learning and responding.
- It's not that hard to have a tweet re-tweeted. Ask for it, share useful links, ask questions, re-tweet the tweets of others.
- Accept that you will be unfollowed at times just as you will unfollow others.
- Be careful not to over-promote your presence on other social media channels when on Twitter.
- Resist the urge to auto-message a new follower. Send personal direct messages instead.
- What to tweet about? The weather, food, where you are now, what you watched on the television . . . congratulating someone for a great achievement.

Conclusion

You have now reached the end of my book. I hope that you feel inspired and empowered to roll up your sleeves and get cracking on the marketing front! Commit to putting marketing at the centre of your business universe. Be prepared to push well and truly out of your marketing comfort zone in the months ahead as you take on the exciting but sometimes bracing challenges that arise when putting an effective marketing plan into action. Set aside any personal fears and pick up that phone to make that cold call; control your nerves, command that stage and inspire the audience with your expertise and charm. Take comfort in the fact that your tenacity, enthusiasm and commitment to marketing will pay off handsomely with more hot prospects converting to loyal clients, and more recommendations as people become aware of your expertise and reputation.

Be prepared to embrace marketing tools and tactics that you've previously ignored and don't shrink from making subtle or dramatic changes to your business plans. On occasion you may need to burn the midnight oil in order to keep pace with your marketing plan and ensure that any actions are implemented to schedule. You will definitely need to treat marketing as a priority and allocate time in your diary to work on your marketing tasks. But when you are presented with the problem of how to service all the new clients that will be coming your way, you will know that your consistent marketing efforts and commitment to running a marketing-focused business are being rewarded.

Remember that in a tough economic climate we need to be relentless in our pursuit of the business out there. Don't assume that last year's marketing tactics are still appropriate and will produce the same rewards this year. Refinements or even significant changes may be necessary. Always keep your target audience at the front of your mind when planning your marketing activities.

And, finally, reassure yourself that by bringing marketing into the heart of your business and following a long-term plan, you are probably stealing a march on your competitors. Building marketing campaigns, creating sparkling, relevant and charming communications, focusing on the needs of your target audiences, developing three-month tactical plans and improving your products and services is something that many of your competitors are likely to be skipping. It is they that will be spending money on untested, ill-considered and sporadic marketing activities, not you.

So, I hope that you look upon each masterclass in this book as a profit-generating exercise for your business. After reading each one, revisit it with your pen in hand and underline those tips that most appeal, make notes in the margins and generally deface the whole book with your marketing ideas.

Then put those ideas into action and watch your sales rise!

About the Contributors

Liz Barnes

BSc, Cert Ed, DipM, FCIM, Chartered Marketer

Website: www.envoca.co.uk
LinkedIn: uk.linkedin.com/in/lizzbarnes/
Twitter: @lizzbarnes

Liz Barnes has amassed a wealth of experience in marketing consultancy using this to great effect to develop marketing strategy for companies including training marketers and management professionals. She works across all sectors including blue-chip multinationals, public sector, education, professional services and SMEs. As a Fellow of The Chartered Institute of Marketing (CIM) and Chartered Marketer, she also serves on the CIM South East Region committee as Education Champion and is on the CIM Steering committee of the Social Marketing (Behaviour Change) Market Interest Group. She has also helped many marketers achieve their CIM qualifications and develop their professional marketing careers.

Robert Clay

Founder of Marketing Wizdom Ltd., Mentor to Business Founders in Top 0.5% of Entrepreneurs

Website: http://marketingwizdom.com
Twitter: http://www.twitter.com/marketingwizdom
LinkedIn: http://www.linkedin.com/in/robertclay

Robert Clay built two global businesses when young, sold them to a division of Astra Pharmaceutical then spent years accumulating and assembling the best know-how for accelerating the growth of any business. Following a ten-year experiment in taking businesses to market leadership, he now runs workshops that are often described as a marketing MBA in three days. He also mentors business founders in the top 0.5% of entrepreneurs, by invitation only, where groups of committed, like-minded, entrepreneurs meet and work with others four days a year to not only learn WHAT to do, but also HOW to do it.

Nicky Kriel

Social Media Coach and Trainer

Website: www.nickykriel.com
Blog: www.nickykriel.com/blog
Twitter: www.twitter.com/NickyKriel
LinkedIn: www.linkedin.com/in/nickykriel
Facebook: www.facebook.com/socialmediafornewbies

Nicky Kriel is passionate about empowering, inspiring and educating company owners and managers to use social media to grow their businesses. She uses her background in corporate marketing to help companies integrate social media into their own marketing strategies. As a Master NLP Practitioner, communicating is her strength, teaching people to engage with the "social" aspect of social networking; it's not all about tools and technology, but about people and relationships. Nicky works with businesses ranging from start-up businesses to multinationals, helping them build and develop relevant social media strategies. She runs jargon free and practical public courses on Twitter, Facebook and LinkedIn.

Ben Locker

Web Copywriting Expert and Professional Copywriters' Network Co-Founder

Website: www.benlocker.co.uk
Twitter: @benlocker
LinkedIn: http://www.linkedin.com/in/benlocker

Ben Locker is owner of an Essex-based copywriting agency and co-founder of the Professional Copywriters' Network, the first and largest association for copywriters in the UK. Ben writes for blue chip and SME clients across Europe and is also a well-known copywriting trainer. Also a journalist, Ben has written for *The Times* and appeared on the BBC's *Moral Maze* as an expert in social media. He has twice featured in the *Guardian*'s live careers Q&A, "Routes into Copywriting" and is author of *Swinesend: Britain's Greatest Public School* (Atlantic Book, 2007), a parody of life in our more archaic educational institutions.

Aneela Rose

Managing Director of Aneela Rose PR

Website: www.aneelarosepr.co.uk
Twitter: @AneelaRosePR
LinkedIn: aneelarose

Aneela set up her agency, Aneela Rose PR, in 2004, having spent the previous eight years working in the publishing, manufacturing and IT industries, and growing their marketing and PR departments. She is a member of various professional associations, including The Chartered Institute of Public Relations (MCIPR) and the Public Relations Consultants Association (PRCA). In 2005 she received the *Success in Business* award from Anglia Ruskin University where she is an active Alumni member and is featured in the new Lord Ashcroft International Business School campuses in Cambridge and Chelmsford. Aneela has appeared on TV and radio as the voice for SMEs and is a regular contributor to industry magazines.

Acknowledgements

It began with a comment from Andy Fernandez, Manager of The Chartered Institute of Marketing bookshop. We were talking about the success of my second book when Andy said "When you're thinking about writing your third book, let me introduce you to Wiley and Sons. They are the world's most renowned business book publishers and I am sure they would be interested in talking to you." Until then, I hadn't seriously considered writing a third book. I was still enjoying the success of my second book but with *that* comment, Andy had sown a seed in my mind. And 20 months later *The 15 Essential Marketing Masterclasses for Your Small Business* is a reality.

There are many amazing people that have helped ensure that my manuscript made it to Wiley on time and that, despite running a full time business whilst writing, I have retained my sanity throughout!

So, without further ado, my thanks go to . . .

Andy – for being so enthusiastic about my ability to write a third book and for his encouraging emails and brilliant advice.

The expert contributors in this book – professional people that I like, respect and trust. The experts in this book have honed their craft over many years. So, thanks to the world class entrepreneur and master of Twitter, Robert Clay; the extremely talented and down to earth PR expert Aneela Rose; the social media expert that other social media experts respect and quote, Nicky Kriel; the warm, generous and inspirational e-marketing guru Liz Barnes; and the absolutely brilliant-beyond-belief-copywriter, Ben Locker. *The 15 Essential Marketing Masterclasses for Your Small Business* is all the better for your fabulous tips and advice.

I would like to say a heartfelt thank you to the team at Wiley. When I was a young girl my dream was to become a published author. As I got older and published my own books, my dream changed to being approached by a publisher offering me an international publishing deal. When Jonathan and Iain from Wiley came to my home to discuss the ideas I had for a third book, nothing could have prepared me for their enthusiasm for publishing my work. They gave me complete freedom to write this book and placed their trust in me with no restrictions. What more could any author ask for?

My husband Malcolm has been a great support, as has my brother Andrew and my Mum Ann.

My two lovely, funny and handsome sons, Steven and Mark have on this occasion shown more than a passing interest in my writing. I'm guessing it's because some of their friends follow me on Twitter which has made me cool in as much as a 51-year-old Mum can ever be.

I would like to conclude with a heartfelt thank-you to the many thousands of readers that have bought my books. Your reviews, and your upbeat, inspiring and cheery messages telling me how you are putting the advice in my books into practice have really spurred me on and encouraged me to keep on writing! I hope that you enjoy my latest book and, most importantly, that it helps you on your journey to success.

Please get in touch with me to let me know how you're putting the tips into practice in your business and the results they produce. I do so enjoy hearing from my readers, so please drop me a line via Twitter or Facebook, connect with me through LinkedIn or contact me via my website, www.themarketinggym.org. I would love to hear your stories. Or why not write to me just to say "Hello?"

With love and gratitude,
Dee Blick

Index